Voyage to the Edge of the World

Voyage
to
the
Edge
of
the
World

ALAN EDMONDS

McClelland and Stewart Limited

The illustrative materials for this book
were provided by R. Belanger, N. Fenerty,
the Atlantic Oceanographic Laboratory,
the Bedford Institute, H. Wiele, the Department
of National Defence, the National
Museums of Canada, and the
National Film Board.

0-7710-3067-3

Printed and bound in Canada

The Canadian Publishers
McClelland and Stewart Limited
25 Hollinger Road, Toronto

For my mother, who gave me the world;
for John, David and Sarah,
to whom I bequeath it;
and to the men of science
who may yet save it.

A.E.

Foreword

On October 16, 1970, css *Hudson* came home from her epic scientific expedition around the Americas.

When announcing the project in January 1969, I said that the Hudson 70 project would have significant value to the development of Canada's, and the entire world's, undersea resources. I also said that Hudson 70 would have global implications that could prove of direct benefit to all nations in meeting the scientific and economic challenges of the day.

Hudson 70 met expectations. It ranks well among the major oceanographic expeditions of the past fifty years. At the foreign ports of call, css *Hudson* was widely admired and her people were warmly received. From all reports, her presence was a credit to Canada. It provided one of the infrequent occasions for marine scientists from several countries to work together in relatively inaccessible and little studied areas of the seas. It has produced thousands of observations and sample collections of excellent quality.

The achievement of the men of the *Hudson* is one of those great Canadian enterprises in which all our people can share. The accomplishments of our todays and yesterdays as a people are the stuff of which the edifice of nationhood is constructed. In the larger context of Canadian nationhood, I think it important that accomplishments such as this be clearly and indelibly recorded.

HON. J. J. GREENE

7

THE HUDSON 70 EXPEDITION

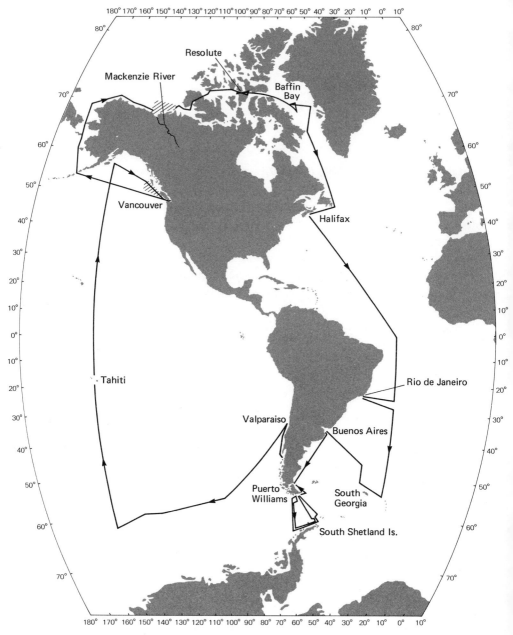

Resolute

Mackenzie River

Baffin Bay

Vancouver

Halifax

Tahiti

Rio de Janeiro

Valparaiso

Buenos Aires

Puerto Williams

South Georgia

South Shetland Is.

Marine Sciences Branch, Department of Energy, Mines and Resources.

Prologue

Larry Griffin's absorbed silence was a measure of the tension on the bridge. Usually he was relaxed on watch. For that matter, Griffin was usually relaxed whatever the situation; lean, boyish, prone to smiling most of the time – and when officer of the watch usually affable, even talkative. Now he was neither. Now he moved quietly, purposefully and repeatedly from bridge windows to port radar set and back again. From the windows he would look down at the fo'c's'le where Chief Officer Fred Mauger stood at the bow, hands thrust in the pockets of a blue government issue parka peering at . . . well, nothing. At least, Griffin hoped it was nothing. On the radar he could see, uncomfortably close, the etched silhouette of land on either side. Segments of the shoreline of Halifax harbour stood out brightly as the radar beam swept around the screen, then faded as the arm of light that represented the beam fingering out from the rotating antenna on the upper deck moved on. Both radar sets were on. Both appeared to have tiny clouds of luminous green suspended above them. The fog that night was so pervasive it had crept into the bridge itself and the green light of the radar screens was reflected from a few million moisture particles.

Dave Butler – Captain David W. Butler to be formal about it – sat where he always sat when on the bridge entering or leaving harbour, on a flip-down seat by the port engine control console and turned awkwardly sidesaddle because there wasn't enough room between bridge windows and seat for his knees and the considerable bulk he was always threatening to diet away. He said nothing, which wasn't unusual, and lit one cigarette from another, which was. He watched as Griffin's shadowy

9

shape paraded briskly between the window and the radar sets. No sailor likes fog. In fact, thought Butler, probably no one did, except perhaps murderers, rapists or anyone else with something to hide. But, beyond a dislike of fog, no deep sea sailor, which Butler and Griffin were, felt comfortable close to land. And now he had both *and* it was night and he and his ship were moving – though just barely, at five knots – between McNabb's Island to the port and the Dartmouth shore to starboard. The fog had drifted in, sudden and unpredicted, as they lay at the fuelling dock, topping up the tanks that held 1,230 tons of diesel fuel when full. Now they were creeping back to their home berth at the Bedford Institute of Oceanography, and Butler felt as though they were being carried along in a cocoon of wispy cotton wool – though that wasn't the right way to describe it; he was Canadian now, not English, and here cotton wool was called cotton batten.

Somewhere far off, out by the Chebucto Light at the approaches to Halifax harbour, a clutch of deep sea ships waited anxiously at anchor for the fog to lift. Every few seconds one of them would let off a blast on her siren to echo the lighthouse foghorn. There were deep, sonorous sirens that sounded like the melancholy bellows of some primordial creature of the kind Butler knew even respectable scientists still believed might live in the ocean deeps. At the other end of the scale there were sirens that gave out high-pitched, tremulous wails. And then there were sirens that ranged up and through the Tonic Sol-fa scale – do, ra, me, fa, so, la, ti, do – that he remembered from school. You could, thought Butler, compose a cantata for ships' sirens and lighthouse foghorns.

Crossing the bridge, again, Griffin changed course to the ship-to-shore radio phone behind the helmsman. He called Halifax Naval Information Centre, traffic control headquarters for the harbour. He went back to the window, turned to Butler and said with the formality reserved for the bridge where there was always an audience of crewmen: "We still have the harbour to ourselves, Captain." Butler replied that that was only because of the fog and as far as he was concerned he didn't want to be sailing around the damned harbour, either, and wouldn't be if he had a choice, which he hadn't. But by then Griffin was back

10

at the radar, and saying: "They were wrong. We've got company. There's something off the port bow. It's in the channel too."

The inshore channel between McNabb's island and the Dartmouth shore is half a mile wide, give or take a few yards. The *Hudson* was hugging the mainland shore, creeping up toward Bedford Basin, the great inner harbour which made Halifax the natural assembly point for the Atlantic convoys during two world wars. Butler carried the chart in his head. So did Griffin. Neither man worried overmuch. There was room for two ships to pass in the channel.

They all saw it at the same moment – Butler, Griffin, the lookout standing in front of the bridge windows, Mauger on the fo'c's'le. A red light suspended, disembodied, in mid-air. It was to port and angling towards them. No one would ever remember the details for sure, but it was barely fifty yards away on the periphery of the cocoon of fog when they saw it first. Within seconds the light ceased to be disembodied; became part of a threat to the *Hudson*; was seen to be fixed to the mast of a fuel barge; a fuel barge that was the hulk of an old 1,000-ton ship and was now heading across the channel; across their bows and on collision course. "Full astern," snapped Butler – but Griffin was already yanking back the engine control to "All astern, full". The coffee cups on the shelf by the radio phone rattled as all four engines, all 7,500 horsepower, took hold. Butler, Griffin, the lookout, Mauger – all stood silent, watching the light and the bulk of the barge heading inexorably toward them. "The tug pushing her – he's on the far side. He can't see us." Butler was talking to no one in particular, offering up an explanation for this insanity.

The mind can run a thousand miles in seconds. Far enough for Butler to first assess the likely consequences of the inevitable collision. The one-and-five-eighth-inches-thick steel plates of the hull – more than twice the usual thickness to enable the *Hudson* to work in ice – would be stove in. The repairs would take anything between one month and three. And in two days – just two damn days – he was scheduled to sail triumphantly out of Halifax with a cargo of computers and magnetometers and sampling bottles and a score or more of some of the world's best known oceanographic scientists on Canada's first major voyage of deep-sea oceanographic exploration. From Halifax, right around South America and back up the Pacific across the roof of the world through the Northwest Passage to the North Atlantic, and then back to Halifax. It was, by any odds, one of the most ambitious expeditions of its kind mounted by any nation at any time. The scientists and his predecessor as captain of the *Hudson,* the late Walter Kettle, had spent almost three years planning the trip. The public relations people from Ottawa – from the Department of Energy, Mines and Resources – had promoted the expedition until the entire nation knew of the project. The Minister himself was coming down to see them off. There was to be a formal lunch aboard which young Claude Durin, the chef, was already planning. Then there would be speeches and people in their best suits and he and his officers in dress uniforms – he'd had a new one made for the trip – and probably a band and a thousand or so sightseers and ... and now he was about to hit a fuel barge that had no right to be charging around the harbour without telling the traffic control centre and which was propelled by a tug that couldn't see what it was doing, and his bows were about to be smashed in.

He had been captain of the *Hudson* for only three months, and it was his first ocean-going command. After a life as a deep-sea sailor he had joined the Canadian government's scientific fleet as a junior officer only thirty months earlier and had been annointed for success when they had given him command of the *Limnos,* the research ship that worked the Great Lakes, within a year of his joining the service. But for all that the *Hudson* was his first ocean-going command; it was the flagship of the ocean-ographic fleet and – dammit – he was only forty and he'd started as a cockney kid seaman when only fourteen and he was proud of himself and his command. And now ... and now he was about to collide with a fuel barge and could do nothing to prevent it.

That red light on the barge's stubby foremast was mesmeric. It was the light that the men on the bridge watched, not the slowly moving bulk of the vessel itself. The *Hudson's* twin screws churned astern, dragging at the water to first stop the 4,800 tons of ship and then haul it backwards. The sea foamed furiously up and around the stern, setting the quarterdeck awash. But still the *Hudson* moved ahead, and the red light hung almost over the port bow, seemingly motionless. And then it was dead ahead, and for a moment Butler thought it was hanging on his own bow jackstaff. And then it was past the bow, moving to starboard. And then the bulk of the barge was directly ahead of them. And still they hadn't hit. And then it was gone, the red light fading into the fog surrounded by a halo for a few seconds until, finally, it disappeared. Butler sighed, and for once didn't have a gentle wisecrack ready to ease the tension.

Later, safely back at dock in Bedford Basin, Butler, Griffin and Mauger, who had been on the fo'c's'le, drank hot chocolate on the bridge, and mourned that the liquor supply was still in bond, not to be opened until they were twenty-four hours out of port. Butler was convinced that *Hudson's* bow had actually scraped the side of the barge. Mauger, who had been standing at the bow and was probably better able to see, said the *Hudson* and the barge hadn't actually touched. "We missed her," he said. "There was maybe six inches in it."

And so the Canadian odyssey called Hudson 70 was saved – by six inches. Dave Butler said he had sweated off ten pounds in ten seconds, but would prefer a less exciting way of losing weight.

1

You cannot actually see Neverfail Shoal. There's no menacing swirl of white water on the surface because the shoal itself, the peak of an underwater hill, is twenty-six feet beneath the sea and to the east of the main channel to and from Halifax harbour. No member of the crew of the Canadian Scientific Ship *Hudson* – and among them there are some relatively ancient mariners – can tell you when the shoal first appeared on navigation charts, and none of them really know why it was so labelled. And that doesn't matter because they have their own entirely satisfactory explanation of the mystery surrounding the name. Neverfail Shoal is well out toward Chebucto Light, which is perched on the last headland before the open sea, and precisely at the point that departing ships first meet the big Atlantic swell that has built up over the 2,000 miles of open ocean between the Caribbean and Nova Scotia. For most of the peak shipping season the prevailing winds are from the south and they sweep across the great expanse of nothing, piling up the sea's surface into the hills and valleys of this legendary North Atlantic swell, the great ripples of the ocean that are born at the equator and go on forever until they hit land and become waves that pour, frothing and spluttering, against rocky cliffs and sandy beaches in the north. And it is as the *Hudson* meets this swell on every outward bound trip that the sailors grin slyly at one another and privately know why Neverfail Shoal was so named: At this point the ship begins to take the swell on the starboard beam and starts to roll, and that never fails to send the cargo of scientists, who have been jauntily looking seaward or backwards at the diminishing Halifax skyline, scurrying for their cabins to suffer the agonies of seasickness.

In the fall the swell is particularly bad because the winds have strengthened and are turning to blow from the north for winter, and on the day that Hudson 70 began – November 19, 1969 – it was worse than usual; bad enough to even send veteran sailor Dr. Cedric Mann to his Chief Scientist's cabin to lie on the bunk. On the bridge Navigating Officer Ray Gould, who also felt squeamish, noted that it was a twenty-foot swell, and on the deck below Mann lay looking out of the porthole, thinking that even with the *Hudson's* vaunted stabilizers – even though she was the only oceanographic ship outside Russia to have such luxuries – it was still a little like being in an airplane one minute and a submarine the next. Rolling one way, all that could be seen through the porthole was the grey November sky; rolling back the other, the sky vanished and was replaced by the heaving, froth-flecked sea. He wondered whether he would feel better in time for dinner. For that matter, he wondered whether it was safe to go to dinner – the captain, Dave Butler, had already told him that Claude Durin, the chef, was French and very temperamental and likely to be suffering a fit of sulks because Joe Greene, the Minister of Energy, Mines and Resources, had cancelled the formal roast beef lunch Durin had spent days planning. Butler said they were lucky to have so good a chef on a working ship, but that the price was paid with the taste buds and digestion when he fell into a bad mood. Butler's gloomy prediction was that because the Minister had failed to keep his date with the chef's roast beef, they were all about to suffer a few days' of gastronomical torture.

The cancelled lunch had, to Mann's astonishment, been the only hitch in the departure of the Hudson 70 expedition that day. In fact, the entire performance had gone so smoothly that he had felt a sense of anti-climax. Somehow this departure, the culmination of two years of his dreaming and scheming, planning and arranging, should have made more impact – on him if no one else. As a scientist and the head of a government research department, he knew he should be hugely pleased that there had been no last minute disasters. As a man, even a determinedly phlegmatic one, he had enough human perversity to wish there had been some last minute drama, some excitement, to send the adrenalin pumping and leave him ready to depart with a heady awareness of the importance of it all.

And it was important, this voyage called Hudson 70. There were good, sound scientific reasons for spending $1,500,000 and tying up the *Hudson* for a year in what must rank somewhere in the top six of major deep-sea expeditions in man's history. The oceans form more than two-thirds of the earth's surface, and are so deep that if you were to raze all the continental land masses to sea level and dump them into the Pacific you still would not fill that ocean's basin. In what he had come to call The Age of Ecology, Mann was a physical oceanographer studying the movements of water around the globe and was, like all his colleagues in oceanography, painfully aware that an ever-hopeful mankind responded to those who predicted the end of the world as a creeping Armageddon of pollution by looking to the oceans and saying in effect: *"They* can save us!" But could they? As the *Hudson* sailed out of Halifax, the u.s. astronauts were paying a second visit to the moon. Yet man still knew so little about the oceans, where all life was thought to have begun, that the Danish *Galathea* oceanographic expedition of 1950 was mounted partly because Dr. Antoine Bruun had whipped up scientific as well as public support by saying it was entirely possible that there really were sea serpents in the depths of the oceans. And still no one could say there weren't. When Hamlet said: "There are more things in heaven and earth, Horatio, than are dreamt of in your philosophy," he might well have been talking about the oceans.

And then there were the important political reasons for Hudson 70. Canada, after all, is bounded by three oceans – Atlantic, Arctic and Pacific – and has more coastline than any other nation on earth. Besides which, Canada has been lucky with its Continental Shelf. That part of the seabed which geologists consider a submerged part of the land mass is more extensive off Canada's shores than in most parts of the world. In fact, Canada's Continental Shelf is almost half as big as the nation itself – 1,400,000 square miles of potential resource riches, all belonging to Canada as long as she demonstrates a preparedness and capacity to explore and develop them herself in accordance with the latest international conventions.

There was also the issue of the Arctic environment. The Americans had found oil at Prudhoe Bay near the Mackenzie River delta, and only weeks earlier the giant 125,000-ton tanker Manhattan had, with the aid of a Canadian icebreaker, crashed through the Northwest Passage just to prove it could be done. Both events made even more urgent the fundamental issue of how the needs of man and those of the environment could be reconciled, if at all. How could anyone answer that while scientists knew so little about the knife-edge balance of nature up there, about the state of the Arctic Ocean and whether it really was navigable to big ships.

All these were good, logical reasons for Hudson 70. But to Canada's scientists there was an underlying emotional significance to the expedition that was beyond practical and political consideration.

This voyage, history's first circumnavigation of North and South America, was probably the best way Canadian scientists could serve notice on the world that as the so-called International Oceanographic Decade began Canada was in the business of oceanography in a big way. And that in itself was a milestone in the life of a nation in which fundamental pure science – that is, research for its own sake; the pursuit of knowledge as an end in itself – had traditionally played Cinderella to the more practical forms of research and development that would lead to cash in the bank, or put you one up over a potential enemy. Such research was described as "mission-oriented" in current political argot – and Ced Mann had had enough of that in his years with the Defence Research Board, studying the oceans with a view of devising better ways of finding and eliminating hostile submarines. He had succeeded, but he had not particularly wanted to devote his life to finding more efficient ways of conducting war, even if – as seemed likely in Canada's case – it were a purely defensive one.

A scientist can never escape that sort of research entirely, of course. And on a project like the Hudson 70 expedition mounted by the federal government's Atlantic Oceanographic Laboratory – part of the Bedford Institute of Oceanography at Dartmouth – it was only proper that all areas of research in which the government was interested should be represented. That was why young Oreste Bluy, a sonar expert with the Defence Research Establishment, was aboard to study ways of detecting the mysterious "scattering layer" of fish that live about half a mile down in the deep. These creatures are like submarine airships; they have gas bladders that they fill or empty to move up and down in the ocean. The bladders distort sonar signals and, in theory, a submarine could hide among them. But aboard the *Hudson,* even Oreste Bluy's project would be dovetailed as part of a research programme that was almost exclusively pure science; research designed to increase man's knowledge of the nature of things, not to find bigger and better ways of making or saving money or waging war.

Before the *Hudson* returned to Halifax almost a year to the day after departing, 122 scientists from four countries would have come and gone as passengers; taken their measurements, collected their samples and specimens and departed. There would be nine separate phases of the voyage, and on each one the scientific personnel would be mostly different.

In a sense the *Hudson* was a Ship of Dreams – as much for Ced Mann as anyone. For him, it meant a chance to break new ground in measuring ocean currents. He would attempt to lay current meters across the 500-mile-wide Drake Passage, that storm-ridden stretch of the mother of all oceans, the Antarctic, between Cape Horn and the northernmost tip of Antarctica. Through this passage swept the circumpolar current which swirled endlessly around Antarctica, mixing waters of the Atlantic, Pacific and Indian Oceans. Later, months later in Valparaiso, Dr. William Cameron, then director of Marine Sciences for the Department of Energy, Mines and Resources, was to think up the catchphrase "taking the pulse of the oceans", and Mann would agree that it was an accurate, if unscientifically colourful, description of the circumpolar current that in one way or another influenced all life on earth. Some scientists had already measured the currents in the upper layers

18

of the Drake Passage, but Mann dreamed of taking measurements from surface to seabed – and where he planned to work the ocean was two miles deep. He refused to dwell on the chances of success – and failure. Three years earlier he and u.s. scientists had attempted something nearly as ambitious – the measuring of the current in the Denmark Strait between Iceland and Greenland – and the failure had been almost total. But that had been three years earlier, and he and the technicians at the Bedford Institute had been working all that time to perfect new techniques and equipment. Perhaps this time . . .?

And the other dreams?

There was grizzled Bill Sutcliffe, brilliant biologist who had given up the directorship of his own u.s.-run institute to go back to pure research at the Bedford Institute and to whom Hudson 70 meant a chance to test his theory that it was possible to measure the productivity of the oceans with unprecedented accuracy by finding out how much ribonucleic acid is contained in samples of zoo-plankton, the insects of the sea. There was Carol Lalli, the leggy biologist from McGill University, who would come aboard at Rio de Janiero to collect samples of two species of tiny creatures called pteropods to see whether they have the same feeding habits in the Antarctic as they do in the North Pacific, and who, in the process, might draw conclusions that could help change the feeding habits of every living creature on earth.

Young Peter Beamish, the acoustics engineer-turned-biologist was aboard because his unpredictable passions had turned him from electronics to the study of the way whales "talk" with one another; he fervently wished the *Hudson* were a sailboat so he could "live" with a school of the great whales, so big that in bulk they can equal thirty elephants . . . though privately Ced Mann thought that trying to make friends with any creature that big, however friendly, would be fraught with disquieting hazards. George Pickard, the man who had been responsible for Ced Mann entering oceanography, would board the *Hudson* at the southernmost tip of South America and take the ship through the uncharted fiord system of southern Chile to examine the water circulation and life-support system of hitherto unexplored territory, and, when asked why, gave the best reason Mann had ever heard for a scientist pursuing his curiosity. Pickard would say that the Chilean fiords were his Mount Everest and quote Edward Mallory, who had written that "Man climbs a mountain because it is there." Well, said Pickard, that was why he wanted to explore the fiords. And that was why Mann wanted to measure currents in the Drake Passage, and why any scientist wanted to discover and define the shape of another piece of the jigsaw that, if ever completed, might enable man to control his destiny wisely and well.

Then there was Bill von Arx, one of the magic names in oceanography, who would leave the Woods Hole Oceanographic Institution in Massachusetts to join the ship in Valparaiso and, with the aid of young Dick Haworth of the Bedford Institute, would try to measure the gravitational "shape" of the surface of the Pacific so one of those typically elaborate American experiments involving satellites might be made to work. Eric Mills, the biologist from Dalhousie, whose attempt to try to prove that a certain flea-like creature that lived on the Antarctic seabed was in fact related to a similar creature that was found at the equator, would come aboard at Buenos Aires. Ced Mann didn't always understand what the biologists were up to, but Mills, who was a dreamer with an imaginative turn of phrase, said that what he was doing was like "studying evolution on the hoof".

And towards the end of the voyage, back in Canadian waters, David Ross and Charles Maunsell would be probing the earth's crust and at the same time finding evidence to support the Continental Drift theory that claimed the continents were like great rafts floating around the face of the earth on the planet's inner core. Then, too, Dave Ross would be trying to prove that the great expanse of water called Baffin Bay in the Canadian north was no such thing, that it was in fact an ocean in its own right. Suppose he was right? Wouldn't that spark a debate between Canada and Denmark, which claimed Greenland on the other side of Baffin Bay, over who "owned" how much of the ocean that had for so long been considered a bay in Canada's coastline?

And then there was Bernie Pelletier's Beaufort Sea project,

in which he would be charting the geology of the Continental Shelf and seabed around the Mackenzie Delta, next door to Alaska where the Americans were mounting a massive effort to bring in productive oil wells. The western world could not much longer depend on the Middle East and South America for its oil supplies, and was now turning to the unexplored north so the u.s., Canada and their western allies would be able to survive on their own resources. Until now no one had really wanted much to do with the inhumanly bleak Arctic. But now the Arctic was being seen as the place where Canada might stake its future. And if Bernie Pelletier and his crew helped prove what was already suspected – that the Arctic and the Beaufort Sea area in partciular are a bonanza of oil and other mineral wealth – what would that do to the map? Earlier that day when formally launching the expedition, Joe Greene, who had made Hudson 70 possible, had said that these yet unde-tected resources could be used to help all mankind by providing the wealth that would help end poverty, right social wrongs and provide economic growth where there was now economic stagnation. There might yet be great cities in the Arctic. There might also be battles over ownership – because it wasn't until someone else wanted what you'd got that they bothered to fight for it.

But most of these questions wouldn't be answered, or the dreams either fulfilled or broken, for months; years even. In the case of the biologists, they wouldn't know the significance of what they'd found while collecting specimens from the *Hudson* for anything up to five years after the voyage ended. For them, the real work was in the long months and years in the labora-tory examining their specimens. What was it Ed Bousfield of the National Museum in Ottawa had said? Something to the effect that Hudson 70 would let him spend a month poking around by himself in the footsteps of Darwin in the Beagle Channel area just north of Cape Horn – and that that month would provide him with work for the rest of his life. And Bous-field was no older than Mann himself, who would have his forty-fourth birthday somewhere at sea in the Antarctic.

That was the trouble with scientific endeavour. It took what, to a layman, was an unconscionable length of time both in the research itself and then in the application of what had been discovered. It had taken thirty years for the quantum leap in man's knowledge represented by Albert Einstein's gloriously simple $E=MC^2$ to result in successfully controlled nuclear fission. Reginald Fessenden, a largely forgotten Canadian whose fame had been unfairly eclipsed by Marconi, had discovered how to transmit the sound of the human voice by radio waves at the turn of the century, yet it was not until a quarter of a century later that radio was in widespread use. There were many such examples in history of the time lag between a discovery and its application.

But apart from the time that would be involved after the voyage had ended, there was the seeming paradox that each question answered, each new piece of knowledge acquired and defined, would itself pose a dozen more question. And that, Mann had long since concluded, was one of the reasons for the widening gulf between scientist and the layman who was, after all, largely responsible for paying for the scientist's work. It was hard for a non-scientist to accept that success in science often meant not so much answering questions as being able to pose new ones – and then to go off in pursuit of more answers that would in turn pose even more questions.

It would all add to the reservoir of human knowledge, which is already too big for any one man to get his mind around and the spawning ground of the new Mandarins of Power – The Experts. It has to do with the rate at which knowledge is being acquired. In the 1970s man would probably learn more about the nature of things than in all the centuries between the birth of Christ and the industrial revolution. In such a world, The Experts have power to a degree that even alarms them. However astute a politician or wise a statesman, their decisions must today be based on the guidance of experts. In a decade in which the quality of life and the future, not the quantity and today, is or should be the pre-eminent concern of any sane government, the scientist finds himself in the front rank of The Experts; the catalyst of the decisions that will shape tomorrow's world. And yet that reservoir of human knowledge is at one and the same time so vast and so full of conflicting answers that no halfway honest man could be sure he was right on a subject he'd spent a lifetime studying.

Man's response to the explosion of knowledge and awareness in the past century and a half has generally been to retreat to specialization; to shut himself off from those areas not of direct concern to him. The scientist, typically, has begun wearing blinkers so he's better able to study one small fragment of the painfully incomplete picture of the universe. Such men rarely look up from their fragment to see where it might fit in the whole. It takes a rare courage to face one's own minor role in the scheme of things, either as a human being or, say, as a scientist. Result: experts working in the same field – two biologists, say, or two physicists – often can't talk to one another comprehensibly because their chosen areas of study may be too specialised for the other to understand. They are Experts, and it is on the advice of such men that the leaders of humanity – desperately reaching for a picture of the whole to measure the consequences of any decision – must depend for guidance.

The Experts are, one way or another, financed by the taxpayer. And yet how can the ordinary man who ultimately foots the bill understand what these new Mandarins of Power are doing and saying if they themselves can't readily talk to one another. Knowledge is power today; ideas the seminal source of wealth. The scientist influences or changes every aspect of the human condition, from a man's sex life through his work ethic (or lack of it) and eating habits to his own sense of *amour propre*. Since he cannot or does not understand what scientists are doing or saying, the ordinary man has largely lost whatever control of his own destiny he once had. He emerged from the feudal serfdom of the Middle Ages to be held in thrall by the induced compulsion to buy a better life; and now he has he is once more in bondage – to The Experts. And yet it's not a monstrous conspiracy. No one, least of all the scientist, really wants to take over the world. It is simply that the obvious dangers of individual man knowing more and more about less and less are coming to pass – and the most obvious danger is that the average man could end up with less free will and control over his own life and the course of the world than he has ever had. And if this is so, it's because of the confusion of the profusion of knowledge.

Yet somehow man must learn to live with and manage the knowledge that his curiosity and imagination – the qualities that set him apart from the animals – will endlessly acquire. If one thing is sure it is that the quest for knowledge will never stop. Hudson 70 was, in a sense, a voyage without end since it was an expedition to explore the new frontiers of this century; the frontiers of human knowledge. And in the end it would probably pose more questions than it actually answered. It was, in a sense, a voyage to the edge of the known world; almost to both north and south poles, and to the borders of man's knowledge of his world. In that sense they were no less adventurous explorers than Champlain or Henry Hudson. Each scientific programme – and there were over forty in all – was designed to find another piece of the jigsaw that would some day add up to a picture of the oceans; of what popular writers were fond of calling "inner space". And understanding "inner space" was becoming increasingly vital as man realized that the earth as a source of life and life-sustaining elements was not inexhaustible.

Lying on his bunk, Ced Mann remembered that as a boy in Auckland, New Zealand, he often saw religious fanatics marching around with placards announcing: REPENT NOW FOR THE END OF THE WORLD IS NIGH. Today's prophets of doom were also the Gods of the age of science who could explain, with alarming scientific fluency, how man was destroying his "oikos" – Greek for home and root of the word ecology – and had already reached the point that within a score or so years there would either be a new ice age, or conversely, a crisis in the atmosphere which would heat up the earth's surface so that it would melt the ice packs and destroy life as we know it. And yet all such prophecies of gloom and doom were based on hypothesis; on conjecture that, thought Mann, might be well-informed but was still conjecture. We need to *know*, and that was what Hudson 70 was all about. It is easy to observe the effect of man's carelessness on land, since it is there to see and to study. But what of the oceans? The oceans provide a large proportion of the oxygen that man needs; they clean the atmosphere of toxic gases that start out as brown smog over New York and Tokyo, Toronto and Moscow. Life on land is possible only because the oceans are there.

As overpopulation becomes obvious man reassures himself with the belief that when all else fails the scientists will find a way to cultivate and harvest the seas. But is it possible? Do the oceans contain enough food? Can they be made to produce more? Have we already polluted them so thoroughly that they, too, are "dying" just as Lake Erie, a great inland sea, is dying from an overdose of man's effluent?

With characteristic caution, Mann was neither an optimist nor pessimist about the fate of the world. His son, who at fifteen was still young enough to regard his father as the font of all wisdom, had asked only a few days before the departure of the *Hudson* whether the world really was likely to choke on its own wastes. Perhaps it was the realization that the boy was one of the legatees of the earth, but Mann found himself saying that while he didn't think things were that bad it was true that there had to be an end to a plundering of the earth's resources and to the population explosion, "otherwise we will be in trouble – we've obviously got to tread warily until we know a few more answers."

And that was what Hudson 70 was all about – finding some answers, or at least clues to them.

The *Hudson* had sailed at precisely 3.30 p.m., November 19, on schedule to the minute. Now it was 5.00 p.m. They had altered course a few degrees south so the swell was now on the starboard bow and the ship was not rolling as badly as it had been. Ced Mann realized his queasiness had disappeared; he was even hungry. He went to the dining room for dinner and found Dave Butler's pessimism unjustified. The chef had obviously not been enduringly upset. The first of the two choices on the menu was roast beef, presumably Minister Joe Greene's beef. It was a little overdone, but good. Sadly, there weren't many people around to enjoy it. Of the twenty-two scientists on board, only seven were well enough to face dinner. Dave Butler was missing, too. He was, he had announced, on a diet to get down from 230 pounds to 190 by the time they reached Rio. He would, he said, follow his own diet in the privacy of his cabin to avoid temptations.

The *Hudson* was built by the Saint John Shipbuilding and Dry Dock Company in Saint John, New Brunswick, and was designed as a hydrographic survey ship – that is, a vessel whose job is to chart the contours and nature of the seabed. All maritime nations maintain fleets of such ships to chart as much of the oceans, estuaries, rivers and other open waterways as possible. Until 1960 it was to this relatively unsophisticated, though necessary, area that the federal government allocated most of the money spent on studying the oceans. But then, on the principle of better late than never, Canada jumped into the business of oceanography, the detailed and systematic study of the nature of the oceans themselves, not just the contours of the ocean floor. As a result construction on the *Hudson* was halted midway through; the ship was redesigned and the vessel that was finally launched in April 1963 was the western world's biggest and most sophisticated oceanographic laboratory; by the time of Hudson 70 only the Russians had a bigger ocean sciences vessel. Oceanography is even now an infant science – indeed, it is not a science in itself; rather it is the marriage of many disciplines, all dedicated to studying the oceans. Canada was belated in its recognition of the need for oceanography, much tardier than the older maritime nations of Europe and several decades behind the u.s., but the *Hudson* was, and remains, a symbol of the nation's determination to catch up.

Only another sailor can really understand the special relationship that exists between a seaman and his ship. Predictably, this relationship increases in intensity in direct proporton to the amount of responsibility the sailor has aboard. Thus the officers have stronger feelings about their ship than the deckhands – and the captain's feelings are the deepest of all. Those captains who have reached the pinnacle of their professions by acquiring an ocean-going master mariner's certificate and command are of necessity men of considerable imagination and intelligence, and such men tend to have love-hate feelings about

26

their ships; the inanimate structures of steel plates, rivets, nuts, bolts, wood, wire, pipes, and engines that leave dockyards and seem to acquire distinct personalities the moment the captain first treads the bridge. They are always female personalities, perhaps because ships and the sea remain a man's world and if you can't take your wife or mistress along the ship makes a handy emotional substitute.

When Hudson 70 began Captain David Butler had been to sea with his ship only three times; once as a junior officer when he first joined the Marine Sciences Branch, Ships Division, of the Department of Energy, Mines and Resources in 1965, then twice during the three months since he had been transferred from the Great Lakes and given command of the *Hudson*. Thus he wasn't yet entirely at ease with his ship. When he thought about it, which wasn't often, he tended to the view that he would have to go through a period of adjustment, just as when he first married. But he had already begun to think of the *Hudson* as a very well-bred, reliable woman, which was more than he was prepared to say about many of the cargo and cable ships on which he had served as a merchant seaman and junior officer.

The *Hudson* is 296 feet long, has a beam of fifty feet and, painted gleaming white, looks like a cross between a high-bowed icebreaker, which she is, and a luxury yacht, which she isn't. With four diesel motors which generate electricity for the two main engines, each of which drives one of the twin screws, she can cruise at fourteen knots, has a top speed of more than sixteen knots and a range of 15,000 miles. She also has a bow thruster – propeller mounted in the bow which can drive the ship to either port or starboard and provide the delicate manoeuvreability which a ship needs when it is vital to stand almost dead still in the heaving ocean, as it is when scientific work is under way. She is equipped with stabilizer tanks, which is part of the reason why she is a relatively comfortable ship to sail in. There are four decks. The main deck houses all the crew's cabins and those of some of the officers and junior scientific staff, plus the crew's mess, ship's hospital, laundry and, among other facilities, one of the two large stern laboratories (the other is below the main deck). The next deck up houses the

27

main accommodation for the twenty to twenty-five scientists usually aboard when the *Hudson* is at sea. The Chief Scientist has a sleeping cabin and a small stateroom-cum-office. The other cabins have one or two bunks apiece, and there is one suite of two cabins separated by the luxury of a private bathroom, so arranged for the occasions on which women scientists are aboard. This deck also houses the officers' and scientists' dining room, the library of scientific reference works and another laboratory. The next deck up houses the deck officers' accommodation, the captain's cabin and the lounge – a large, comfortably if chintzily furnished place that is both scientists' club, officers' mess and communal bar, where liquor and beer cost the same – seventeen cents a shot or a bottle. The bridge is on the upper deck, and aft of the bridge itself is another large laboratory used mainly by physical oceanographers, geophysicists, geologists. Aft of that is the ship's computer room which houses the complex electronic recording equipment used by geophysicists, geologists and hydrographers. Since the *Hudson* constantly charts the contours of the seabed and also never stops making other electronic measurements, there is always someone on watch at the control console. If it grows lonely you can always challenge the computer to chess, tic-tac-toe, blackjack or poker; someone programmed it for these games just before Hudson 70 began. The same scientist was also presumably responsible for feeding it a random word selection programme. On activating this particular corner of the computer's memory bank, it starts producing prose by selecting words at random from a vocabulary stored in its memory bank. Since the words had to be put there in the first place and it is aboard an oceanographic vessel, the computer leans heavily toward oceanographic subjects. It works on the same principle that once prompted a statistician to claim the law of probability meant that a thousand orang-outangs playing with a thousand typewriters would among them eventually produce all the plays of Shakespeare, or at least the words he used. Sometimes the computer's prose is gobbledegook, but it is said that it once accused a rather pompous senior scientist of having an affair with his secretary and of planning to run off with the mess funds.

Even when compared with the accommodation aboard a

modern freighter, the *Hudson* is not luxurious. Most crewmen and scientists sleep two to a cabin. The cabins are small – two men standing up in them constitute a human traffic jam – and in some the plumbing is incessantly noisy, producing an arpeggio of glugs and gurgles when the ship rolls even gently from one side to the other. The nearest evidence of governmental extravagance is four paintings hung in the upper decks. They are of the Chateau Frontenac, Lake Louise, Algonquin Provincial Park in Ontario and the foothills of Alberta. All look as though their artistic origins were in one of the paint-by-number sets which are the second most popular off-watch pastime of the crew. (The first is playing elaborate hi-fi sets very loudly; the third is assembling plastic model boats, cars and planes.) Even the air-conditioning is not a luxury item, since much of the scientific equipment must be kept at constant temperatures and a cooling system is vital for equatorial work.

As the ship passed Bermuda, headed south-east toward the equator, the scientists slowly began emerging from their cabins, seasickness ended but, as Navigating Officer Roy Gould said, "looking like little green men." And, anyway, their cabins had become more uncomfortable than the gently heaving open decks; the air-conditioning system appeared to have broken down. Butler wasn't particularly suprised. The system had been used only a couple of times in the ship's life since most of its work involved relatively short cruises to the North Atlantic and the Arctic, where heating was more important than cooling. It was, however, a minor crisis. The scientists were complaining about the heat to Ced Mann; the temperature in the room housing the gravimeter – the delicate piece of equipment which measures variations in the earth's gravitational field – soared to 108 degrees centigrade, and Sam Lambert, the burly and explosive chief engineer, who was said to be able to curse for thirty minutes with Shakespearian inventiveness, poured abuse on scientists and shipyard with exemplary impartiality. Then he found that most of the air-conditioning vents had been stuffed with newspapers, rags or old clothes by sailors and scientists who used this technique to control the climate in their cabins. Ced Mann found his cooling vents plugged with a three-year-old copy of the Halifax *Chronicle-Herald*. The gravimeter was cooled off by borrowing the portable air-conditioner from the ship's hospital, with ship's surgeon Dr. Louis Rustige warning that, science or not, he'd want it back if he had patients in the tropics. In fact, he never was to have a patient in the hospital itself, but there would be other, more complex medical problems to haunt him and the entire ship.

By now the *Hudson* was three days out. That evening the lounge was filled with recovered scientists who felt less ashamed of their reaction to the Atlantic swell when Captain Butler told them that the stabilizing tanks had not been working. They felt even better when Navigating Officer Gould owned that he too was always sick the first two days at sea, though he called it "landsickness – a nostalgia for the land". And they discovered, too, that the reason they hadn't known earlier that Dave Butler had brought a pet German Shephard puppy aboard was because the dog had also been seasick. Butler appeared, pale and bleary-eyed, explaining that he had had to get up every hour during the night to feed pablum through an eyedropper to the three-week-old puppy. He had dubbed it Nicodemus, which was singularly appropriate in view of the trouble it was to cause later. That evening Mann and Butler met on the bridge, as they did most evenings, and both felt for the first time that Hudson 70 had really begun. For three days the ship had been quiet; the companionways deserted, the lounge empty. Now everyone was up and about and even their complaints – mostly about the air-conditioning and the fact that only heads of departments would be issued bottles of liquor for consumption in their cabins – were somehow evidence that the voyage was really under way.

They made an improbable picture leaning over the polished wooden rail on the open wing of the bridge. Ced Mann is not only small (five feet eight inches), he has the small-boned, lean and flat-bellied frame of a jockey. His face is thin and bony, its planes angular, almost geometric, and because he smiles rarely it is the more attractive and infectious when he does than if he were among those to whom smiling and laughing is as much part of their conversation as talking. When Ced Mann smiles the whole sombre face cracks open and his forehead furrows into four great creases and companions are suffused with pleasure:

Ced Mann has smiled in their company. It is, however, a misleading emotion, since Mann is a warm, thoughtful and occasionally gregarious man. It's just that it doesn't show on him the way the same qualities do on, say, Dave Butler. Which is one reason why the two men mostly responsible for Hudson 70 presented such a study in contrasts whenever they were together. The other reason is that Butler is over six feet tall, and at the time of the departure of the *Hudson* was, as his wife complained, almost as wide. Even when not overweight he is a big man, inclined to be paunchy, with a fleshy, mobile face that has puffy eyes that look sleepy but aren't, as though the eyelids have swelled up to defend eyeballs that have spent a lifetime squinting into a never ending grey horizon.

Leaning on the rail Mann and Butler smoked, gossiped, tried to anticipate tomorrow's problems, agreed that it was sad that Walter Kettle, the former captain of the *Hudson*, had died a few months earlier when in his mid-forties. Dusk was coming, bringing that magic, melancholy light of a dying day. Suddenly, for no good reason, a rainbow appeared. The sky was clear; there were no showers; the sea was calm and the *Hudson* moved easily, comfortably, making almost no bow wave. And yet there was a rainbow which, as Mann would record later in his diary, seemed to enter the sea just off the starboard bow. Ced Mann, scientist, thought it probably had something to do with humidity, the amount of moisture in the air. Ced Mann, the architect of Hudson 70 who had dreamed about the voyage for two years, thought that there might be some less rational explanation. Rainbows were omens of good luck, weren't they? Well, there was a long way to go and they'd need all the luck they could get.

In fact, Hudson 70 really began almost a week later, at 6.00 a.m., November 30, when the ship reached its first station, the point at which the equator and longitude 30 meet. It was there that the first of the daily scientific programmes was conducted. From now on there would be at least one "station" a day. The ship would heave to while the scientists went to work. On station, that work followed a pattern that would vary only a little throughout Hudson 70. It was built around a routine of measuring the temperature of the oceans, collecting samples of ocean water from different depths to determine its chemical structure, and collecting specimens of plankton, the minute plant life and creatures that are the grass and the insects of the seas. All these procedures take hours, but are relatively simple. The hard work of analysis takes place in laboratories, sometimes years later. The oceans' temperature is taken by lowering a bathysonde, a complex electronic thermometer, to the seabed. As it descends, it records changes in temperature. Physical oceanographers trying to determine the way the ocean waters circulate around the world can, from the temperature variations, draw conclusions about the source of the water at that point on the charts. It is this kind of information, for instance, which confirms the belief that the Atlantic is made up of four distinct moving layers of water which originate in both Arctic and Antarctic.

Collecting samples of water at different depths so its chemical structure can be analysed is a much longer process than that of taking the ocean's temperature. To do this a cable is lowered from the ship and open-ended containers, or bottles, are fixed to the cable at pre-determined points. Once the cable is extended the bottles are closed automatically, trapping a sample of the water at a known depth. Since the ocean is sampled from surface to seabed, these water casts are usually done in two stages; one cast for the upper layers and another for the deeps. At times in the South Atlantic and the Pacific Iver Duedall, the ship's resident chemist from Halifax round to Vancouver, collected water samples from almost four miles down. Each day's station would also involve collecting samples of plankton either by towing a trawl on the surface or by lowering an open net into the ocean, closing it at the required depth. This sampling of the oceans by the same people and the same techniques over the 58,000 miles the *Hudson* sailed during the Hudson 70 voyage was to be one of the expedition's major contributions to ocean science. Many such measurements have been taken in the oceans, even in waters sailed by the *Hudson*, but they were all taken by different expeditions and different people using different techniques. Thus comparisons of, say, the chemical analyses of water samples taken at the same depths but by different men using different methods are suspect; the element of possible error is, in scientific terms, perilously large. The Hudson 70 measurements were, however, standardized and often taken by the same scientist: Iver Duedall, for instance, would sample and then spend years analyzing and defining the chemical structure of the Atlantic, Antarctic and Pacific. Hudson 70 measurements would therefore be what scientists describe as "internally consistent".

This, too, was true of the Hudson 70 measurements of the ocean bed along its course, which for long stretches included recording the magnetic and gravity variations in the earth's crust, and in the Pacific these would lead to a discovery which would change the face of the earth as drawn on marine charts and leave the name *Hudson* indelibly engraved on those charts for the first time since explorer Henry Hudson, for whom the ship was named, earned his niche in history in the seventeenth century. Still later in the voyage these same measurements would play a part in changing the nature of resource exploitation in Canada's Arctic, and at the same time spark political repercussions that would radically affect the long-term planning in both Ottawa and Washington, and other capitals where raw materials and their accessibility are regarded as weights to put on the balance of power.

But on November 30 the work on station was the start of what would become a routine, its ultimate significance unpredictable. That routine was often supplemented, depending on the scientists aboard and their requirements, but in itself it never varied. The additional work on this first leg of the voyage mostly involved setting a young Korean scientist adrift in a small boat – and being awakened for breakfast by a series of loud bangs somewhere between 6.00 a.m. and 7.00 a.m. Oreste Bluy was firing sound waves at the so-called scattering layer of fish life by dropping charges of dynamite overboard in the hope he would learn more about the effects on submarine detection equipment of the little-known creatures that live in the eternal dusk of 300 feet to a mile beneath the surface.

The existence of this scattering layer of marine life was unsuspected until the last war, when scientists testing anti-submarine sonar equipment off California found they were picking up interference from a point well above the sea bed. On sonar screens it looked like snowflakes, and was so extensive that even if there had been the solid blip of a submarine on the screen it would have been lost in the bewildering pattern of interference. Submarine detection is never as easy as it may sound to the layman. Apart from the obvious difficulty of finding a submerged object in the wastes of any ocean, the layers of water in the seas vary in temperature and salinity and so distort the beam of sound from the sonar transmitter. A submarine within range of a warship's sonar equipment may go undetected because it is beneath a belt of cold water which deflects the beam of sound. These problems had been bad enough during a war dominated much of the time by submarines. The discovery that there was an additional source of interference was a further blow to the efforts of scientists trying to improve submarine detection.

Marine biologists went to work and found that the "fish" that scattered the sonar signals (hence the name "scattering layer") were a hitherto largely unknown family of marine life rarely longer than eight inches and never more than eighteen. They are bizarre creatures, some of them nightmarish in appearance and all of them without any apparent resemblance to the fish that man knows and eats. The one thing all have in common is a gas bladder which they can inflate or deflate at will. At dusk, the tiny zoo-plankton on which they feed move up toward the warmer, lighter waters of the surface and the scattering layer fish move up with them by taking oxygen from the water, converting it to air and inflating the bladders so they keep pace with their food supply in its daily vertical migration. A sonar sound wave sent probing the ocean hits these bladders and the membranes distort different frequencies of sound in different ways.

When the scattering layer was first discovered sonar equipment was relatively uncomplicated and used only one or two higher frequencies of sound waves. It was possible to predict and offset the effect the layer would have on these frequencies. Since the war, sonar has grown vastly more complex and generally uses a wider range of low frequency sounds. These low-frequency sound waves are more susceptible to distortion by the scattering layer, and because of its vital anti-submarine role in the defence of North America, Canada has made a major investment in studying this particular freak of nature. Over what area does the layer extend? How thick and just how deep is it in different parts of the ocean at different times of the year? How far up and down does it move during the day? Does it flourish in waters of a particular salinity level or temperature? And, above all, how does it affect the different sound frequencies used by anti-submarine sonar? It is this last question that Oreste Bluy was trying to answer although, by correlating his work with the other routine measurements taken during Hudson 70, Defence Research Establishment scientists will be able to at least partially answer the others. In fact, Bluy's work posed more questions for biologists: He found several areas where there are in fact three distinct levels of the scattering layer.

Bluy, a slight and shy bachelor of thirty with a master's degree in electrical engineering, had devoted years to measuring the effects of the scattering layer in the North Atlantic – but had never actually seen one of the fish. Until Hudson 70 that had somehow not seemed important; all that mattered was his ability to record the distortions of sound through the low-range sonar frequencies. The tidy rows of calculations were exquisite in themselves; the life forms that they represented meant little. Aboard Hudson 70 he was meeting men in other fields of science – biologists, chemists, geologists, physical oceanographers, palaeontologists. During the four years he had been working at the Defence Research Establishment, he had at times been disturbed by the fact that he was, in a sense, blinkered by his own expertise. He had consoled himself with George Bernard Shaw's remark about man growing to know more and more about less and less – and with the belief that it was inevitable. Now, aboard ship, he began to comprehend the staggering complexity of oceanography as a science. And he also saw for the first time the kind of creatures that make up the scattering layer.

Two biologists from the Royal Ontario Museum in Toronto, Richard Beamish and Dick Zurbrigge, were on board to catch samples of the creatures in the scattering layer. On October 30, the day of the first station, and five hours after Bluy had let off his first pre-breakfast explosion, the ship dropped a sampling net down into the depths where Bluy had located the layer. As it was upended and the wriggling creatures slithered around the deck – tentacles, whiskers, huge eyes, monstrous mouths, unimaginable shapes, colours that changed in the light – Oreste Bluy saw for the first time what those tiny snowflakes on his sonar screen actually were. Beamish began sorting through the specimens, giving the crew who clustered round a running commentary, explaining what the scattering layer was, exclaiming when he found a specimen that was new, at least to him. Later, in the library where scientists gathered in a ritual coffee klatsch twice a day, Bluy the electronics man and Beamish the biologist discussed ways they could work together. Bluy's early morning experiments would locate the position of the scattering layer and he had perfected his measuring techniques to the point where he could even tell biologists the size of the creatures that were in it, though he had never seen the creatures themselves. Bluy told Beamish: "You know, I'm in the business of making measurements. For some people that's enough; I suppose in an overall way that's enough for me. It's a problem, defining the effects of these creatures, and I like the challenge of solving it. But now I'm getting some idea of what the whole picture is. Just a glimpse now and again, but that's enough to be a bonus. Though how you tell the difference between a hatchet fish and a myctophid I'll never know. To me most of them look like something out of an attack of the DTs."

Ced Mann was privately pleased to see the flowering of Bluy's interest in oceanography as a total field of scientific exploration, largely because he himself had spent a large slice of his career working on anti-submarine sonar. Mann also found himself wondering whether Bluy's awakening interest in those "other parts of the picture" might lead him to the same feelings about military projects that had once disturbed him. Perhaps so. Months later, after many weeks talking with scientists of other disciplines, Bluy was not only to report the findings of military value – but also to produce charts that showed where the scattering layer was heaviest and could most readily be harvested for food. There were, he found, three and a half tons per square mile at the equator in the Atlantic and about eight tons per square mile in the area of the Antarctic convergence, where Atlantic and Antarctic waters meet and cause an upwelling of water from the ocean bottom, water rich in life-sustaining nutrients from the deeps. No one is likely, however, to see a hatchet fish or myctophid on their dinner table. As Bluy told Beamish: "You couldn't give a ton of them to a starving man in Canada – he'd run a mile at the sight of them." Even so, these creatures are a potential source of fish protein – though they look so unappetizing they'd have to be mashed up and turned into fish cakes, perhaps to be marketed as Bladder-burgers.

In one way or another, the potential of the oceans as a food source was to be a concern of most of the biologists aboard the several legs of Hudson 70. The microscope may have been focused on, say, the *Cosomatous pterapod* (which is, anyway, too small to see clearly with the naked eye) or on the amount of ribonucleic acid in a given quantity of zoo-plankton, but ultimately all the biologists were seeking scraps of evidence that, given the state of world food supplies and the burgeoning population, is needed to determine just how much food mankind can expect to harvest from the sea. And of all the scientists, Chung Choi was the one most clearly dedicated to trying to determine just how well the hungry can be fed from the oceans – and fed now.

Chung Choi is a botanist from Seoul, South Korea. At twenty-nine he had been in Canada studying for an M.Sc. in oceanography at Dalhousie University, Halifax, for two years prior to Hudson 70, and he was aboard as an assistant to Dr. Walton Watt, whose aim was to study the "sweat" of the primary, and smallest, life form on earth – phyto-plankton.

Science does not know how life began. Perhaps the moment of Creation came with a flash of lightning – a sudden burst of electrical energy – at a point in the earth's history when the necessary chemicals were present; perhaps it was that which was the genesis of the long chain of happenstance and evolution which produced man. What science does know is that it is vegetable matter that makes life possible, and the smallest and most primitive vegetable matter (and therefore probably the first life on earth) is the phyto-plankton that is often called the grass of the oceans. It grows in the surface areas (or aphotic zone) of the oceans where sunlight penetrates, and it is like snow in that it comes in all the shapes that man can dream of: squares, oblongs, strips, stars, triangles. All phyto-plankton is uni-cellular – that is, it consists of one living cell which reproduces by dividing itself. Much of it floats alone in the oceans, and these specimens you cannot see with the naked eye: a bottle of water containing a rich crop of phyto-plankton simply looks cloudy. Other phyto-plankton live in colonies; cling together to form masses of green that appear to be one large floating plant.

All of it survives by the process of photosynthesis, by which phyto-plankton uses the energy of the sun to convert inorganic chemicals, which fish and animal life cannot use, to organic chemicals, which they can. For instance, the sun's rays stimulate phyto-plankton to absorb inorganic carbon (carbon dioxide, which is poisonous to oxygen-breathing creatures) and convert it to organic carbon, which then becomes one of the basic building blocks of all other life forms, perhaps the most important element of all. In gross oversimplification, this process of photosynthesis carried out by all plant life on land or in the oceans takes inorganic chemicals from water and air and turns them into carbohydrates and proteins on which all animal life, man included, lives.

On land, insects and birds and some larger animals eat grass, leaves and other plants; in the oceans the tiniest and simplest animals, the zoo-plankton, live on phyto-plankton. So do some larger creatures. And so, in the prey-predator relationship that exists throughout nature, those organic chemicals created by phyto-plankton are passed up the food chain from the smallest and weakest creatures to the biggest and most aggressive, the latter being man. In the process of photosynthesis all plants absorb the gases in the atmosphere and elements in the waters that are potentially lethal to animal life – carbon dioxide, nitrogen, et al – and convert them so they become nutrients, not poisons. In doing so, the plants cleanse the air and water and manufacture oxygen and other life-support elements. Plants and animals, then, co-exist in mutual interdependency. Plants live on the waste products of animals and the earth itself, and their principle waste product is oxygen, which all animals, birds and marine life must have.

Fairly recently, however, it has been found that phyto-plankton not only gives off oxygen as a waste product, it "sweats" as well. This "sweat" is also made up of organic chemicals, and becomes part of the total food supply of the oceans. And it was this which Dr. Walton Watt and Chung Choi, who earned a place in the history of the Hudson 70 as "the jolly green Korean", were studying aboard the *Hudson*.

Watt had adapted an established method of measuring the rate of photosynthesis and phyto-plankton growth for his purposes. In an experimental technique which originated in Sweden, two sampling bottles are suspended on a cable into the ocean. One bottle is plain transparent glass; the other is painted black. At the required depth, the necks of the bottles are opened and seawater from that level floods in. They are left suspended there during the peak sunlight hours – 10.00 a.m. to 2.00 p.m. Photosynthesis takes place in the plain glass container, but not in the opaque bottle because no sunlight reaches the phyto-plankton it contains. The customary procedure is to have a tiny isotope of radioactive carbon in both bottles, so that as the phyto-plankton consumes the inorganic carbon in the water it also absorbs some of the radioactive carbon. The growth rate is determined by pouring the water away and measuring the amount of radioactivity in the phyto-plankton against that in the opaque bottle.

Watt had turned the last stage of the experiment upside down – he wanted to pour away the phyto-plankton and keep the water from the plain glass bottle. By analysing its chemical and nutrient structure and comparing it with the sample from the opaque bottle he hoped to determine the degree to which phyto-plankton "sweat" had enriched the water.

It was Watt's experiment, and Chung Choi played the part of scientist's apprentice. His job was to take the samples. On November 30, he suspended the sampling bottles from a buoy, lowered the buoy to the ocean and tethered it to the side of the ship. But to stay as nearly as possible in precisely the same location the *Hudson* had to manoeuvre, and that broke the tether. The buoy drifted away and had to be retrieved by launch. The next day Chung Choi put to sea in a ship's lifeboat manned by three sailors from Newfoundland. By the time the four-hour experiment had ended, Chung Choi had suffered and recovered from his second bout of seasickness – and the boat had drifted eight miles from the *Hudson*. Worried, Dave Butler ordered that in future the lifeboat should be tethered to the ship – and for the next ten days Chung Choi and the three sailors sat in the lifeboat as it bobbed and heaved at the end of a 1,000-foot line, and when he wasn't lying down beneath the awning rigged up to protect them from the tropic sun the Korean botanist and the seamen talked.

He had little in common with them, but as he later wrote to a friend: "They are a strange, fine people, the Newfie. They are humble people, not well educated, but magnificent. Their language is foul and they are not learned, but they have full hearted minds." He also grew to admire their courage. On Wednesday, December 10, there was a line squall, so called because such storms march across the sky as a line of sullen clouds set in limitless blue. Within three minutes sheeting rain hid the lifeboat from the *Hudson* while a seventy m.p.h. wind whipped the sea, calm just minutes earlier, until the waves were fifteen to twenty feet high, and foaming. The *Hudson* deck crew began hauling the lifeboat in, and doing it oh, so slowly, for fear of pulling its bow into one of the waves and so causing it to be swamped. In the lifeboat, coxswain Frank Durnford had the engine running and was able to keep the lifeboat bow-on to the waves.

Through the rain Butler could see the lifeboat bobbing around, corklike. He ordered the *Hudson* swung around so the wind would break on the ship's superstructure, and slowly the lifeboat was inched alongside. At one moment a wave would toss it high so that it was almost level with the main deck and in danger of being splintered against the ship's plates; the next it would sink in a trough and seemingly be almost level with the ship's keel. Struggling, the seamen in the lifeboat caught and attached the cables from the lifeboat davits on the *Hudson*'s deck, and slowly they were winched up and inboard. As Butler told Ced Mann later: "I was really worried, and so was Chung Choi – God, he was green with seasickness or fright, or both. But Durnford seemed to think it was about as exciting as a joyride around St. John's harbour. It's almost impossible to worry a Newfie in a small boat." Chung Choi freely admitted

40

his terror. He sat down to write to his parents in Seoul: "On all the stations the boat was so little and the swell of the ocean so big that I felt quite ill. During the storm there were streams of rain that got into our eyes so we could not really see the *Hudson*. The waves were very high, and it seemed we would climb the mountain of one side and then slide down the other. The crew all seemed very confident, but I must confess to being very afraid. The canvas awning under which we sheltered from the sun was ripped away by the storm and these men from Newfoundland showed they were fine seamen. We could hear the siren of the *Hudson* and it got louder and louder as we got nearer. It was most difficult when we reached the ship because we bobbed up and down as much as 20 feet at a time. The next day was the last station I was to do, and although I went out in the lifeboat to do it and there was no incident, I was very glad that it was the last station."

In the event, Chung Choi never sent that letter for fear of worrying his parents. His father is a Seoul high school teacher who approved when Chung Choi decided his post-graduate work should be the study of oceanography even though it meant studying in North America. South Korea is not a maritime nation and there is an almost superstitious fear of the sea, even among the sophisticated middle classes to which Chung Choi belongs. Indeed, Choi himself could not honestly claim to have any love of the sea. He had chosen oceanography as his post-graduate study area because of the awareness that food is shorter in South Korea than in many nations, and that the population explosion meant the country would have to look for alternative sources of food. As a botanist, he remained convinced that within the foreseeable future South Korea would be forced to break the natural food chain in the oceans and harvest the bottom, the phyto-plankton, instead of the top, the higher life forms of edible fish. Phyto-plankton *au gratin* may not sound very appetizing, but that's what Chung Choi believed the world was coming to – and South Korea sooner than most nations.

That last day out in the lifeboat Chung Choi spent more time talking with the three seamen. He had little in common with them but, since he wasn't much older than they, he felt obliged to try to be one of the boys. Which was difficult, since their conversation tended to dwell on Rio de Janiero, the amount they were going to drink there and the girls they were going to meet and pay with bonus vouchers from the Canadian Tire store in Halifax instead of real dollars. It was, for Chung Choi, an immersion course in the more rudimentary relation-ships that can exist between men and women in non-Asian societies. In South Korea, the social strata to which he belonged had long since abandoned the practice of the arranged marriage, yet even now parents had great influence on their children when it came to the choice of companions of the opposite sex. In Chung Choi's case it was expected that his parents would seek out friends with a "suitable" daughter, and then both sets of parents would create opportunities for their children to meet and, perhaps, mate. Chung Choi pondered this system of finding a wife, and measured it against the polarized extreme – the random, promiscuous selection of a female companion that the seamen were discussing. This, he felt, was not appealing. On the other hand, he could see merits in the more casual relation-ships he had observed in Halifax between men students and emancipated Canadian girls, though the divorce rate seemed to be so high that it would indicate the "true love" system didn't work particularly well either. It was a difficult situation for a man thrust from one culture in to another, and while he had not been lonely these last two years in Halifax he had found relationships with Canadian girls difficult. And as his father pointed out, it was about time he began to think of marriage.

Chung Choi was to leave the *Hudson* at Rio de Janiero. Back in Halifax he would find a letter from his parents saying they had met a charming couple who had a daughter, Sung Hee, whom he should meet. Chung Choi replied that she sounded nice. With their next letter his parents sent photographs. Chung Choi replied that, yes, he too thought Sung Hee very beautiful but that he must wait to meet her until he finished his work in Halifax and returned home to Korea. A few months later he received a phone call from New York. It was Sung Hee's father, who said that he and his wife had decided to travel to see some-thing of the world and that Sung Hee was with them. Would Chung Choi, the son of their friend at home in Seoul, care to visit them in New York? Chung Choi went; Sung Hee was as pretty as her picture, as charming as his father's description. Three weeks later Chung Choi and Sung Hee decided that their parents were right; they should marry. And they did.

The first leg of Hudson 70 was idyllic. Much later, taking stock of the catalogue of near disasters, conflicts, dramas that were the handmaidens of the expedition's considerable achievement, Dave Butler and Ced Mann were to look back on the voyage between Halifax and Rio as a period of blissful calm. After only four days sailing from Halifax the weather had become tropical. By day, off-duty scientists baked brown in the sun on the monkey island – the open upper deck above and behind the bridge. Flying fish danced across the deep blue sea. Idle seamen caught sharks, and Dr. Rustige shot them. By night there would be movies in the helicopter hangar aft – "The Girls of Pleasure Island", "How Green Is My Valley", "The World of Suzie Wong" – with the doors left open to catch the trade winds that sough through the tropics, cooling the night. After dinner, Ced Mann, other scientists and sometimes Butler would set up chairs on the open wing of the bridge, smoke, talk, try to spot the Green Flash.

The Green Flash is either myth or freak of nature, depending on your level of scepticism. It is said that in the tropics on a clear night, just as the last arc of the sun slips below the horizon, there is for one brief second a flash of brilliant green in the far sky. Ced Mann saw it first – Ced Mann, phlegmatic sometimes to the point of being taciturn, a man of whom the irrepressible technician Bruce Carson once said: "If they gave him the Nobel prize, his face would open up in that big grin and he'd just say, 'That's nice'." At the time Mann was standing at the bridge rail with Dave Butler. They were gloomily discussing the fact that Mann had been ordered by Ottawa to label "Made in Canada" all the appropriate scientific and electronic equipment aboard. It was to be for the benefit of visitors to the ship when in port, and because of the order Mann faced a dilemma. The idea was to show foreign government officials the products of Canadian industry, but of all the complex instruments aboard he could find only three that were Canadian-made. Suddenly Mann, who had been gazing abstractedly out to sea, paused and then said: "You know, Dave, I saw it. The Green Flash. Just then." Butler had missed it, but having seen it several times in his career at sea, he congratulated Mann – and the Green Flash Club was born.

Each night the scientists on the wing of the bridge would devote part of the evening to watching for the Green Flash. Before Rio only Russ Melanson, the hydrographer, claimed to have seen it – and the Green Flash Club was to thereafter be dormant for a few months until the *Hudson* reached the tropics in the Pacific. The membership list never would extend beyond a half dozen names and its benefits were dubious; Mann was later convinced that any scientist who did see it was probably wary of admitting the fact for fear of the derision that would be heaped on his head by sceptical colleagues.

With the Green Flash Club a major non-scientific preoccupation aboard, it was hardly surprising that the Case of the Captain's Pregnant Wife should assume more importance than, in retrospect, it deserved. The *Hudson* was steaming between stations one evening when the alarm bell in radio officer Philip Rafuse's cabin shrilled. The receiver in the radio shack had picked up a call on the distress frequency. Under international law radio officers spend two hours on and two hours off watch throughout the day, so an alarm bell was located in Rafuse's cabin in case he was off watch when a distress signal was picked up. Rafuse dashed to the radio room aft of the bridge, and found it was not a distress signal but an "urgent" message; the receiver was chattering out the morse code urgency call letters XXX – dash-dot-dot-dash repeated three times. He acknowledged the signal and took the message: URGENT ALL SHIPS. ANYONE HAVE DOCTOR ABOARD? Rafuse requested the other ship switch to the normal working frequency, and on doing so, the other ship identified itself as the Indian freighter *Jalakala*, then added: CAPTAIN'S WIFE ILL LAST TWO DAYS WITH FEVER 101-102.3 DEGREES STOP ASPIRIN GIVEN DAILY EVERY SIX HOURS STOP DIFFICULTY SWALLOWING STOP ALSO SUSPECT PREGNANCY STOP REQUEST MEDICO ADVICE WHETHER TO GIVE SULPHA TABLETS AS PENICILLIN REACTION UNKNOWN STOP END MESSAGE.

44

Rafuse called Butler, then Dr. Rustige. With Rafuse's finger on the morse key as interpreter, Rustige established that the captain's wife had never had penicillin before; that the *Jalakala* had penicillin injections aboard. Then Rustige sent his advice: DOCTOR ADVISES PENICILLIN REACTION IMPOSSIBLE FIRST TIME STOP GIVE HER TWO SHOTS MORNING AND NIGHT FOR FOUR DAYS AND NO MORE THAN EIGHT ASPIRINS DAILY STOP PUSH FLUIDS AND GOOD LUCK STOP.

And that, they all thought, was the end of a routine medical consultation at sea. Two hours later however the captain of the *Jalakala* was back on the air asking: MEDICO MESSAGE PATIENT HAD PENICILLIN BEFORE BUT ORALLY STOP REQUEST CONFIRM OK TO GIVE PENICILLIN INJECTION STOP HAVE ALSO ADRENALIN ABOARD STOP. Rustige, Butler and Rafuse began grinning. As veteran fathers they concluded that the problem wasn't a sick woman at sea, but a frightened husband whose wife was pregnant. Rustige dictated: IF PATIENT HAD NO REACTION BEFORE BELIEVE REACTION NOW UNLIKELY. Then Rustige left, saying that he hated to think what would happen when the lady started ordering pickles and ice cream at 2.00 a.m.

It hadn't ended though. Four hours later – by now in the middle of the night – the *Jalakala*'s anxious captain-cum-husband was back on the air pointing out his wife was probably pregnant and asking whether penicillin was safe in the circumstances. By now a little weary of it, Rustige told the Indian freighter: PENICILLIN OF ANY KIND BETTER THAN LEAVING SERIOUS INFECTION UNTREATED. He then went on to give elaborate instructions about the symptoms that would appear if the lady were penicillin allergic and the name of the drug that was an antidote to the allergy.

And with that the drama ended – to the annoyance of Rustige, Butler and Rafuse. They had gone to elaborate lengths to treat a sick and pregnant woman at sea, and to calm her worried husband. They expected a progress report by radio within a day or so, but the *Jalakala* called no more. "I hope," said Butler maliciously, "that the lady has quads. He deserves it."

2

Dave Butler decided he was happy, and then with a natural pessimism nourished by years at sea decided that it was time something went wrong since nothing had yet. The *Hudson* had sailed into Rio de Janiero on December 10 and now – at noon on December 20 – was sailing out, course almost due east, to pick up the 30th meridian again and turn south, bound for the treacherous latitudes called the Roaring Forties, where the winds are rarely less than forty-knot gales and the *Hudson* would sail in convoy with the great, eerily flat icebergs spawned by the glaciers of Antarctica that end in ice cliffs bordering the Weddell Sea.

The weather was still tropical: hot, hot days when seamen and scientists worked shirtless and in shorts, and cooler, sensuous and mostly starlit evenings. Apart from the unscheduled departure of a Polish oceanographer, Ced Mann's assistant, because of a stomach ulcer, and of a cook who had had to return to Halifax to tend to family problems, Butler could count no major problems. By Rio he had, by sticking to a high protein diet, lost thirty pounds and had weighed only 190, which meant he had to get the laundryman to cut his new dress uniform down to size. The *Hudson*, flying the Maple Leaf flag so rarely seen in South American ports, had almost become a must on sightseeing tours during the stopover in Rio Harbour. Gleaming white, she had inspired a rare flight of fancy in Ced Mann, who said that she looked like "a beautiful great yacht and you half-expected the Queen to come strolling down the gangplank." The principal social function, the reception for senior

46

Brazilian officials and the Canadian ambassador, had been enormously successful. It had been held on the open deck aft of the bridge one comfortably cool evening, and between them Bill Shaw, the Chief Steward, and Chef Claude Durin had staged a party that for elegance and food rivalled any that Butler could remember from his days sailing aboard cargo-liners on the run between the Caribbean and Britain. Butler assumed that in Rio Chef Durin had found a stack of letters from his girl in France. They were, he knew, unofficially en-gaged and Durin was travelling the world for a couple of years saving while he gave the relationship time to prove itself. But-ler had always thought that Durin's moods were in part dictated by the way he felt about his absence from the girl at any given moment.

The reception had in some ways been the high point of Butler's career. He had stood there, a tall and newly slender man with a slightly fleshy face, sun-crinkled brown eyes, and mop of still healthy hair, welcoming Brazilian ministers and ambassadors to his ship and a reception he was convinced would have done justice to the royal yacht Ced Mann had compared her to. In a brief moment between conversations with his guests, Butler had paused and looked at this group of some of the world's most elegant and influential men and women and thought that it was a long way to have come, beginning as a fourteen-year-old boy seaman fresh out of Exmouth naval training school in Britain, up through the years in freighters, tankers and cable ships and one ticket after another to being Master of the *Hudson* and, as receptions like this demon-strated, a part-time diplomat as well. As a boy seaman he had not been ambitious. Above all, he had not even daydreamed of becoming master of his own vessel; the Exmouth school was not the place to go if you seriously aspired to such heights. True, many of its pupils had gone on to become ship's captains, but Roy Gould, the *Hudson*'s navigator and stand-in Chief Officer, was the only other Exmouth pupil who had become an officer Butler had ever sailed with. And Gould had graduated to the mercantile marine through the Royal Navy. It was Britain's better-known Dartmouth Naval College that produced most of the successful career officers who, it sometimes seemed, largely ran the world's merchant fleets and navies.

There had been a time when Butler, newly married, had left the sea and taken a job as management trainee with an engineering firm in southern England. He had grown increasingly unhappy as he spent six months working his way through the machine shops. He remembered operating one machine that drilled holes – the same holes in similar pieces of metal, one after another. Grab metal blank; place beneath bench drill; pull lever to actuate drill; hold steady until hole drilled; raise lever; remove metal; place on conveyer for passage to next operator who would drill another hole; grab another metal blank; place beneath bench drill . . . . A faceless army of numbed humans working with, or for, another army of remorseless robots. Butler had withered. Even Maria, his bride, said he seemed to have visibly shrunk, and she sent him back to sea. Standing in some splendour, chatting with the Canadian ambassador on the deck of his ship that night in Rio harbour, Butler was eternally glad that she had.

At sea anything could happen and usually did, which is why Butler was suspicious as they left Rio. Hudson 70 was thus far worry-free. Butler had only two minor problems on his mind. One was that he had already completed his longest voyage to date in command of the *Hudson* and now that he felt comfortable with his ship he began to wonder how the crew felt with him. They were still referring to him as "the captain", which was unusual on so small a working ship. In such circumstances he expected – indeed, he hoped – the crew would find some other less formal, even slightly disrespectful, way of referring to him. The second minor problem was the ice cream: there wasn't any. Chief Steward Shaw had grown accustomed to using the large refrigerator designed for storing big marine specimens as an ice cream storage container. But in Rio harbour that slightly eccentric young man Peter Beamish had caught a dolphin that he claimed was little known to science and he had insisted that it be cut in two and stored, deep frozen in the refrigeration cabinet. For a day there had been an ice cream orgy – and now there was none left and no alternative storage place.

48

Had the ice cream been cut off because another, less notice-able scientist needed the specimen refrigerator there would probably have been no comment on the matter. But since it was Peter Beamish who was involved, there was inevitably a stir. Beamish had been aboard since Halifax, trying to eavesdrop on whales, and his passionate enthusiasm was such that it had in-fected and at times infuriated the whole ship. By Rio the watch-keeping officers had even begun looking for whales and, on seeing them, would pipe through the loudspeaker system: "Dr. Beamish to the bridge, please. Whales off the port bow." And at such times Peter Beamish would leap up, chair flying and sometimes cutlery, plates and food as well, to dash to where he stored his cameras on the bridge and yell: "Where? Where?" Once he had had to go to his cabin for a long-focus lens, and by the time he reached the deck the off-watch crew and scientists were already there, watching the whales swoop through the water. Beamish rushed out with a camera bearing a 1,000-millimeter lens so big that it looked like a machine gun. He was shooting pictures as he ran and didn't stop until Bruce Carson, Ced Mann's technician, tapped him on the shoulder and said: "Stop it, Peter. Not there – here. You've got the camera pointing at the wrong place."

Beamish's passion was relatively recent, and its strength surprised even him at times. He was a physicist, specializing in acoustics, employed by the Fisheries Research Board at the Bedford Institute and while he had freedom to choose his own project the FRB undoubtedly hoped he would use his expertise to help measure the productivity of the oceans. But he was, at the time of Hudson 70, just twenty-eight, a bachelor and deter-mined to find his own mountain to climb. It was while he was seeking an area of specialization that by chance he met Dr. Edward Mitchell, a biologist with the FRB Arctic Biological Station at St. Anne-de-Bellevue, Quebec. The two met at the Bedford Institute, talked over coffee in the Institute's bleakly barren basement cafeteria and, as Beamish put it later, "found to our astonishment we could talk one another's language." In an age of increasing specialization it grows more and more difficult for scientists in disparate disciplines to communicate on a scientific level. In Beamish's words: "I know it's not unusual for one man to be able to explain to another the broad aims and directions of his work. What is rare is for men in different fields to be able to talk to one another with enough expertise to see how those fields overlap and complement one another. When it does happen, fundamental ideas from one science are often found to fit neatly with those of another, and new and exciting hypotheses emerge. I knew enough biology to be able to talk to Mitchell, and he knew enough physics and acoustics to be able to talk to me. The result was the hypothesis that baleen whales use ultra-sonic radar, and that was damned exciting."

The accidental teaming of Beamish and Mitchell was, in fact, the sort of pairing the senior scientific echelons sought to bring about by establishing the Bedford Institute. At the rambling blue grass and glaze Insitute building on the shore of Bedford Basin, men and women of many disciplines work together, examining the same problems from different viewpoints. It is obvious the Fisheries Research Board knows it needs biologists, but the fact they hired Beamish the physicist and permitted him to choose his own area of research is evidence that Ottawa recognizes the need to cross-pollinate the sciences. In the main these scientists are left to find their own goals, their own challenges, and in a sense the government simply acts as the patron of the scientist, much as the princelings of Europe were once patrons of artists, writers and musicians. Today it is the arts that go begging. The challenge that physicist Beamish and biologist Mitchell accepted and sought to answer on Hudson 70 was: "Do baleen whales use ultra-sonic sound, and if so, what for?"

In itself, the answer to that question will put no bread on any table, will save no lives, will not enrich the human spirit. But it will be a completed part of the puzzle of the nature of things which, when completed, could do all those things.

There are two families of whales, the toothed and the baleen, and they may be the best examples of the evolutionary law of the survival of the fittest in the history of life on earth. It is widely assumed that both are former giant land creatures that, somewhere before known time began, returned to the oceans to survive, while others like the dinosaur grew too big for the land to support and so became extinct. Unless there really are monsters in the deeps (and there may be; deep-sea explorers tell of seeing great shadowy creatures a mile or more down) , whales are the biggest creatures on earth, and probably survived because in the weightless world of the oceans their size and bulk are not handicaps. They are, in a sense, living fossils from the dawn of life, when giant beasts roamed the land that man would one day inherit, and while land monsters vanished the whales survived and evolved over an uninterrupted period of somewhere between 30,000,000 to 80,000,000 years. By comparison, the period of time in which man has evolved to his present imperfections is just a flicker of an eyelid in time.

Few, if any, life forms have been as intensively studied as the whale is today and, since it is handiest in size, the dolphin, one of the toothed whales, is the creature researchers focus on. Studying other whales, the great blue whale which is roughly the size of two suburban houses, for instance, presents certain difficulties when you're trying to keep it captive in a laboratory. It was from studying the dolphin and the way in which its blubber and glossy skin change shape at different speeds that the u.s. navy learned how to build nuclear submarines that could travel faster submerged than any sub ever had before. And if we could find out how the whale uses underwater sound – natural sonar – to find food, navigate and communicate, and then duplicate it electronically, mankind would be better equipped to harvest the oceans. And yet, for all its potential practical value, the concentrated study of dolphins seems to have a most unscientific underlying motive: mankind is eager to communicate with another species, and to many it seems that of all life on earth we are most likely to be able to "talk" to the whales.

With laudable scientific caution, Peter Beamish always refused to discuss the whale's intelligence, though he did explain to Butler once that whales, or dolphins rather, seemed to "be about as bright as household pets." Less cautious scientists would regard this as a massive understatement. Most dogs or cats, or any other domestic animal for that matter, will bite or scratch any human who hurts or threatens them. The dolphin,

51

enormously powerful and with double rows of sharp teeth, has never yet turned on man, even when in captivity. In fact, some species – notably the *Tursiops truncatus,* or bottle-nosed dolphin – seem to regard mankind with almost inexhaustible goodwill. The lore of the sea is made up in part of stories about the way dolphins sense mariners' needs and then help them. For years one dolphin used to guide ships through a particularly hazardous strait along the coast of New Zealand.

Years ago, when scientists used the ratio of brain weight to body weight as a measure of intelligence, it seemed certain the whale was an intelligent creature. The conclusion was based on the fact that average brain weight in a dolphin was three and three-quarters of a pound compared with three pounds in man – and three-quarters of a pound in the chimpanzee. Even though this simplistic line of reasoning has been abandoned, more sophisticated investigation shows the dolphin brain is complex: it is, like man's, rich in densely packed cells. Along with other observations, this suggests the dolphin (and therefore perhaps all whales) may be the brightest creature next to man on earth.

In captivity, even in travelling carnival shows, the dolphin's tricks have none of the dreary, repetitive trained-seal routine of the circus animal. His trainer is a friend. In fact, the dolphin isn't trained as are other animals; he is shown what is expected of him, and once he understands he needs no practice; it simply becomes a game he enjoys playing, and he frequently varies the rules to add to the fun. If, as many contend, a relatively complex "language" is a sign of true intelligence, then the whale may be demonstrating that intelligence through the sounds that Peter Beamish was so eager to record on Hudson 70. The sounds a whale makes are far more complex than those of, say, any dog or bird; they run through a spectrum of sound that suggests to many researchers that their communication with one another is vastly more complex than the growls of disapproval, snarls of anger, and yelps of delight made by dogs. Their direction-finding sonar is infinitely more sophisticated than any yet devised by man.

But for all this, man knows relatively little about whales; about how they live, die, mate, reproduce, find food. The two families of whales – the baleen (*Mystecites*) and the toothed (*Odonocetes*) – probably came from two totally different families of land based creatures; the baleens probably from vegetarian animals and the toothed from carnivores. Instead of teeth the baleen whale has a mouthful of large overlapping plates called baleen (hence the name) and eats vast quantities of tiny shrimp-like creatures called krill by lowering its bulbous lower jaw as it swims through the water. When its gargantuan mouth is full of krill it closes the lower jaw, then forces the seawater out through the plates. In this manner it is believed to eat a ton of krill each day – and that means the world's largest creature lives on one of the smallest; krill are rarely larger than one and a half inches long. The toothed whale, on the other hand, preys on fish. The great blue baleen whale is around 110 feet long in the Antarctic and about ninety feet in the Arctic, where krill seem to be less plentiful. Other baleen whales aren't much smaller; they range down to the Fin, which is seventy feet long in the Antarctic and again slightly smaller in the north. The bigger toothed whales are all smaller, though only slightly, but range down to the small dolphins of four feet long which mostly live in inshore waters.

We know enough to be fairly sure that whales communicate with one another and may even be able to detect food hundreds, even thousands, of miles distant. We know that they do this with sonar – underwater sound waves. We know some whales transmit sound in not only the frequency range audible to humans, but in the sub-sonic or ultra-sonic frequencies – sounds either above or below the range of the human ear. But we don't know how or why it works; which sounds are for communication, which for navigation, which for food detection. The great body of man's definitive knowledge on the subject of whale sonar fits neatly into a three-foot-long bookshelf in Peter Beamish's hazardously cluttered Dartmouth office.

Among the accepted wisdoms at the time of Hudson 70 was the belief that the great baleen whales did not use ultra-sonic sound. Whenever scientists have picked up ultra-sonic sounds near baleen whales it was always explained away by the claim that dolphins, members of the toothed whale family that are known to use ultra-sonic sounds, were in the vicinity.

Peter Beamish was to be frustrated throughout the two phases of Hudson 70 when he was aboard ship. His attempts to record the sounds made by baleen whales, in a bid to prove that they do in fact make ultra-sonic sound, all failed. Early on, when the ship was on its first station, he lowered his hydrophones (underwater microphones) into the ocean – and immediately yelped with excitement. He was picking up and recording an ultra-sonic sound. Whales? Oreste Bluy, the other specialist in sonar, tried his own equipment. He, too, could pick up the sound. But it was a constant noise, singularly unlike the sounds made by whales, which usually come in short bursts and may within a second range from the sub-sonic through the audio range to the ultra-sonic. The entire ship became involved in the mystery. Dave Butler ordered the ship to be made totally quiet. First the engines were shut down. Then every electrical appliance aboard; cabin fans, air conditioners, lights, ovens, toasters, coffee urns. By a slow process of elimination they found Peter Beamish's "whale" – an engine room fan that was squeaking, though the noise it made could not be picked up by the human ear.

Beamish was digusted. He had long contended it was impossible to study whale sounds from a modern ship and had bought a schooner, the *Oceanus,* to do his own research in the belief that with a totally noiseless craft there would be no sound to interfere with recordings or frighten the whales. It was, he argued, quite possible for a sailboat to join a school of whales and "live" with them for a time as they wander the ocean. But the *Oceanus* was back in harbour at Dartmouth and so, after much wrangling, Beamish persuaded Chief Officer Mauger to let him use one of the ship's two launches with a three-man crew. In this Beamish moved a mile or so away from the ship. There, with the launch engine silent, Beamish set up his equipment for a test run. He lowered the hydrophone over the side, clamped headphones to ears and began adjusting the receiving equipment. He had not then hooked up the tape recorder. Suddenly he heard a distinct sound in the ultra-sonic frequencies: *Chick, chick, chick.* Beamish looked up; saw a Bryde's baleen whale perhaps thirty feet away, heading straight for the launch, its long grey body barely humping out of the water, the dorsal fin about two-thirds of the way back from the head, cutting a wake. The sound it had made lasted barely a second. But Peter Beamish had actually *heard* a baleen whale produce ultra-sonic sound when there were clearly no dolphins in the area. He was both elated and depressed. Back aboard the *Hudson* he told Ced Mann: "I know that ultra-sonic sounds came from that Bryde's whale, I know damn well there wasn't a porpoise or any other kind of toothed whale around to explain it away – God, the thing was swimming right at the hydrophone. *But I can't prove it.* The tape recorder wasn't hooked up." Mann sympathized. Peter Beamish had seemingly come across an important piece of scientific data – and couldn't proffer it to the scientific community because he had no proof.

The dolphin he later killed in Rio harbour was no consolation. At the reception aboard ship Beamish met Brazilian scientists and learned that once a year dolphins came into the harbour and stayed about two weeks. The *Hudson* and the dolphins had arrived together. Curious, Beamish again took off in a launch to find the dolphins – and was excited to find they were the species known as *Satalia brasiliensis,* one of the least studied of the sixty or so types of dolphins. He decided to kill one, deep freeze it and get it back to Canada where his biologist collaborator Mitchell could dissect it at leisure, studying particularly its head and ears, the transmitter and receiver of those incredible sounds that have fascinated biologists and zoologists for a century or more. He collected a 12-gauge shotgun loaded with a heavy lead slug instead of shot. Then he went hunting. The launch inched close to the dolphins; Beamish shot; missed – and the dolphins, alarmed, scattered. As Dave Butler noted, this incident reinforced the scepticism among his colleagues about Peter Beamish's talents with firearms. His efforts to harpoon porpoises from the bow of the *Hudson* were never successful. And when Dr. Louis Rustige, a self-proclaimed crack shot, had tried to use Beamish's shotgun to fire a marker tag into the blubber of a passing whale there was a comic disaster that everyone remembered. Usually the whales would sense the presence of the *Hudson* and then the great, grey back would heave up; the water would boil and the whale would vanish beneath the surface to reappear, unpredictably, too far away for useful observation. This time the *Hudson* had stalked a whale for forty-five minutes, slowly overhauling it until ship and whale were parallel, the whale still seemingly unaware it had company. On the wing of the bridge Beamish busily shot pictures while ship's surgeon Rustige levelled the shotgun loaded with a special charge and the marker dart. His skill with firearms was unquestioned since he had several times shot sharks caught by idle crewmen who fished from the main deck with a meathook and hunk of raw meat. By now almost everyone aboard had ceased to work and lined the port side of the ship, watching. Carefully Rustige took aim midway along the whale's back, low down where the blubber is thickest and the dart unlikely to be even felt. Even more carefully he squeezed the trigger. As Dave Butler described it later, "there was a phutt – half sigh, half burp – and the dart just barely got out of the barrel and plopped into the sea alongside the ship." Beamish was dismayed, Rustige annoyed. "You should keep your powder dry," he told Beamish. Before there was time to reload, the whale vanished, perhaps disturbed by the laughter of the ship's company.

So when Peter Beamish set out dolphin hunting in Rio harbour for the second day few people expected him to return with a trophy. They were wrong. He killed a prime specimen of *Satalia brasiliensis,* six feet six inches long and weighing 300 pounds. It turned out to be a pyrrhic triumph. As the dolphin was hauled alongside the launch, Beamish was saddened. Then he dismissed sadness as anthropomorphic – the dolphin was, after all, just an animal and studying it would add to man's knowledge. And yet, sitting in the launch in mid-harbour, he resolved he would never again kill if he could help it. Back aboard he explained: "It was a graceful creature. When I realized what I had done I suddenly felt very glad that I'm a physicist. I won't kill animals again, and I won't have to. What I do is study the sounds they make, and that makes my science beautiful."

There were two reasons why everyone aboard was particularly aware of Peter Beamish's successes and failures. The first was that his work on whales could be seen and everyone could be involved, while other scientific programmes mostly involved collecting data or specimens for later examination, both relatively undramatic and, to the lay crew, usually invisible activities. There was however a second, more subtle explanation why Beamish emerged as one of the more memorable characters of that stage of the voyage. A ship at sea is an emotional pressure cooker: people are thrown in one another's company and on their own resources in a relatively confined space, and to an unnatural degree. "You can't escape yourself or anybody else," one biologist wrote home. Men work, play, eat and even sleep in constant companionship.

In such a climate the basic character of a man, flaws and virtues, stand sharply etched. Friendships are close, enmities strongly felt. Men behave improbably. One usually amiable electronics man, losing at chess, picked up board and chessmen and hurled them across the lounge. One biologist went on a hunger strike; at least, he refused to eat the regular meals that others found acceptable on the grounds that they were "swill". At one stage the crew began breaking one another's coffee mugs. These were usually hung on racks in the mess, and it became a point of honour to see whether you could smash someone else's mug by breaking the china cleanly at the handle. This game went on so long new mugs had to be bought, and crewmen were still hiding mugs in their cabins at the end of the voyage. Soon after the *Hudson* left Rio there was a confrontation between a group of scientists and Ced Mann and Dave Butler because the scientists claimed that while paying for their seventeen-cent drinks in American dollars they were entitled to a five per cent discount. They got it – and afterwards their drinks were seven-tenths of a cent cheaper per ounce. Those involved in this penny-ante rebellion were later embarrassed by it, but the fact that it happened makes the point that a ship is an abnormal environment and that in it men – even sober, responsible scientists – can behave abnormally.

It was in this context that Peter Beamish stood out. Most scientists are reserved about their work. It is almost a point of honour to maintain the role of the quietly dedicated academic. Beamish was openly and publicly enthusiastic with a passion that was contagious to many and distasteful to some, and so he became an *enfant terrible* within the Hudson 70 family.

And it was a family of sorts by the time the ship had left Rio on the second leg of the voyage. It was because he anticipated this that Ced Mann had a year earlier decided that the ship should spend Christmas at sea. "Christmas is a family time and down here we're the nearest thing to family any of us has got around," Mann told Butler. "If we spend it in port everyone will be lonely and as miserable as sin." In his journal, however, Mann was characteristically phlegmatic in describing Christmas Day itself. He wrote: "Cut down on the number of observations today to allow time off for Xmas dinner and to allow us to get to next station in good time. The Isaac Kidd [trawl] and Bathysonde were not done. At 10:00 the cooks put on a magnificent spread in the coffee room. Pears, grapes, Xmas cake, sweets. At noon Xmas dinner. Had drinks in the lounge before dinner. Stopped work at 10:30 and recommenced at 14:30. Did acoustics, a shallow cast and tow for Bob [Conover] in the morning. Then the deep cast and Bob's multiple tow using three nets on the hydrowire in the afternoon. In evening we had a punch bowl (actually a large glass demijohn) in the lounge. Then played liar dice. A rather quiet evening."

That day – as he had been on Christmas Eve – radio officer Philip Rafuse was busy sending Christmas telegrams to towns and cities throughout North America, to England and – for Chef Durin – to his girl friend Elaine in Gironde, France. As with all Durin's monthly cables home it was in French, which Rafuse could transmit in morse code but not read, and ended as did all Durin's cables: "Amour – Claude". Some members of the crew and scientific staff actually spoke to their families from the ship during the Christmas holiday. Fred Muise, the ship's senior technician, had on December 22 received a cable from his wife in Halifax saying that the youngest of their two children, a year-old boy, had died in hospital of a malignant tumor on the brain. Muise had been using his ham radio set mounted in his cabin to try to reach another radio ham in Halifax who would hook him up by phone to his wife. He spent the day finding his wife in Ottawa, where she and their eldest child were staying with her parents. In the process he arranged radio-telephone links for others aboard. Butler had offered to put Muise ashore at the first opportunity so he could fly back to be with his family, but Muise refused on the grounds that he had left on Hudson 70 knowing, as did his wife, that the child was mortally sick. There was, he insisted, no need for him to return. Butler accepted the explanation, and would later regret having done so.

The four-hour Christmas Day itself was not quiet. Butler and Ced Mann donated several bottles of liquor to the crew's mess on the main deck, where usually only beer was available. The crew had bravely decorated the mess with Christmas cards and Christmas wrapping paper and the ribbons from gifts they had either brought with them from Halifax or received by mail in Rio. There, at midday, they had Christmas dinner and drank and when Mann and Butler and Chief Officer Mauger made a visit, they danced the Newfie Stomp. It was this that was probably the noisiest event of the day because the Newfie Stomp is a men-only dance like no other in the world. It has none of the rhythmic grace of the traditional Greek and middle-European dances for men; none of the vigour of the traditional sailor's hornpipe; none of the mystic inner meaning of the Mayan rain dance, the Indian victory dance, the Zulu mating dances; its steps are neither intricate nor symbolic nor rooted in traditional or religious significance. The Newfie Stomp is a dour, generally slightly alcoholic performance danced to Maritimes music or rousing country and western songs or, for that matter, anything with a beat, which is not necessarily followed. Big, burly men drape their arms around one another's shoulders and prance around – stomp really is the right word – approximately in time to the music, and since they're usually wearing work boots and are a little drunk besides it's a hazardous undertaking, particularly aboard a ship at sea. Butler and Mauger and bo'sun Joe Avery and Chief Steward Bill Shaw danced and the ship rolled in a heavy sea and they would be stomping, or staggering, from one end of the crew's mess to the other as the ship canted first to port, then to starboard and back again.

It was a good party, and the life and soul of it was bearded, bear-shouldered Chief Steward Bill Shaw, formerly a cook and commissary officer with the Royal Canadian Navy. He's a drinker, a carouser and – say his friends – a devil with the girls ashore. But beneath it all that day, and on many others like it ashore and afloat, there was a melancholy in Shaw that was revealed rarely, and then only to old shipmates and in the wee small hours when the glasses are empty and it is dark and the dog-watch men on the black and silent bridge feel the breath of mortality on their necks. At such times Shaw would explain that he was one of the few who had signed on for the entire Hudson 70 voyage, from Halifax to Halifax, because there was no reason not to. Three years earlier his wife had left him, run off with his best friend and left him with the big frame house in St. Margaret's Bay forty-five miles from Halifax where, he was fond of saying, he could only "rattle around like a pea in a bottle", or take the dory and go fish in the bay itself. Midway through that Christmas party, sensing a false gaiety among men who would rather be home with their wives and families, he felt a quiet melancholy because he himself was actually happy. At least, he was happier spending Christmas at sea with good companions than at home in the empty house in St. Margaret's Bay. Later he and bo'sun Joe Avery sat quietly in Shaw's cabin and he said: "You know, Joe, it's not leaving port that bothers me. It's going back that does it. There's no one there. Look at those guys at the party. A lot of those guys had a sad, lost look. I think half of them would have rather been alone to think about the family and stuff, the people they've got to go home to." He sat silent for a moment. Then he got up, poured another drink – a stiff one – and turned up his hi-fi tape deck and said that since it was now evening it was time they had another party.

There were several more parties that night in the crew's quarters, and Carol Lalli went to one of them. Dr. Carol Lalli, a biologist and at thirty-one a singularly attractive, willowy woman with long brown hair, patrician face and startling aquamarine eyes, was one of two women on board the *Hudson* during that leg of the voyage; indeed, one of only five women who would take part in the entire expedition. She and Dr. Georgina Deevey, another biologist, had boarded the ship at Rio and were to leave it at Buenos Aires after four weeks of collecting their own specimens for future study. And it was Christmas and the presence of women reminded both scientists and crew of wives and mothers and girl friends left behind, and both Carol Lalli and Georgie Deevey agreed to visit the party in one of the steward's rooms. In the event Georgie Deevey felt ill and Carol Lalli went alone, and, later, when he heard about it, Butler was to nearly have conniptions. "God, a good looking woman on her own at a sailor's party," he groaned. "Anything could have happened." But, as Carol told him, he was foolish to worry since she drank only ginger ale and the crewmen treated her as though she was the mother or at least the sister of every one of them, and even stopped swearing – well, almost – for the half hour she spent there. Mostly she talked to Steward Larry MacDonald about the girl he had been going out with for two years and had taken for granted until now, when he'd spent almost two months away and was beginning to think he had been wasting time, that he should get engaged. Another older sailor told everybody who would listen that the socks he was wearing had been knitted by his twelve-year-old daughter for Christmas, and when Carol Lalli left she went to her cabin and wrote to her husband in Montreal that she thought it was all rather sad; that it was a rotten way to spend Christmas.

Chung Choi, the young Korean who conducted experiments with phyto-plankton on the first leg of Hudson 70, had left the ship at Rio and so had not met Carol Lalli. Had he done so he would have found more than customary sympathy for his dream of short-circuiting the food chain and drawing human food supplies directly from the bottom of the chain – the plankton life forms – instead of waiting for it to be passed along through a series of complex prey-predator relationships to the fish we now find palatable. For Carol Lalli is a specialist in one tiny link in the complex food web of the world, and was aboard the *Hudson* to pursue her studies into the prey-predator relationship between two species of zoo-plankton, the *Gymnosomatous pterapods* and the *Cosomatous pterapods*. The word plankton comes from the Greek, and means "wandering". It was long ago applied to the two smallest life forms on earth. Both phyto- and zoo-plankton drift around the upper layers of the ocean as wind, tide and current dictate. The first of the creatures Dr. Lalli studied is the *Cosomatous pterapod*, a snail-like creature slightly bigger than a pinhead. It feeds on phyto-plankton. The second, the *Gymnosomatous pterapod,* feeds exclusively on the *Cosomatous pterapod,* for which information the world is indebted to Carol Lalli: proving that fact earned her doctorate.

And when asked at cocktail parties why she studies the inter-relationship between two of the world's tiniest creatures, she explains – with a by now well-rehearsed little speech – that apart from the acquisition of knowledge for the sake of knowledge, her work may ultimately have a bearing on the decision whether to do as Chung Choi advocates and try to feed man from the bottom of the food chain instead of the top.

It began when Carol Lalli was a child in Ohio, where she caught the enthusiasm which fired her amateur naturalist father, a furrier who preferred watching living creatures in their natural habitat to working with the pelts of the dead. She went on to study biology at university, and then bacteriology for her M.Sc., during which she learned she didn't like bacteriology; working with cultures in laboratory dishes was hardly satisfying to a girl with a passion for the outdoors. But while studying for her master's degree she was taught invertebrate zoology by a young professor who passed on his interest in marine biology. And so, for her doctorate, Carol Lalli went out to the University of Washington in Seattle near the Pacific, and there was fired by another enthusiasm – the study of marine molluscs. Both the tiny creatures who were to become her special interest are molluscs, which are among the most diverse of invertebrates and are found on land, in fresh water and in the oceans. The giant octopi and squid of the Pacific are molluscs; so are the snails of the land; the slugs of the forest and the oysters and snails that are on the menu of any good restaurant. Molluscs have demonstrated an astounding ability to adapt and evolve in to different species to survive in changing and widely different environments, yet they have one common characteristic: all have a barbed tongue – that is, a tongue with built-in teeth – used to haul food directly to the gut.

Other biologists aboard collected specimens to be preserved in formalin for later study. But Carol Lalli did not like working with dead creatures. It was this which had led her to study the food chain relationship between the two particular species of molluscs in which she had become an acknowledged world authority. To determine the prey-predator relationship between them, Carol Lalli had to spend her time studying the behaviour of the *Gymnosomatous* and *Cosomatous* pterapods while they were living in a laboratory mock-up of their natural environment. When she began her studies it was known that the larger *Gymnosomatous* pterapod – it is roughly three-quarters of an inch long and does not have a shell – and the tiny *Cosomatous* pterapod, which does have a shell, were always found in the same waters at the same time. It was presumed the larger ate the smaller. But to what extent? And how? By studying the creatures in their natural habitat – she spent days as a doctoral student lying on fish docks in the San Juan Islands peering down into the water – and in tanks in laboratories she was able to conclusively prove that, in the north-eastern Pacific anyway, the bigger pterapod fed exclusively on the smaller. She was also able to say how they did so; the bigger has six tentacles around its mouth so it can grasp the shell of the smaller pterapod while its barbed tongue lashes out, probes into the shell and winkles out its prey. Now she was aboard Hudson 70 in an attempt to collect samples of similar creatures from the southern oceans to find out whether they, too, had an exclusive prey-predator relationship.

Months later she was able to say that yes, the exclusive prey-predator relationship between the pterapods was the same in the Antarctic as elsewhere. And that posed another set of questions, such as: how did it happen that almost identical species with identical feeding habits ended up in the Arctic, the North Atlantic, the north Pacific and the Antarctic?

Even so, by Hudson 70, that line of research was almost a side issue to Carol Lalli. Having earned her doctorate, she continued to study this easily definable link in the food chain – definable because she had already proved that one pterapod fed only upon the other – in an effort to determine just how much energy is wasted within it. The basic energy on which all life depends comes from phyto-plankton, whose growth is stimulated by the sun's rays. Phyto-plankton is eaten by zoo-plankton; zoo-plankton is eaten by bigger life forms and so on up the food chain until it reaches man. Science has long worked by the rule of thumb that ninety per cent of the potential energy – that is, the calories, or units of heat energy – is lost in each link in the food chain because the big fish that eats the little fish uses some of that energy to move, to hunt, to live. Actually proving this has been more difficult and to many biologists demonstrable proof of the amount of energy lost as it passes up the food chain has become a Holy Grail; Carol Lalli wasn't the only scientist on Hudson 70 working in this area. She, however, had the advantage that she knew of the exclusive prey-predator relationship between the two pterapods. In this one link it is at least theoretically possible to make precise energy loss measurements. In gross oversimplification it could be done this way: take a given number of the tiny *Cosomatous* pterapods and measure the amount of calories in them. Then take a similar number of these pterapods and place them in a tank with the larger *Gymnosomatous* pterapods and measure the rate at which the larger eats the smaller. In theory it is subsequently possible to measure how much of the original energy is left to pass up through the food chain when all the smaller pterapods had been eaten. If you mash up the larger pterapods that are left and measure the number of calories in them you should be able to determine the calories that, in the oceans, would be available to pass on to the next link in the food chain. But the techniques for making this measurement are imprecise, and at the time of Hudson 70 it was the need to perfect such a technique that seemed likely to occupy the next few years of Carol Lalli's life.

Chung Choi is from a part of the world where food is already so short that he has visible proof that it may be necessary to short-circuit the food chain and take protein from its source, the plankton. Carol Lalli, living in a more affluent and better fed world, recognizes this need only as an intellectual abstraction. Both, however, are aware that, from the brutally selfish standpoint of a hungry man, it is wasteful to wait for energy to pass up through the food chain. Carol Lalli's major work was producing a piece of evidence that would prove just how wasteful. Intellectually, at least, she too had faced the fact that overpopulation means that at some point we may have to eat plankton – not wait until the original energy generated by the sun's rays passes up the food chain to end up in Dover sole muniere, lobster thermdor or Gaspe salmon avec fines herbes.

As a scientist, Carol Lalli had the respect of all the men aboard, as did Georgie Deevey, who was older and whose reputation was more established. But it still wasn't possible to forget they were women – though neither would have wanted to – and both were aware that as a minority of two among eighty men they were more noticeably women than they were on either the Dalhousie or McGill university campuses, where they then were teaching. They weren't aware of it until later, but the presence of women prompted the men – scientists and crew alike – to pay more attention to their appearance. With Carol and Georgie wearing dresses for dinner, the men would be sure to shave, would often change for the meal, and some even wore ties.

For a few days after leaving Rio the weather remained tropical, and Carol and Georgie joined other scientists sunbathing on the bridge deck – but always together, and with Carol wearing an archaic, and comfortingly modest, one-piece swim suit. Even so, several sailors to whom the bridge deck was out of bounds tried to press cameras onto scientists, asking them to photograph the women sunbathing. Both women were a little irritated by being made so conscious of their sex, though Carol reflected that it was inevitable since women scientists were still something of a rarity aboard Canadian oceanographic ships; indeed, older sailors still considered them bad luck. She rebelled, however, when biologist Bob Conover of the Bedford Institute knocked timidly at her cabin door asking for a needle and thread, saying he had to sew a seam in pants that had split. She knew he hoped she would take pity on him and do the needlework herself, but, as she told Georgie later, she probably wasn't any better a needlewoman than Conover. So she did what he asked – just gave him the needle and thread. A couple of hours later she went down to the biologists' laboratory and found Conover peering through a microscope focused on the eye of the needle and the thread, trying to bring the two together. Even then Conover's tactic failed; Carol took pity on him to the extent of threading the needle, then handed it back saying that she was sure sewing was easy for a man who had mastered all the complex electronic equipment that Conover used in his research.

Conover, in fact, is a biologist who sounds strangely like an electronics engineer, largely because much of his zoo-plankton work on Hudson 70 would ultimately involve the use of complex electronic equipment to produce any conclusions. A rumpled, lanky, laconic American of forty-two, he had embarked on Hudson 70 dreaming of finding a piece of biological evidence that might prove or disprove many of the theories about the speed and depth of ocean currents carrying water from the Antarctic north up the Atlantic. He hoped a tiny creature called *Rhincalanus gigas*, one of the thousand or so species of zoo-plankton, would provide this information.

The *Rhincalanus gigas* is about a quarter of an inch long, and lives in zero degree water in the Antarctic. In the southern spring it surfaces, gorges itself, mates, and then as the surface waters warm up it sinks down to spend the summer in comfortably cold depths. But, while they're doing this, some are caught up in the currents where the South Atlantic and the Antarctic waters converge, and are carried north toward the equator in two of the four separate layers of the ocean. They eventually die, either from starvation or because they get swept up in to water too warm for them. But en route they live off their fat, and Conover's theory was that by catching them at different points as they are carried up the South Atlantic and measuring the amount of fat left on them it would be possible to tell how long they had been travelling north from the Antarctic. This in turn would indicate to the physical oceanographers – men like Ced Mann, who study ocean currents and structure – how fast water from the Antarctic moves up through the Atlantic.

What was vital in this experiment was that the samples of the *Rhincalanus gigas* should be taken at precise depths. Conventional sampling equipment has a depth error of about 500 metres, too great for Conover's experiment. But since 1966 technicians at the Bedford Institute had been working to perfect a net designed to collect samples with great precision. It has three compartments, each with complex electronic equipment operated by sonar signals from the ship. The net constantly signals the ship, telling the depth at which it is being towed.

At the required depth a sonar signal is sent from the ship to open one compartment; the plankton sample is taken and the procedure is repeated with the two other compartments at different depths during the same tow.

On Hudson 70 it didn't work – at least, not often.

The sampling was to take place down the South Atlantic, around Antarctica and up the southern Pacific, and early on Conover and his biologist colleague Mahdu Paranjape tried to rescue their experiment by adapting older, less precise sampling techniques. In the event Conover's experiment was to be a fine demonstration of the delay between biological sampling and "working up" the results. Two years later he would be saying gloomily that he didn't know what he and Paranjape would be able to prove, if anything, and anyway "Hudson 70 was about typical as expeditions go – you achieve a quarter or half of what you'd hoped."

The failure of Bob Conover's sonar-operated zoo-plankton sampling net was just one of a series of incidents that, in the two weeks bridging Christmas 1969 and New Year 1970, justified Dave Butler's pessimism when leaving Rio harbour. The first phase – Halifax to Rio – had gone so smoothly he felt things had to begin going wrong, and they did. There was one day which even Mann described in his journal as a "Day of Disaster"; every scientific undertaking seemed to run into trouble at once. One of the sampling bottles on the cast into the deeps was insecurely fixed and slid down the cable prematurely, tripping the mechanism of all other bottles so that the cast had to be done again. The cable towing Oreste Bluy's hydrophone, which picked up the sound waves bouncing back from the scattering layer, fouled one of the *Hudson's* two propellers, wound itself round the shaft and had to be cut clear. That day the only scientific work that seemed to go right was Peter Wangersky's sampling of the air for subsequent analysis of carbon dioxide content. To take these daily samples Wangersky simply walked to the bow and held a hypodermic syringe at arm's length and drew back the plunger, thus trapping a sample of the air at that particular point on the map. Even the ship's dogs – the captain's growing German Shepherd puppy, Nicodemus, and the ship's surgeon's amiable Doberman Pinscher, Mark – were causing problems. The captain's dog could not be house-trained, large-ly because there was no "outside" for him to go to, and the companionways became so fouled they were a hazard for those not accustomed to looking where they put their feet. Dr. Rustige's Doberman became an alcoholic. Early in the voyage he had been freely admitted to the lounge, and had learned a new trick. He would collect a deep glass ashtray in his large mouth, approach someone drinking beer or rum and coke, lay the ashtray down on a seat nearby and then sit back, tongue lolling, asking for a drink. When he had done the rounds of the scientists and officers in the lounge he would go down to the crew's mess and repeat the performance. Just before New Year's Day Dr. Rustige posted a handwritten notice on the crew's notice board. It read: "Friends. Please stop feeding Mark. He is getting too fat and his drinking problem is serious." The lounge was made off limits to both dogs.

By New Year the *Hudson* was south of latitude 40, and into the Roaring Forties, dreaded by old seamen because of the violent winds which even today's steam sailors, less prey to the vagaries of wind and high seas, regard with some dismay. The weather closed in, but it remained fairly calm until they reached 47 degrees south. Then it began to blow. And it stayed blowing from the north-east as the ship ploughed down the line of longitude 30 – the 30th meridian – planning to reach 55 degrees south, about 300 miles east of South Georgia, a remote and desolate British-owned island almost due east of Cape Horn. Work on deck was difficult, cold, uncomfortable. After weeks of tropic sun, scientists and crew were cooped up between decks, and Iver Duedall, who was to be the resident ship's analytical chemist for another four months, wrote his wife: "One thing this trip has taught me is that the optimum time one should spend at sea is about two weeks, never greater than three weeks." Despite Claude Durin's efforts, Duedall echoed the feelings of everyone when he added that "the food aboard is really not much to write home about. By now all that they serve, no matter if it's fish or steak, tastes the same. At first the food was great, but now it's lousy." The weather and the mood it induced tainted everything, taste buds included.

For one stretch of two weeks they saw neither sun by day

nor stars by night, and it was during this period that ship's officers and scientists began to appreciate the true value of the Satellite Navigation System installed aboard the *Hudson* for the Hudson 70 voyage. The U.S. Navy has five satellites constantly circling the earth about 600 miles up. Each one circles the earth every ninety minutes, which means there is always one either "rising" or "setting" on the ship's horizons. Each satellite constantly transmits coded information about its precise height and location. The information is fed into a computer that calculates the ship's location on the face of the earth to within 1,500 feet. It is this staggering degree of accuracy which helped make the Hudson 70 expedition so valuable to the world of science: the ocean scientist must know exactly where he is at all times so that he can tell just where it was that a particular sample or piece of data was acquired. For this reason the *Hudson* took satellite navigational "fixes" every thirty minutes. The traditional methods of navigation, the sextant observations of sun, moon and stars which have been used for centuries, can be almost as accurate as satellite "fixes", but for them a navigator must be able to see the sky. And since the *Hudson* sailed the Roaring Forties beneath sullen cloud such navigation would have been impossible, and the scientific work therefore less valuable. Dave Butler calculated that, with winds rarely below forty knots, his ship drifted twenty miles during each eight-hour station, which meant that at the end of that one fifteen-day period of heavy cloud the ship might have been as much as 300 miles off course had it not been for the satellites.

New Year's Day came and went almost unnoticed, and at dawn on January 2 the first Antarctic iceberg was sighted. Second Officer Peter Reynell, officer of the watch, noted that it was massive – about three miles long, and perhaps a mile wide and 400 feet high, and as the *Hudson* passed in its lee the men on the bridge heard the lingering groans punctuated by sudden squeaks as the great mountain of ice heaved in the ocean. This would remain the biggest iceberg seen from the *Hudson* in the Antarctic, but even the smaller ones were fascinating because the icebergs of the Antarctic are different from those of the Arctic, the *Hudson*'s home waters. The Arctic iceberg is mountainous, complete with valleys, plains and rugged terrain.

Antarctic icebergs are flat, regular, almost geometric in shape. They are carved from the great plateau-like icefields of Antarctica which slide down into the sea and in summer – which it now was in Antarctica – shed great shards of ice. The biggest iceberg ever seen in the Antarctic was reportedly sixty miles long.

But it was growlers, not icebergs, that presented the greatest threat to the *Hudson*. A growler is an aged iceberg, one which time and winds and waves have worn down until almost nothing projects above the sea's surface, and what does is round and smooth. By day growlers are not a threat to navigation, since they can be seen from the bridge or the crow's-nest, which aboard the *Hudson* is a comfortably heated cabin stuck atop the swaying mainmast. But at night the ship must depend on radar, and radar will rarely pick up growlers since it relies on sharp edges that will bounce the radio signal back to the ship. Growlers are either so low there's nothing for the radar transmission to bounce back from, or else they're so smooth and round that the radar beams glance off at an angle, skywards, and don't return to warn the ship of the hazard that may lie ahead.

By January 3 the icebergs and growlers were, as Butler told Mauger, "as thick as palings on a fence". Even so, he decided to steam slowly during the four-hour Antarctic summer night. It was a mistake. Butler spent that first night among the icebergs on the bridge himself. There was a twenty-five-knot wind and pellets of ice as big as a man's thumbnail whipped across the decks. Seaman Gerald Dwyer in the crow's-nest could barely see his own ship's bow; he sat as isolated as an astronaut in the cabin atop the mast, his only contact with reality being the occasional muffled sounds heard through the voice tube to the bridge. On the bridge itself watch officer Reynell, aged twenty-two, stood at the whirring disc of the clear-screen – a motor-driven circle of glass which throws off snow, rain or sleet as it spins – peering through night glasses. Bill Dobson, at forty-one the oldest of the ship's four quartermasters and a clerkish man with a reputation for imperturbability, was at the wheel. David Butler alternately sat at his flip-down seat at the bridge window and wandered restlessly from one radar screen to the other. All he could see on them was sea clutter: the signals registered by the radar beam bouncing off wave tops. The lights were dimmed to aid night vision, and Butler was reminded of another occasion on which the tension had been as great; the night of the near collision with the fuel barge in Halifax harbour just before Hudson 70 was to begin. At 2.00 a.m. there was a flood of light as the man on watch at the Satellite Navigation System computer opened the heavy bridge door curtain to bring in the navigational fix. With a curt "Thanks" Butler took the print-out paper and went to the chart room to make the appropriate notation on the chart.

As he bent over the chart table the engine note suddenly changed. Reynell had grabbed the engine telegraphs and thrust both to full astern. The ship began to shudder. Butler dashed the fifteen yards back to where Reynell stood at the clear screen. Reynell said, with frightening economy: "Growler. Dead ahead." Butler looked and there, perhaps 300 feet away and coming closer by the second, he could see a line of white foam where waves broke off the surface of a massive block of age-hardened ice. Barely ten feet of it showed above the surface.

In the chief scientist's cabin on the deck below Ced Mann awoke to the sudden roar of the engines, the vibration that jolted every rivet as the engines went into full astern. He looked at his watch. It was exactly 2.00 a.m., the time at which a routine temperature and salinity reading was to be taken. Had the man taking the reading fallen overboard? He jumped up, struggled into his plaid dressing gown, ran for the bridge.

On the quarterdeck at the stern Oreste Bluy had just completed the temperature and salinity measurement for Mann and, cursing the stinging sleet, was about to head for his cabin and sleep. Suddenly the steel deck plates began shuddering, and within seconds the water astern began to boil as the twin screws took hold. The sea foamed up over the stern in a great spray and showered the quarterdeck. Bluy was soaked and frightened. He too ran for the bridge.

On the bridge, Butler, Reynell and Dobson at the wheel stood frozen as, slowly, the line of white foam where the sea broke over the growler came nearer. For the second time in three months Butler found himself estimating the damage to his bows; the efficiency of the seven sets of watertight doors;

the problem of limping 2,000 miles back to Buenos Aires to have the bows patched up so they could return to Halifax. Ced Mann and then Bluy reached the bridge in time to see the threat. And the ship throbbed and slowed and finally stopped. That ominous line of breakers was just fifty feet ahead. Someone – no one remembers who – sighed and said that a miss was as good as a mile, and the *Hudson* went astern for 1,000 feet and Butler ordered the shipe hove to. "No more steaming at night," he said bleakly, and went below to have a drink.

Later, much later, he would talk with Chief Officer Mauger about their junior officers. The question of Peter Reynell's antics came up. He had grown to become part of what was called the "terrible trio"; the others were young scientists' assistants and all three were involved in minor pranks aboard ship. Butler said: "What Reynell does off duty isn't important. Look at that night – the night of the growler. There's a lot of kids who would have seen that growler and, knowing I was on the bridge, just yelled for me to do something about it. That would have cost us twenty seconds, maybe more. And that's all we'd have needed to have a disaster. Twenty seconds lost just then and we'd have hit the bloody thing, at three or four knots. But he jammed the engines into reverse on his own initiative and that's why we're here now, going on with the voyage, instead of wallowing back to Halifax with our tail between our legs." And then he paused, and remembered it was his decision to steam at night among the icebergs and added: "Besides, it all happened because I made the decision I did. That's the trouble with command. You have to make decisions and sometimes they're wrong, and if you're the captain of a ship they can be lethal."

There were, however, no more disasters to bedevil this second leg of the voyage. A few days later the *Hudson* finally reached 55 degrees south and turned north-west, back to the South American mainland and Buenos Aires, the next port of call. And it was then that Peter Beamish acquired another piece of scientific data which to him helped justify his participation in the expedition.

At 8.45 a.m. on January 11, while the scientists lingered over breakfast and anticipated the pleasures of Buenos Aires five days away, the loudspeakers crackled and the voice of the officer of the watch piped the now familiar words: "Dr. Beamish to the bridge, please." Beamish leapt up, scattering bacon and eggs, climbed to the next deck where the bridge crew pointed to a solitary black and white dolphin arching through the water alongside the ship. It was the scout of a school of the rarely seen *Lagenorhynchus cruciger*. Of all the dolphins these are perhaps the shyest. Some dolphins, particularly the common Atlantic bottle-nosed dolphin, ride the bow wave of any passing ship and seem to enjoy the attention they receive. But the *Lagenorhynchus* is ship-shy and, typically, travels in schools with scouts ahead to investigate anything alien. In this case it seems the scout that encountered the *Hudson* decided the ship was harmless. As Beamish explained: "Whales seem to be able to sense your intentions, and we were friendly." In any event, the scout dolphin did not alarm the school because within minutes there were a half-dozen of the five to seven foot long dolphins alongside, arching playfully out of the water, plunging along in great leaps as they passed the ship, which was doing 13.5 knots at the time. They were in view for barely a minute. In that time Beamish shot a roll of thirty-six exposures using a long-focus lens on his camera, and he was to later pronounce that these were invaluable because, greatly enlarged, they would enable biologists to study the pigmentation of the species.

Beamish was jubilant. It was, to him, an important piece of research material, and he had obtained it at almost the last minute. Along with most of the scientists who had been aboard since Rio, he would be leaving the *Hudson* at Buenos Aires. Most were glad to be doing so. Ced Mann recorded in his journal that by the end of that particular four week phase of the expedition spirits were low. The weather had been bad, the stations closer together and the work load therefore more time-consuming. "There was less time and inclination to relax," he wrote. As they sailed north the weather warmed again. Dave Butler went briefly back on his diet because his wife Maria, who he had met and married in Argentina when a merchant marine officer more than ten years earlier, was flying down from Halifax to spend a few days with him. Bob Conover announced that he knew of a night club in Buenos Aires where the band still played 1950s jazz, of which he was devotedly fond, and made Carol Lalli and Georgie Deevey promise to join him and other scientists who planned to visit it. "We've got to have someone to dance with," he said. Ced Mann let his thoughts turn to his own experiment, the attempt to measure the currents in the Drake Passage between Cape Horn and Antarctica, which would be the major scientific work on the next leg of the voyage.

Fred Muise began to brood.

3

For all that it is the largest city in the southern hemisphere, Buenos Aires is an unimpressive sight when leaving harbour or entering it. At a distance it is a lazy, shapeless fungus that stretches back to the horizon of the great treeless plain that runs down to the turbid waters of the River Plate. In closer, it emerges as a strangely European-style city distinguished by great wide avenues and a skyline serrated with church and cathedral spires and the great dome of the Congressional Palace. The *Hudson* left the man-made harbour at 10.15 a.m. on January 22. By 7.00 p.m. she was passing Montevideo, capital of Uruguay, on the north shore of the river mouth, and was preparing to turn south to hug the coast down to Cape Horn and to what Ced Mann privately feared might be his own scientific Nemesis.

As the ship met the increasing ocean swell at the river mouth Dr. Eric Mills stood on deck and noted that "the high buildings of Montevideo . . . rose white above the water and had an unearthly, unreal quality about them, as if by enchantment cleansed of all people, evil-doing and defilement. Such is the power of the sea over a city built by man and seen at a distance." As he wrote this in his diary, Mills paused and thought of the power the sea seemed to have over him. It was the first day of his voyage and he felt strangely content. He knew it was a feeling that would not last; that before long he would be sated with shipboard life, would start pining for Anne and the kids. But now he was happy, and he wondered whether this was because of the sea itself, or because it was the start of another adventure. He fancied it was the sea.

His first clear memory, from the age of three, was of the ocean lapping the beach at Buzzards Bay in Massachusetts, whence the family had been taken on holiday from Toronto by his father. And another of the persistent, almost uncomfortably clear memories that shone through his thirty-four years was of seeing the Pacific for the first time, when he had gone to British Columbia to work one summer as a student assistant to a marine biologist. Prior to that he had thought he would be an ornithologist, but the Pacific had changed that and he had become a marine biologist instead. The ocean had stirred in him shadowy forebodings that were unsuspected and which he was unable to articulate, even to himself. It was so vast it imposed no sense of restriction on a man as the land did, yet it was also deep, dark, mysterious, brooding – waiting, it always seemed to him, for the right moment to rear up and, in storms and tidal waves, prove to man that he really is a puny creature who should be penitently humble before the might of nature. This feeling about the sea was not a particularly scientific reason for having turned from birds to marine biology, but it was as good a motivation as any for a life's work, and Mills was content.

The sea was a magnet and, while he accepted and enjoyed that fact, the trained scientific mind of the biologist considered possible explanations. The ratio of the chemical components of both blood and seawater were intriguingly alike. The quantities weren't the same, of course, nor the consistency but the actual ratios of sodium, magnesium, sulphate, chlorine, potassium and other components of both seawater and human blood were so similar in both that many biologists regarded it as proof that man had evolved from creatures that, millenia before, had come from the seas. There were even some biologists who believed (privately, more often than not) that the ongoing march of evolution of which man was the current apogee had begun when the invertebrate creatures of the deeps, like those which filled so many jars at Mills' laboratory at Dalhousie University in Halifax, had trapped part of the ancient oceans inside them and that this became the juices of changing life forms. There were even some scientists who suggested – again privately – that the blood of man might be of the same consistency and structure as those first waters that sloshed around the earth in the days of Creation. Supposing they were right? It would explain the lure of the sea, its fascination for man. It was simply chemical attraction.

In any event, it was at least possible that the ancient seas ran in the veins of modern man. While collecting his benthic organisms – the tiny creatures that live on the seabed – in the Antarctic they would undoubtedly pick up a collection of tunicates, worm-like creatures sometimes three feet long and usually tubular. They live by taking in seawater at one end and passing it out the other. Somewhere in between a membranous filter traps the plankton in the seawater. These then drop down into the primitive digestive system and the filtered water goes on out the hole in the other end. They have only the most primitive circulatory system of their own, but perhaps some similar creatures had, a few billion years ago, closed off the orifices through which the seawater passed and trapped a portion of the ancient oceans inside them to use for their own evolutionary development into more complex creatures. Even today, in the larval stage, tunicates seem to have the beginnings of a primitive backbone though this disappears by the time the creature is full grown. And at the base of all Creation it was those creatures that grew spines that were able to flourish, to become great fish and then amphibians crawling on to land and then – if the theories were right – eventually set in motion the chain of evolutionary events which ultimately produced man.

Evolution was much on Eric Mills' mind as the *Hudson* left Buenos Aires because he and Dr. Fred Cooke, a geneticist from Queen's University in Kingston, Ontario, had spent two weeks tramping around the pampas of southern Chile trying to study the Lesser Magellan Goose in the hope they would get some clue to the unique evolutionary processes taking place in Canada's own Arctic geese. Barely twenty years ago the literature on North American birds had defined the Snow Goose and the Blue Goose, both abundant in Canada's Arctic, as separate species. Since then ornithologists and geneticists – Fred Cooke among them – had proved they were in fact of the same species, as were thousands of grey geese of the same shape and with the same cry: a short, high pitched sound once described as being like the bark of a chihuahua dog.

The problem had been the distinct colour differences. The Arctic Goose was a snowy white, the Blue Goose clearly blue. Since distinct colour differences within a single bird species are rare it was understandable that they had been classified as distinctly different. But the growing numbers of grey geese – birds neither white nor blue – had posed the sort of haunting question, a massive "Why?", that provides the motive power for pure scientists like Mills and Cooke. The final conclusion was that the two birds were of the same species; that they and the growing numbers of grey geese should be re-classified as the Arctic Goose – and it seemed that in the great flocks of these Arctic Geese man could actually see evolution taking place, a species mutating to survive in changing circumstances before mankind's very eyes.

The possible reasons for the change are fascinating. Perhaps the geese were all white when the glaciers stretched farther south, and white would have been the colour most suited for survival. But over the past fifty years Arctic temperatures have been going up; there's been a five degree increase in places. Coincidentally, the glaciers in the far north have, almost imperceptibly, been receding. For instance, somewhere around the turn of the century the waters around Greenland warmed up a couple of degrees and for that reason great schools of cod moved in and flourished. For most of this century those cod-fishing grounds have been important to the world, but now the cod are vanishing, not through overfishing but because the water appears to have begun to grow colder and the cod don't like it. In any event, if the geese were white during the ice age, it is possible the species mutated to produce some blue geese because blue would be a less obvious colour against the background of forest and field. Thus the blue goose would be a less easy victim for predators. With the Arctic glaciers receding in the wake of a temperature increase, this mutation procedure might be accelerating. But then perhaps the geese had always existed in both colours, and the great increase in cross-breeding between the colours was because today grey was a better survival colour. And then again, the increase in human predators –

duck hunters – could also explain the increase in grey geese. Duck hunters, faced with a flyover of a mixed flock, would shoot the white birds rather than the blue for reasons a psychologist might have fun postulating. That would reduce the pool of white goose genes in the species, and *that* meant the blue geese would impose their genetic structure – their colour – on the white ones and produce the greys.

In an effort to find a clue to the real reason for changes in the appearance of the Arctic Goose, Mills and Cooke, both due to work on Hudson 70, set out early to spend two weeks studying the Lesser Magellan Goose, one of the few species of birds known to have distinct colour differences within it. The females are all brown, but some males have pure white breasts while others have white breasts with black bars on them. Mills and Cooke spent the time on a sheep farm about fifty miles inland from Punta Arenas, the world's most southerly city, and found failure. They had arrived at the end of the breeding season, and the great flocks had broken up into small groups, all wary of man. Mills and Cooke spent days traipsing over bleak countryside burdened with binoculars, telescopes and cameras. Their one near success came when they caught some chicks, took them back to the farm and made plans to rear them in captivity. That night a farm dog killed all the chicks. And so, no wiser, they left to join the *Hudson* in Buenos Aires. Mills and Cooke would continue to study birds, while Mills would also be collecting benthic organisms from the deep Antarctic with Allan Michael, a graduate student from Dalhousie University, as his assistant and Bob Hessler, of the Scripps Institute of Oceanography in California, as his partner.

For them, as for all the scientists, the six day voyage down to the land that might be called the edge of the civilized world – Patagonia (which means "big feet" in Spanish) and Tierra del Fuego (the land of fire) was uneventful. Little scientific work was done. The major work of Phase Three of Hudson 70 was to be in the Antarctic.

Patagonia is the name given by the Spanish to the most southerly tip of the South American mainland. Tierra del Fuego is separated from the mainland by a tortuous waterway discovered by Magellan and named after him as the Straits of

Magellan. Most of Patagonia is in Argentina, and the remainder is part of Chile. The area was settled in the 1860s by the Welsh and the English who not only imported sheep but also diseases which were fatal to most of the natives, tribes of tall, athletic people who wore oversized boots stuffed with grass to keep them warm in a bleak and unfriendly climate. Tierra del Fuego earned its name from the fact that it is a storehouse of natural gas as well as other fossil fuels. When the first explorers came they saw, as did the men of Hudson 70, great bushes of flame where the gas escaped from the rocks below and, ignited perhaps by lightning, burned merrily through time to be fanned and occasionally extinguished by the howling pamperos – the winds of often seventy miles an hour or more that howl abrasively across a land that is largely arid (less than ten inches of rain annually) and therefore sterile, the fecund river valleys and mountain slopes standing out as slashes of green in a bleak world.

The *Hudson* headed first for Punta Arenas to pick up a pilot to guide them down through the labyrinthine inland waterways and fiords to Puerto Williams, the most southerly outpost of civilization on the continent. It is a Chilean naval base in Tierra del Fuego occupied by 200 officers and men and perhaps a dozen or so senior officers' wives. It is the focal point of the dispute between Argentina and Chile over the ownership of islands in the archipelago, the most southerly of which is the mountainous rock which rears with brutal suddenness from the sea and is called Cabo de Hornos – the dreaded Cape Horn.

From Punta Arenas, which would subsequently figure largely in the crew's recollections of the expedition, the *Hudson* sailed in the wake of history's best known oceanographic expedition, that by the sailing ship *Beagle* whose principle scientist passenger was Charles Darwin. It was here, in the islands north of Cape Horn as well as in the Galapagos, that Darwin found much of the evidence on which he based his theories of *The Origin of Species* and of the history of the world as well. To the biologists aboard it was an awesome moment when the ship passed Darwin Island to the starboard. Eric Mills, whose stubborn streak of romanticism insisted on intruding on his scientific detachment, wrote in his diary: "The Darwin Range rose rugged and snow-capped, with massive white and blue snowfields. The top of Mount Darwin itself was hidden in cloud, but gleamed out occasionally. I wonder if Darwin now sits there, like Zeus on Olympus, watching biologists pass through the Beagle Channel, following not only his footsteps but trailing in the wake of his work?"

In the event, it was to be another biologist, Ed Bousfield from the National Museum in Ottawa, who would spend the most time treading in Darwin's footsteps. He would be dropped at Puerto Williams and spend almost a month in the archipelago with another scientist collecting specimens and data from beaches and rocky shorelines. In the meantime the *Hudson* would be off across the Drake Passage between Cape Horn and Antarctica where Ced Mann would at last be able to do his own major work. But first there was a courtesy stop at the Puerto Williams base, where Dave Butler gave a party for Chilean officers and their wives.

The ship anchored offshore and guests were ferried out from the base. In its own way this party was every bit as successful a social occasion as the more glittering receptions staged in major ports. As Butler described it in his official cruise report to the Bedford Institute: "We were well received by the Chilean Naval authorities at Puerto Williams. The Commanding Officer of the base and some 30 of his officers and their wives were entertained at a cocktail party on board on the evening of 28 January. This went off very well. Only four of the guests, including one lady, fell into the harbour on their return ashore."

And then it was time for the Drake Passage and Ced Mann's attempt to achieve what had until then been impossible: to "take the pulse of the oceans".

It was Francis Bacon who first said, almost 400 years ago, that knowledge is power, and in his rare idle moments Ced Mann was prone to think that Bacon was a good man for the pure scientist to quote when questioned by laymen about the expensive and time consuming pursuit of knowledge for its own sake. Yet when his thinking turned in this direction there were

81

two other familiar quotations that also came to mind. First the one about power corrupting whoever possesses it. Then the one about a little knowledge being a dangerous thing.

Mann's own work, the study of ocean circulation, was as good an example of the problem as most, and better than many. Since what happens in the three-quarters of the world that is ocean affects the growth of wheat on the prairies, of potatoes or apples in England, of rice in Asia or cattle in the Kootenays, it was obvious that greater knowledge of the oceans would give mankind power to manipulate his land environment to his greatest benefit. For instance, the climate in any part of the world is in part dictated by the oceans. If man has enough knowledge of those oceans and how waters circulate and change temperature it should be possible to advise farmers in, say, Britain, that a particular year will produce weather that is good for fruit growing and cabbages, but not for potatoes and root crops. With that kind of advance information it should be possible to use the world's food productivity potential with maximum efficiency.

But then there is the disquieting thought that a little knowledge is dangerous. Man has very little knowledge of the oceans. He does not know exactly what is happening in the oceans. He cannot yet define the natural laws and influences that affect the oceans and thus the weather. Even so, the little real knowledge that man does have of his environment has corrupted him. His knowledge is inadequate to give him the power over his fate that he needs to survive in a world already facing famine through over-population. Yet he has just enough knowledge and superficial power to be arrogant, to assume that he is the ultimate Creation and therefore master of all. Truth is, in many fundamental areas – and again the oceans are a good example – man is only now reaching the frontiers of real knowledge. There are many theories about the ways in which the waters of the world circulate around the oceans, but theories are not knowledge. Man does not *know*.

And what Ced Mann wanted above all else was to know. More precisely, down in the Antarctic, the mother of all the oceans, he wanted to know which way and how fast the water moved from one ocean to the other.

The three major world oceans – Pacific, Atlantic, Indian – can be seen on a world map as three great bays in one vast ocean, all linked in the south by the Antarctic, which surruonds the continent of that name. Around that southern land mass swirls the circumpolar current, carrying water from one ocean to another. In this sense it is the main artery of the world. Of the three oceans the Atlantic is the youngest – it's only a few billion years old – and the most complex and interesting as well, largely because it extends further north than either Pacific or Indian oceans, providing an uninterrupted water link between the ice pack that covers the North Pole and the continent of Antarctica, on which is located the South Pole. Much of the deep bottom water of the Atlantic comes from the Arctic, while the colder deeper water – the abyssal currents – of Pacific and Indian oceans largely comes from the Antarctic.

The Atlantic has four distinct layers of water. The surface layer has definable currents, called gyres (from gyration) created by prevailing winds and the west-east rotation of the earth – the coriolis effect. There are two main gyres, one north of the equator, one south. The northern gyre, for instance, swirls in a roughly circular motion between Europe and North Africa in the east and North America in the west and forms a "fence" around a great mass of relatively static water in the central North Atlantic called the Sargasso Sea, a name inspired by the great floating beds of Sargassum weed that are carried along in the current of the gyre itself. Since the waters of the Sargasso Sea are almost motionless and there is very little mixing between the surface layer and the colder, lower layers, the surface retains the heat of summer and this helps ensure that Bermuda, sitting in the western edge of the Sargasso Sea, has year-long temperate weather while those parts of North America on the same latitude are swept with snowstorms in winter and bake in broiling sun in summer.

Bermuda's climate is also partly due to the fact that for part of its journey the western edge of the gyre is joined by the Gulf Stream, that benign and unexplained current of warm water that flows up from the tropic waters of the Gulf of Mexico to make parts of Europe more habitable than the land on similar latitudes in North America. It is because an arm of the Gulf Stream wanders across the North Atlantic and bathes Britain with warm water that you can grow palm trees in southern England while Newfoundland, most of which lies south of Britain, languishes in winter beneath thick layers of snow and nourishes only the hardier sub-arctic trees. Another extension of the Gulf Stream fingers north to disappear near the southern coast of Iceland. Labrador lies on the same latitudes as Britain and well south of Iceland, but Labrador is a brutal land so inhospitable to man that even Indians have rarely ventured inland. Yet Britain's weather is mild and southern Iceland has a climate so comfortable to man that the Vikings settled the area centuries ago. Reykjavik, the capital of Iceland, is a pleasant place to be when Toronto, much further south, is frozen in for the winter. The water off Iceland's southern coast rarely goes below forty degrees Fahrenheit – and yet the northern coast that is unaffected by that errant finger of the Gulf Stream is bleak, forbidding and always almost as frigid as the polar north itself.

The second layer of the Atlantic is centred at about 2,500 feet and consists of colder water from the southern Antarctic. It becomes part of the Atlantic at a point known as the Antarctic Convergence. It is at this point that the South Atlantic current, or gyre, which performs a circular motion south of the equator in much the same way as the North Atlantic gyre does to the north, meets the Antarctic circumpolar current. The South Atlantic gyre is of relatively warm water; that of the circumpolar current is colder and slightly more saline. It is therefore "heavier" and sinks beneath the warmer Atlantic surface waters. There it forms a current that streams slowly north as a second layer toward the equator, mixing with both the warmer surface waters and the colder lower layers until it disappears somewhere around the Caribbean.

The third layer of the Atlantic comes from the Labrador and Norwegian Seas in the north. Both these Arctic seas are deep and their cold waters flow down into the Atlantic between Labrador and Greenland, between Greenland and Iceland (an area called the Denmark Strait), and between Iceland and Scotland. This third layer of cold water never really becomes warm. It passes down the Atlantic at a depth of around 11,000 feet and may take between two and three hundred years to finally reach the Antarctic at the other end of the world, where it becomes part of the circumpolar current and eventually is redistributed through all the oceans.

The fourth, lowest and coldest layer of the Atlantic comes from the Antarctic. It hugs the ocean bed at depths of up to 15,000 feet, slowly mixing with the upper layers until it finally disappears somewhere not far south of Newfoundland in the west and off the coast of Spain in the east.

Here and there these deep waters rise to the surface in what are known as upwelling areas. Either the wind blows the surface waters aside and the deep waters well up to replace them, or the deep waters meet an undersea mountain or shoal and are forced to the surface. And in a third situation that causes upwelling, the deep cold waters meet a layer of still colder water and rise above it. This happens in the Antarctic convergence, where the cold waters of the circumpolar current sinking to the seabed to travel north up the Atlantic meet the upper layers of the Atlantic, which are then forced toward the surface. Man knows some of the upwelling areas, but is constantly discovering more. It happens on the Grand Banks, where it is possible that the undersea shoals of the banks themselves force water upward. And when and where upwelling takes place there is an abundance of life-sustaining nutrients. As all marine life dies it falls to the deep waters, gradually decomposing on its way to the seabed. The organic nutrients released by this decomposition process are brought to the surface in the upwelling areas. The nutrients stimulate the growth of phyto-plankton, and wherever this happens there is an abundance of life. The Antarctic convergence may be one of the most fertile areas on the face of the earth and is a feeding and breeding ground for creatures of all kinds, from the great Blue whales through to microscopic zoo-plankton and tiny seabirds.

If the circulation of the oceans were thoroughly understood it should be possible to chart all the areas where upwelling takes place. The abundance of marine life in these areas would make them all potentially great new sources of fish food and could help the world solve its food shortages. Not long ago an upwelling area was discovered off the northwest coast of Africa, where prevailing winds push surface water aside. This is now being exploited. There are almost certainly many other such areas yet unknown and to find them some marine scientists try to examine charts that have existed in fishing families for centuries. Generations of fishermen have had their own private, and secret, fishing grounds. For centuries a fishing skipper's charts were his most valued possession, for on them was marked the areas he had found most productive. The charts were long considered a more important legacy than the boat itself.

All human activity is affected by ocean currents. Increasing pollution problems make it a matter of urgency to understand them, since pollutants are distributed around the world by these currents. Sewage streaming out of the St. Lawrence, put there largely by Montreal which still has no adequate sewage treatment system despite a 1932 court order, could be carried off by the Gulf Stream and end up fouling the shores of Iceland or Europe. And an enduring pollutant, like DDT, can end up anywhere: the lemmings of the Arctic and the penguins of the Antarctic, both creatures which are born, live and die thousands of miles from civilization, are infected with the residues of pesticides, fungicides and other chemical aids to more productive farming.

The Gulf Stream may be the best example of the mystery of the oceans. That warm, astonishingly blue band of tropic water has for untold years nourished western Europe and provided it with a climate that enabled the Caucasian races to flourish there and emerge as one of the focal forces of civilization. Although scientific interest in the Gulf Stream is relatively recent, its existence was known for centuries to sailors who plied the Atlantic. They learned to avoid it on the way from Europe and to seek its aid on the way back: the five-mile-an-hour current running northward and then east would hinder them one way and help carry them along in the other.

Until recently it was thought the Gulf Stream was a surface current but in 1960 U.S. scientists suspended floats 9,000 feet down along the path of the stream and tracked them by sonar. They found the floats moved in the same direction as the Gulf Stream on the surface, though more slowly. This suggests the current reaches down to the abyssal depths and may be influenced by the undersea mountains and ridges. This, then, might explain why the Gulf Stream meanders around the ocean without apparent rhyme or reason. Southeast of Newfoundland it splits, so that part of it heads north and east towards Britain and part of it turns south to join that North Atlantic gyre that enfolds the Sargasso Sea and Bermuda. This split may be caused by an underwater ridge known to exist 10,000 feet beneath the surface off the Newfoundland coast.

Like so much of that postulated when Ced Mann and other physical oceanographers discuss the oceans, this is simply a theory. But it is a theory with enormous implications. Suppose the temperature of the Gulf Stream is found to change cyclically over a period of years. In that event meteorologists might be able to predict the weather years ahead. If the same information were known for all ocean currents other parts of the world could equally be made more productive. The potential benefits of knowing just how – and how fast – the available storehouse of life sustaining nutrients are moved around the world by the oceans are equally dramatic. Man will never "harvest" the oceans until he knows what they can produce. It is believed – largely on evidence acquired by measuring temperature and salinity of the several distinct layers of all the oceans – that the water in the deeps is almost still, that it moves sluggishly at about one-quarter of a mile an hour. But does it? It is at least possible that if oceanographers really knew how fast those deep waters do move around the globe, the u.s. might have reconsidered its decision to dump concrete containers holding sixty-seven tons of surplus lethal nerve gas, enough to destroy all life on a continent, in the deep Atlantic 282 miles off the Florida coast as it did in August 1970. Dumping toxic materials into the ocean, even in containers, carries unknown hazards. One day that nerve gas will end up in the oceans, and without knowing precisely how fast the deep waters move it is impossible to accurately predict the consequences.

By the time Hudson 70 left Halifax the u.s. had developed techniques to measure the sluggish deep currents of the open ocean. However, no one had produced and used equipment that had been successful in areas where the currents were stronger – places like the Drake Passage, where the circumpolar current funnels through the 500-mile straits between the north-ernmost tip of Antarctica and the southernmost tip of South America. For all Ced Mann knew the currents might be so strong they would sweep away the new equipment that Bedford Institute technicians had spent two years developing. The chances of success or failure were imponderable. The irony of the situation was that the Hudson 70 expedition had its genesis in 1967 aboard the *Hudson* during an earlier attempt to measure deep currents in the Denmark Straits between Greenland and Iceland, where water from the Norwegian Sea streams down to form that third layer of the Atlantic. That experiment had been unsuccessful. And yet it had given birth to this, one of the most ambitious scientific expeditions ever mounted by man.

It was February 1967 and Mann was chief scientist aboard the *Hudson*, heading through the whiplash end of the northern winter to the 200-mile-wide Denmark Straits where the ship was to lay six strings of current meters. They are secured to a cable weighted at one end so it will drop to the seabed and supported by a buoy at the other which keeps it upright. The equipment was developed by the u.s. and this experiment was jointly mounted by the Woods Hole Oceanographic Institution in Massachusetts and the Bedford Institute, where Mann heads the ocean circulation division. The director of the Atlantic Oceanographic Laboratory at the Bedford Institute, Dr. William Ford, was aboard the *Hudson* because, he told Mann, "I need to get some sea time in so I can stay in touch. When you're in an administrative job you get no time to do your own science, and if you don't go to sea once in a while you get stale."

The two men, old friends who had once worked together in defence research for the federal government, began talking of future projects for the Bedford Institute's fleet, the *Hudson* in particular. Mann unashamedly began to think of projects for the ship that would also enable him to go south to study the Antarctic convergence. Bill Ford had an abiding interest in the western Arctic; the Beaufort Sea was little explored, and he was conscious of Canada's need to know more about its continental shelf in the potentially resource rich Arctic. The *Hudson*'s captain, Walter Kettle, joined the discussions as the voyage progressed, and to them he brought his own dream of making the Northwest Passage. Three men with three ambitions, all of which could be dovetailed neatly into a voyage circumnavigating North and South America, something no ship had ever done before – and that alone was important. All three men were aware of the need for Canada to establish itself as a leading nation, and the Bedford Institute as a world centre, in the field of marine science. The Institute had been opened in 1962 by the then newly-formed Marine Sciences Division of the Department of Energy, Mines and Resources, a division set up to bring the fragmented marine science work by several government departments under one umbrella. For the first five years the main task had been to seduce the best available scientists into oceanography, then leave them to find their own projects to work on. By that February of 1967 both Ced Mann and Bill Ford believed the nascent years had ended; that it was time for Canada and the Bedford Institute to undertake a dramatic major project.

After the current meters had been laid in the Denmark Straits the *Hudson* put into Reykjavik so Bill Ford could fly back to Halifax. By then it had been decided to sound out Canada's scientific establishment to see how interested they were in doing work on such a major expedition. Precisely six weeks later the *Hudson* returned to the Denmark Straits – and failure. Four of the six strings of current meters (they cost $4,000 each, plus an additional $1,000 for an attendant temperature meter) had disappeared, presumably swept away by currents stronger than anyone had suspected. Mann's disappointment was, however, to be tempered during the next year by the progress of his planning for a major oceanographic expedition. Other scientists within the government and at university departments of marine science were enthusiastic if not optimistic. The reaction of George Pickard, head of the pioneering University of British Columbia Institute of Oceanography, was typical. The idea of circumnavigating the Americas, working all the way, excited him because he wanted to look at the largely uncharted and scientifically unexplored Chilean fiord system. But he was also sceptical; he did not believe Ottawa would ever approve so ambitious an undertaking.

In the fall of 1968 Bill Ford carried Ced Mann's working plan of the projected expedition to Ottawa. There it was presented to Joe Greene, then Minister of Energy, Mines and Resources, and the scheme was approved. "It's the sort of thing Canada should be doing more of," said Greene. And that was how Hudson 70 was born.

In the meantime Tom Foote, a taciturn senior technical officer at the Bedford Institute, had been tinkering with existing current measurement equipment. He had re-designed the equipment to the point that he told Mann there would be a better chance of success next time. Thus encouraged, Mann decided to add to his own scientific programme during Hudson 70. As well as taking temperature and salinity measurements throughout the depth of the ocean around the Antarctic convergence, he would also attempt to measure the strength of the circumpolar current in the Drake Passage. And when the *Hudson* left the Chilean base of Puerto Williams on the 29th of January, 1970, the course was south-south-east, bound for Cape Horn, the Drake Passage and . . . what? Ced Mann feared another Denmark Straits disaster, and hoped for the best.

From the moment the ship had left Buenos Aires, Dave Butler had been a prophet of gloom. He was, he said, a veteran of several passages around Cape Horn and he promised the weather would be foul. Just laying the meters would, he said, be an ugly, uncomfortable job fraught with possible disaster. Argentinian naval oceanographer, Roberto Rebaudi, who had joined the *Hudson* at Buenos Aires, was equally pessimistic. As the ship neared the Magellan Straits both Butler and Rebaudi, a small, dark and normally cheerful man, daily announced that the weather might be passable at that moment "but just wait until tomorrow!" The pamperos would howl in the Magellan Straits, they promised. They didn't. There would be storms and violently capricious winds in the Beagle Channel. There weren't. Both men were quite emphatic about what to expect when the ship cleared Cape Horn itself. Gales. Heaving

90

seas. Sleeting rain that would in seconds turn into an ice storm. Mann, however, had studied the few available weather reports for the Antarctic summer, which it then was. He knew there were often stretches of a week at a time when the weather was, if not pleasant, at least tolerable. And so he hoped.

By supper time on January 29 the *Hudson* began to clear the last of the archipelago islands at the tip of South America. At 7.00 p.m. Ced Mann stood on the open wing of the bridge gazing to starboard. In the distance, perhaps ten miles away, was the hazy hump of the island Cape Horn itself. The wind blew at about twenty m.p.h. The movement of the *Hudson* was gentle. He went below and wrote his journal for the day: "Left Puerto Williams at 0800. Mills had a good sled haul as we left [and] we did two more hauls east of Wollaston Isle. In the evening we were south past Cape Horn in good weather and headed for the first current meter station." Later, in the lounge, after the showing of the film "Girls of Pleasure Island", he greeted Dave Butler and Roberto Rebaudi. "Terrible weather," he said. "We might not be able to sunbathe tomorrow."

Tom Foote, the technical officer who had developed the current meter system Ced Mann was using, had been aboard since Buenos Aires working on the equipment he had designed back in Halifax. And, as the *Hudson* steamed in bright sunlight for the place where the first string of meters was to be laid, even the stoic Foote, a man of six feet three inches and broad to match, began to show signs of tension. If the experiment failed in the same way as the Denmark Straits experiment had failed – that is, because of a failure of the equipment – Ced Mann would be disappointed, but would not have to hold himself directly to blame. Tom Foote, the equipment specialist, would. The moment they started laying the current meters would be the beginning of the end of two years' work of design, research and testing at the Bedford Institute.

The attempt to measure the circumpolar current was the most ambitious undertaking of its kind ever. In the Denmark Straits the sea had been only 1,200 feet deep. In the Drake Passage it was more than 8,000 feet – almost two miles. All the world's oceanographic institutes had been successful in measuring currents in relatively shallow waters, largely because working in such depths it was always possible to recover the meters by dredging, or trawling, from the surface to hook the synthetic ropes to which the metering equipment was attached. That wouldn't be possible in the Drake Passage. It was too deep. The system devised by Foote depended totally on the use of sonar-operated release mechanisms never tried in such conditions.

The meters were to be attached to a single steel wire, not synthetic ropes, which would be anchored to the seabed and kept upright by a specially designed buoy. Finding an anchor, or ballast, heavy enough not to be dragged out of position by the currents was easy. Foote simply obtained a supply of old railway wagon wheels, bolted two together and tied them to one end of the wire. The wire itself was a problem since it had to be strong enough to take the battering in the deeps – but only just strong enough. The heavier the wire the bigger the buoy you must have to keep the wire upright. Foote regarded this as a heads you win, tails I lose engineering problem. The bigger the buoy the heavier the wire must be to weigh it down: the balance of buoyancy and weight is delicate. If the buoy isn't big enough it can be swept down by the currents either to the point where the wire isn't sufficiently upright for the meters to work, or to a depth at which it implodes, crushed by the weight of water. If the buoy is too big it can provide to much buoyancy and, affected by those same currents, can haul the meters out of position. The buoys themselves must be so designed that they will "fly" through the water; in the Denmark Straits the American equipment had involved the use of globular buoys which were swept around willy-nilly by any change in the current. Foote was using specially designed aquadynamic buoys which looked, said Ced Mann, like a cross between pregnant torpedoes and wartime barrage balloons. They would stay nose-on to the current, the fins providing directional stability.

To recover the meters it must be possible to release them from the ship. The sonar-activated release mechanism Foote used was located near the seabed, and must be able to stand up to the ocean's battering and still work. But no one knew just how bad a battering they would have to take two miles beneath the surface. The shackles used to secure one piece of equipment to another must be able to survive rapid sea water corrosion, so Foote was using shackles of stainless steel. The current meters must be mounted in housings that would survive the ocean – but just how rough would be the treatment they would receive?

In the lounge of the *Hudson* on January 29 Foote and Mann reviewed the procedures they were to follow the next day in laying the first of the four strings of current meters, three meters to each string. Foote said the trouble with Ced Mann's experiment was that, in contrast to most of the scientific work done aboard Hudson 70, they were faced with the extremes of total failure or total success. "Only one shackle has to give, those currents down there only have to be a couple of knots more than anyone expects, and the whole thing is a bust," said Foote. Silently Mann agreed, but added: "Well we've done all the homework we can. There's no point worrying now."

The next day, January 30, was anticlimactic. The ship reached the point that Mann had, back in Halifax, chosen as the best location for the first string of current meters and the sonar showed that the bottom was too rough to risk trying to moor the string there. If it fell into a deep undersea fissure or valley, of which there were many, it would go so deep the buoy would implode. The equipment is designed so that the buoy is only around 150 feet beneath the surface, its buoyancy tugging it toward the surface. There is a safety margin of almost 2,000 feet, because the buoy can be swept down to that depth before imploding. Thwarted on its first day by a mountainous seabed, the *Hudson* headed west toward the Pacific, its sonar mapping the ocean floor. Ninety miles from the first and unsuitable location the undersea mountain range ended. Through the morning of January 31 the *Hudson* sailed a criss-cross course in a grid pattern across thirty square miles of ocean. A level area roughly the size of an Arctic landing strip was located. That afternoon the first string of meters was laid. First the bright red buoy was lowered overside. Then the two miles of steel wire with the three packages of measuring instruments attached. Finally the two wheels from the caboose of an old freight train that would rest on the seabed were lowered gingerly into the water. One of the refinements of Tom Foote's equipment was that this great weight of metal would go to the bottom slowly to avoid violent movement that might damage the meters. Two small parachutes were fixed to the wagon wheels so they would float gently down through the Antarctic to land where they had been intended to land – on that flat area of seabed found by sonar.

As the wheels vanished, Foote went to the laboratory where his own special sonar equipment was located. To find out what had happened two miles down he had to "interrogate" the transponder, the electronic device which "talks" to the ship and which also operates the release mechanism located near the wagon wheels. When "interrogated" the transponder replies with a single "bleep", which means it is at least within 45 degrees of the vertical, which is acceptable. If there are two bleeps it means it is either at a greater angle than 45 degrees – that would mean that either the whole string had collapsed, perhaps because the buoy had imploded, or that the currents were so strong they had swept buoy and cable along to the point where the angle was too acute for the current to work. Mann stood watching as Foote manipulated the equipment. Outwardly Mann is always calm. When he doesn't feel that way inside he rolls a cigarette instead of smoking a ready-made one. That way his hands are busy. As Foote sent the "interrogative" signal Mann rolled a cigarette. It took between one and two minutes for the signal to reach the seabed and for the transponder to reply. It did so with a single "bleep". Both Foote and Mann grinned, and Foote said: "One gone, three to go."

Next day, February 1, they laid the second string of meters one hundred miles to the south. The weather was worsening. Fred Cooke and Eric Mills, up early to count birds, found ten inches of snow on the bridge deck, but it soon melted. The third and fourth strings were laid on successive days. The first, third and fourth strings were laid without a hitch. But when Foote had "interrogated" the transponder on the second string there had been no answering signal. What had happened down there? Had the whole string been swept away almost before it had been put in position and the transponder crushed or in some way damaged? Or had the transponder just failed? And if it had failed, was it a total failure? Would it still operate the release mechanism? They would have to wait two weeks before

94

there was any hope of answering these questions because it was planned to leave the meters in position for about that length of time. But these questions were themselves overshadowed by the bigger one: would the current meters and their mooring equipment stand up to whatever happened down there, and could they be recovered?

On the night of February 3, the last string of current meters laid, the *Hudson* set sail for Antarctica to continue the sampling programme for Cooke, Hessler and the other biologists. It was cold and the wind blew at a steady forty knots, though the sea remained relatively calm – much calmer than anyone had expected in the Drake Passage. Fred Muise, looking strained and pale, told ship's surgeon Rustige he had not been able to eat for almost a week without vomiting and that now he had "a skin disease". Rustige gave him tranquilizers and ordered him to rest. Rustige told the captain Muise wasn't really fit for work and had been complaining of stomach pains and sickness that in his opinion were psychologically induced. In his complaints, said Rustige, Muise did not mention the death of his year-old son in Halifax just before Christmas. Like Muise, Eric Mills was a radio ham and the two men had grown friendly. But in the preceding week Muise had grown increasingly withdrawn, complaining of his physical condition. He thought he was either seasick – which was surprising in a man accustomed to the sea – or that he had food poisoning. Strangely, he had not talked to Mills about the death of his baby son, though Mills had seen photographs of two small boys – the five-year-old and the baby – on the locker in Muise's cabin. On February 5, when the *Hudson* was in the South Shetland Islands, Mills wrote in his diary that "the condition of Fred Muise is going downhill." The night before Muise had noisily rambled and moaned in his cabin and next door Mills had heard him through the bulkhead. Ced Mann, worried, said that if Muise's condition did not improve they would have to head back across the Drake Passage to Puerto Williams and fly him to hospital.

On February 7 the *Hudson* put into Admiralty Bay on King George Island, a storied name from the annals of whaling and

Antarctic exploration, for in the southern winter pack ice forms a bridge across the Bransfield Straits between Antarctica and the South Shetland Islands. More recently it had been Base G of the Falkland Islands Dependencies Survey occupied in the late 1950s and early 1960s by groups of men working for the British, for whom the islands were claimed in 1819 by Captain William Smith. It was a remote, unlovely place even now in the high summer of the south. Eric Mills wrote: "We went ashore on to the rocky beach to a land of stones, greenish-yellow carpets of moss and crumbling slopes of volcanic rocks. A pair of Trenton penguins was standing by the shore and we stalked them for photographs in superb close-up views of the features, almost mammalian tail and strong yellow-pink feet and legs. The *Hudson* lay offshore in a setting of cold grey water, floating ice, black rocky slopes and blinding white snow slopes and glacier fronts. Snow flurries passed across the bay and between flurries a weak sun half-heartedly glowed through the overcast." Directly inland from the mouth of the bay there is a glacier. The half dozen huts of Base G, widely separated as are the buildings of all Arctic and Antarctic bases for fear of fire, are to the west of the glacier. Behind them towers a pinnacle of rock about 1,000 feet high.

Tom Foote was in the first launch ashore. He carried a "time capsule" fashioned from a cylinder which once contained scientific equipment. Into it he had thrust two booklets, one in English and one in Spanish, which described the Hudson 70 expedition. With them he included a slip of paper on which was written his name and address. He set about climbing to the top of the pinnacle of rock where he would eventually bury his capsule beneath a cairn of rocks. He clambered across loose boulders and scree and, more gingerly, traversed a patch of aging, crumbling ice about half a mile wide. Half way across he looked back; saw four wooden crosses behind the huts. "What the hell am I doing?" he said out loud. "There are already four graves on this island and doing this sort of thing is probably what killed them." But he reached the summit, built his cairn and gazed down at the white-painted *Hudson* at anchor, looking, he said later, like a Mediterranean yacht that had strayed wildly off course. From where he stood the huts of the

A
VOYAGE
WITHOUT
END

The Canadian Scientific Ship *Hudson* spent almost a year
sailing from Halifax down to the Antarctic, up the Pacific
to Vancouver and then – in an unexpectedly dramatic climax
that subtly changed the future of the world – up to the Arctic
and through the Northwest Passage. She travelled almost 58,000
miles and carried more than 120 scientists studying the oceans.
It was a voyage to the edges of the world: To the physical edges
of the inhabited world, and to the borders of man's knowledge
of that world. And since every question the scientists answered
posed a dozen more for future explorers, the voyage of the
Hudson was a voyage without end.

Capt. David Butler

Dr. Cedric Mann spent two years organizing the Hudson 70 expedition, one of the most ambitious exploration programmes of its kind ever mounted. When the *Hudson* left Halifax, N.S., on November 19, 1969, without there being any apparent hitch, Dr. Mann felt almost cheated: There should, he felt, have been some unforseen oversight or drama at the last minute to cause some real excitement. Captain David Butler, on the other hand, was over-joyed. What Mann did not know was that a couple of nights earlier, in thick fog, there had been drama to spare on the ship's bridge. The *Hudson,* and the entire expedition, had narrowly missed being wrecked. The first scientific work was scheduled to begin at the equator, but acoustics expert Peter Beamish got half the ship involved in his experiments before then. He was aboard to eavesdrop on whales talking to one another. His enthusiasm was compelling, if not infectious, and as soon as the *Hudson* reached the tropics he had most of the off-watch officers and scientists whale-spotting on his behalf.

Dr. Cedric Mann

The bridge, with Butler at the clear- screen window.

Whalewatchers' corner

The captain's dog

From the equator on, sonar expert Oreste Bluy announced breakfast and started each day's scientific programme by tossing a stick of dynamite over the stern. As it exploded the sound waves travelled deep to bounce off the night-marish creatures in the Scattering Layer, great colonies of grotesque marine life that live between 300 feet and a mile below the surface, moving up and down by inflating or deflating air bladders that provide buoyancy. It was an experiment designed to help track down enemy submarines. Daily, the *Hudson* stood "on station" to take samples of the ocean at various depths and take the ocean's temperature as well. Daily, too, biologists would collect samples of phyto- and zoo-plankton – the "grass" and the "insects" of the sea. In the picture far right (bottom) biologist Bob Conover, hydrographer Russ Melansson, Chief Officer Mauger and bo'sun Joe Avery watch as a mess of plankton is about to be emptied into buckets before being preserved for study. An occasional addition to the daily routine was the taking of a seabed sample by lowering the giant corer to within twenty-five feet or so of the ocean floor, then dropping it. From one ten-foot core of sediment scientists can often trace a million years of natural history. At the time, however, the entire ship had a more immediate problem to solve: How to housetrain the captain's puppy, Nicodemus, when there was no "outdoors" to send him to.

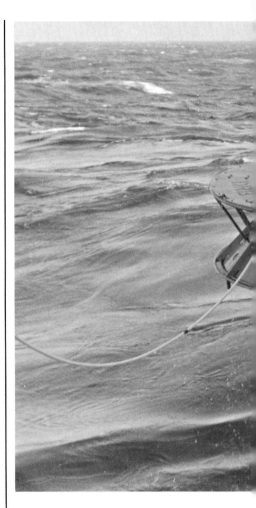

The seabed corer

Oreste Bluy's sonar cone for receiving signals from the Scattering Layer

A plankton tow

Korean botanist Chung Choi and Montreal biologist Dr. Carol Lalli never met aboard the *Hudson* because he got off at Rio de Janiero before she went aboard. Yet they had much in common. He was trying to measure the "sweat" of phyto-plankton, the smallest life form on earth, and she was studying the prey-predator relationship between two types of tiny zoo-plankton called pterapods. The results of the work of both will help prove whether it is practical to short circuit the food-chain and take our food supplies from the bottom. Scientifically speaking, it's wasteful to wait for the sun's energy to be turned into solid matter by phyto-plankton and pass up the food chain until it ends up in a fish form palatable to humans. If the population explosion continues and food supplies go on diminishing, man could one day find it necessary to eat Planktonburgers just to stay alive. Aboard Hudson 70 Chung Choi did his work from a lifeboat tethered to the ship. Carol Lalli and biologist colleague Dr. Georgie Deevey were the first women to take part in Hudson 70, and although they weren't aware of it their presence did much to improve the low spirits of a shipload of men at sea over Christmas. Some sailors, however, still held the old superstition about women at sea being bad luck.

U.S. biologist Bob Conover tried to take advantage of their presence by playing strong man in distress. He had, he piteously explained to Carol Lalli, a seam that needed stitching. Graciously she lent him a needle and thread. When she went to her laboratory she found Conover trying to thread the needle – with the aid of a 25-power microscope. She fell for it to the extent of threading the needle for him – but he still had to do the sewing job himself.

Whaleman Peter Beamish

The women biologists in stern laboratory

Chung Choi returning aboard after weathering storm in a lifeboat

Carol Lalli (right) and Georgie Deevey in lounge

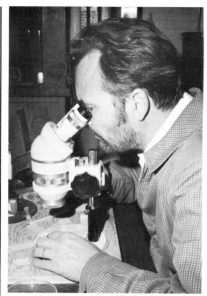

Biologist Gus Vilkes

Main geophysics laboratory aft of bridge

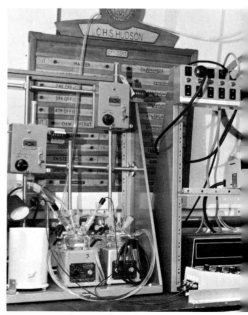

Seawater chemical analysis equipment

To look at, the main computer aboard the *Hudson* during Hudson 70 was a typical humanists' nightmare – spinning tapes, chattering teletype print-out mouthpieces, dancing lights and all those inevitable, implacable, inexorable dials. And in truth it was a bit like that during the busy periods of the day. But come the night watch, when there was just a pool of bright light in a dark and muted world, the duty operator could lean back in the comfortable reclining bucket seat borrowed from a European car and twinkle his fingers across the right buttons and – presto! – it turned out that computer played a pretty mean game of poker. Or blackjack. Or chess. Or even tic-tac-toe. The machine was even comfortingly abusive because if, in blackjack say, you touched the wrong keys its chattering print out would roundly abuse you with: "Come on, you damn fool, play up or pay up and get out."

That computer console

"... south past Cape Horn in good weather. ..." – Ced Mann's Journal

There are scientists who believe the blood in your veins may be a sample of the ocean waters as they were at the time of Creation. No one will know for sure, but science has proved that there is a startling similarity between the chemical structure of blood and seawater. And certainly the world has a circulatory system which distributes waters around the globe. The main artery – the pulse – of this system is the Antarctic ocean, which swirls around that continent, mixing the waters of Pacific, Atlantic and Indian oceans. It was Ced Mann's dream to measure the speed at which water passed through this artery, and he and the *Hudson* did so in the Drake Passage – that legendary 500-mile-wide stretch of storm-wracked ocean between Cape Horn in the north and Antarctica in the south. The results astounded the world of science. Current meters designed in Halifax were lowered two miles to the ocean floor. In Antarctica, an abandoned British base in Admiralty Bay was visited; "an unearthly, inhuman sort of place" was the way one scientist described it. Inside the shuttered hut were the debris of living left behind by the last survey crew to stay there. They included an ancient record player found by Tom Foote and Iver Duedall, a collection of books ranging from *Dr. Jekyll and Mr. Hyde* through scientific reference books and first aid manuals to a copy of *Grimm's Fairy Tales*. Behind the main hut of what had been Base G of the Falkland Island Dependencies Survey were the four graves of young Englishmen who had died in the area which Charles Darwin described as "enough to make a landsman dream for a week of death, disaster and shipwreck." The *Hudson* had its disaster.

Lowering current meter

Part of Hudson 70 ashore at Admiralty Bay. From left: Roger Smith, geologist; Iver Duedall, chemist; Hugh Henderson, technician; Dr. Ced Mann; bo'sun Joe Avery; Fred Cooke, Queen's University; Tom Foote, technical officer, and Bob Hessler, Scripps Institution of Oceanography. Squatting in front: Eric Mills, biologist from Dalhousie University in Halifax; Dr. Louis Rustige, ship's surgeon.

and Duedall with Base G record player

One of the four lonely graves

Ced Mann

A few days after visiting the abandoned
British base at Admiralty Bay, the
Hudson visited Deception Island,
another in the Antarctic South Shetland
chain, and there they "went ashore in
Hell," as biologist Eric Mills described
it. Until 1967 Deception was the
location of weather bases set up by
several governments, British, Chilean
and Argentinian among them. That
year the island volcano erupted and the
bases were abandoned. When the
Hudson steamed in to the great natural
harbour the island was still smouldering
and lava-covered. Biologist Mills
thought it looked much as the world
must have when the earth cooled and
life began. The waters around the shore
steamed eerily, so hot from volcanic
action the paint on the ship's dory was
blistered. The Hudson 70 party went
ashore at the site of what had been the
Chilean base. Wrote Mills: "We went
ashore through a steaming sea to a
warm shore of volcanic ash. Ash fields
led up to a cross leaning on the remains
of a shrine, and the twisted, bent
skeletons of radio antennae stood
sentinel over a pile of twisted sheet
metal which had once been huts. Even
in the level ash fields we saw the
pockmarking of conical depressions.
How they formed I can't imagine, but
they gave me a sense of insecurity even
in the flattest parts of this newly formed
landscape. The skeleton of the camp
itself adds to the feeling of impermanence, disaster and death."

Antarctica

A Chilean weather station

"Going ashore in Hell"

Few if any ideas have had such impact on the mind and history of man as that put forward by Charles Darwin in *The Origin of Species*. Darwin made only the one major voyage – aboard the tiny *Beagle* in the 1830s – and from it came evidence to support the theory of evolution. Hudson 70 literally followed in the footsteps of Darwin in what was probably the most intensive programme of biological research done in that area since the *Beagle* had passed that way. Hudson 70 biologists, working in the brief Antarctic summer that was still bleak, cold and uncomfortable, hauled dredges along the ocean floor collecting samples of benthic organisms, creatures that live on the seabed. Their quest was for a clue as to just where life began and how the first primitive life forms spread around the earth. And while shipboard biologists were doing this, Dr. Ed Bousfield of Ottawa was running "the pup of Hudson 70" – a two-man expedition aboard the ship's launch Redhead that wandered the channels and bays of the archipelago islands. Of all the biologists, Bousfield most closely followed Darwin's footsteps; much of his work was almost within sight of the peak called Mount Darwin. Most biologists collected specimens, often of creatures unknown to science, that would occupy them for years to come, classifying, describing, analysing. But Ed Bousfield made one instantly identifiable major find. From one beach in the archipelago he collected four species of amphipod, a tiny creature you'd call a beach flea if you met one sunbathing. One of the four turned out to be at the stage of evolution from marine creature to land creature that amphipods elsewhere in the world had reached and passed several million years ago. He called it "a living dinosaur."

Sled dredge used to collect deep-sea benthic creatures

Ed Bousfield's "living dinosaur" – a multi-million year-old amphipod, or beach flea.

Contents of the dredge

When the Chilean Fiord phase of
Hudson 70 was over Captain Butler
decided it should never have begun.
The *Hudson* was the biggest ship to
have ever navigated the labyrinthine
fiord system on the Pacific coast off the
tip of South America. The fiords are so
poorly charted they were never sure
the ship would not run aground, and
the *Hudson* was also in peril from
winds that could whip from a breeze to
a 100 m.p.h. gale within hours and
howl down the mountainous funnels
of the narrow fiords. The first civilian
pilot assigned to guide the expedition
through the fiords refused to even
board the ship because he thought she
was too big for the job. But with Dr.
George Pickard, of the University of
British Columbia, aboard as chief
scientist, a pioneering study of the fiord
system was completed during a month
of steaming up, down, across, through
and round the maze of fiords and
channels. The navigation hazards were
such that one night Dave Butler and the
two Chilean pilots went out and got
very drunk – to celebrate the fact that
Butler had not had to kill one of them.
And when the fiord phase was ended
the ship called at Robinson Crusoe
Island, a tiny paradise where the village
has two front-parlour bars that serve
only beer. Hudson 70 drank them dry.

Canadian, U.S. and Chilean
scientists who studied the
fiord system

Long hours whiled away
in ship's lounge bar

" . . . Hudson 70 drank them dry"

The Pacific leg of Hudson 70 to measure the "shape" of the world's largest ocean was the longest and, for most, least exciting phase of the entire expedition. The *Hudson* left Valparaiso, turned southwest almost to the coast of Antarctica again, then changed course to due north and steamed with painstaking care 7,200 miles up the 150th meridian almost to the coast of Alaska. The main scientific aim of this leg of the voyage was to measure the gravitational variations in the earth's surface along that 150th meridian so that an elaborate U.S. experiment involving the use of a space satellite might have a better chance of working. There was excitement in the early days, when geophysicist Dick Haworth made a discovery that was to leave the name of the expedition forever marked on charts of the Pacific. But then crew and scientists grew first weary of the Antarctic bleakness, and then comfortably lazy in the South Pacific sun. Oreste Bluy, the sonar expert, lost his receiver cone overboard and his technician made a new one from scrap metal. Crewmen fished from the main deck; U.S. scientist Bill Von Arx revived the Green Flash Club and the ship called at Tahiti. But the most exciting moment came near Hawaii, when crewmen picked up a U.S. hit-parade radio station and heard Anne Murray singing "Snowbird".

Bluy's home-made receiver cone

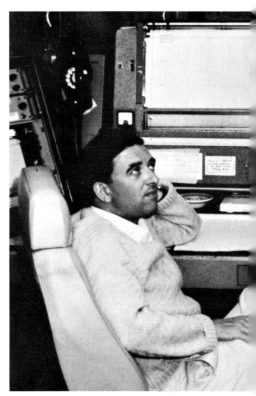

On watch at computer console

Tahiti – and the Hudson

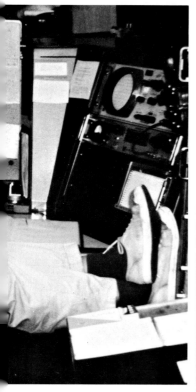

Science? Off-watch scientists making fishing nets.

And then there was the Arctic and the Northwest Passage.

Long afterwards, Dave Butler was to say with rare poesy: "It hung there at the top of the world and at the end, or almost the end, of the whole expedition as the ultimate challenge to me, the *Hudson* and all the men aboard." To the sailors, then, the Arctic leg was a professional challenge, an ultimate achievement for all deep-sea mariners. To the scientists, led by geologist Dr. Bernard Pelletier, it was equally a challenge – a chance to fill in gaps that still yawned on the maps of the north. When Hudson 70 was first planned, it was intended that work in charting the contours of the Continental Shelf of the Beaufort Sea should occupy only two weeks. By the time the *Hudson* left Victoria to head north the Americans had demonstrated a determination to reach the newly discovered Arctic oil reservoirs by sending the supertanker *Manhattan* through the Northwest Passage. For this and other reasons the Arctic phase of Hudson 70 was promoted and perhaps became the most important part of the entire expedition. In the Arctic the *Hudson* was the flagship of a fleet of four Canadian scientific ships. In less than a month the discoveries made by geologists and geophysicists aboard those ships were to change the face of northern development, and cause subtle changes in attitude among those politicians whose greatest concern is the balance of power in the world.

Dr. Bosko Loncarevic at geophysics console

Dave Butler on his bridge going through pack ice

*Plotting course: from left,
Gus Vilks, Butler,
Dr. Pelletier, Roy Gould,
Navigating Officer*

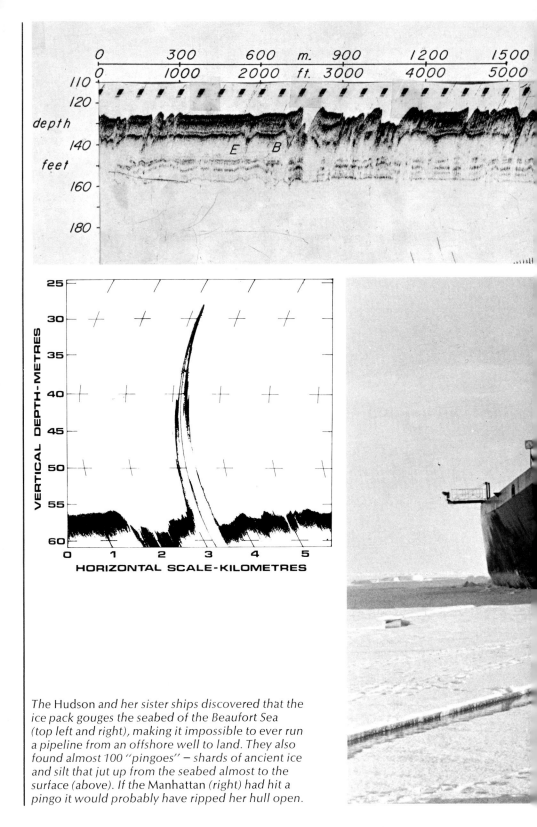

The Hudson and her sister ships discovered that the
ice pack gouges the seabed of the Beaufort Sea
(top left and right), making it impossible to ever run
a pipeline from an offshore well to land. They also
found almost 100 "pingoes" — shards of ancient ice
and silt that jut up from the seabed almost to the
surface (above). If the Manhattan (right) had hit a
pingo it would probably have ripped her hull open.

PORT

500 ┌ 150

ft. | m.

0 └ 0

PINGO-LIKE FEATURES

0 — 0

1000   feet   2000   3000

300   meters   600   900

SHIP'S TRACK

0 — 0

ft. | m.

500 └ 150

STARBOARD

ICE SCOURING ?

MANHATTAN

Gus Vilks collecting samples

Geologists had long suspected the Arctic was a potential bonanza of oil, gas and minerals, but until the 1960s the U.S. was sufficiently rich in such resources to have ignored the fact. However, by the time of Hudson 70 the U.S. and the rest of the western world needed to know just what reserves there were in the Arctic, and how they could be got out. Thus the discovery of ice-gouges on the seabed and of a whole forest of undersea pingoes (see previous page) introduced a new element into the equation. First, offshore wells and conventional tanker transport were shown to be either impossible, or fraught with peril for the fragile Arctic ecology. It was at least partly because of Hudson 70's discoveries that Canada later laid a firm claim to great stretches of the Arctic ocean; that the Americans decided on pipelines to get the oil and gas to southern markets and that Ottawa announced it would not again readily give permission for tankers to use the Northwest Passage. The threat to the ecology of oil exploration was underlined by ex-gold miner turned geologist-biologist Gus Vilks, whose study of the *Orbulina universa* (seen right, magnified 370 times) proved Arctic waters flow in from the Atlantic and that the Canadian north is consequently affected by any pollution in the North Atlantic.

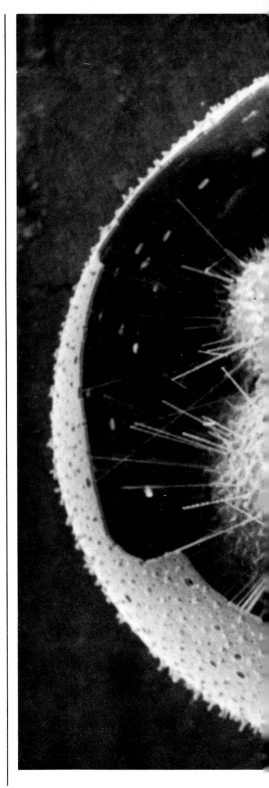

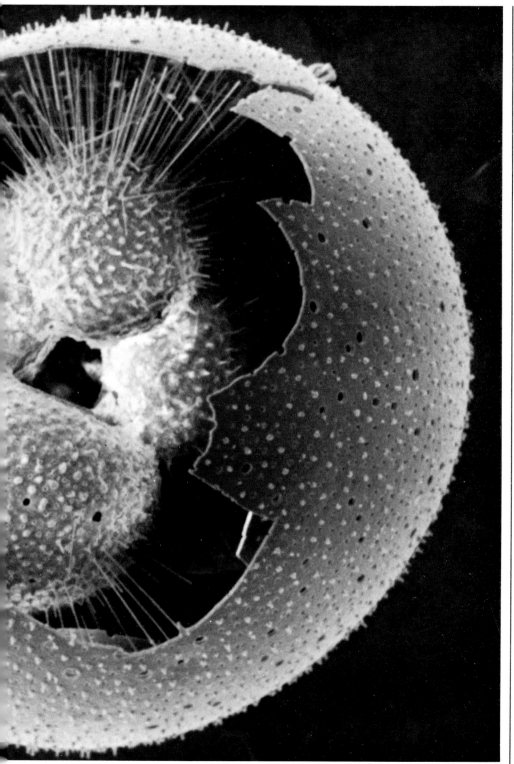

Orbulina universa *as seen through scanning electron microscope.*

Shipboard science has little in common with clinically clean laboratory research. You want to find out what's on the seabed? Then dredge for a magnificient sample of ocean floor sedimentary mud, dump it out on deck and sift through it for the creatures that live there.

Bo'sun Joe Avery made this plaque (right) as the Hudson headed down to the Antarctic. Unable to find a place to erect it there, he finally set it up a few miles outside Resolute in the Canadian Arctic. Aided by Dr. Pelletier, he drilled holes in the top of a massive rock, cemented steel posts in place, then rivetted the plaque to the posts.

There was a mini-mutiny as the *Hudson* left Baffin Bay, scene of the final experiment in the Hudson 70 expedition, and steamed south for home. Dave Butler took the shortest route and set course to pass through the Strait of Belle Isle between Labrador and Newfoundland. But the third of the crew who were from Newfoundland began to rumble their discontent. They pointed out that if the ship did not sail round the *outside* of Newfoundland, it would not have truly circumnavigated the Americas. Ced Mann, who had returned to the expedition to ride with Hudson 70 through the Northwest Passage, could see awesome political embarrassments. Dave Butler did not want to offend a large slice of the crew who had made the expedition possible. So he ordered an abrupt change of course; the ship headed due east and then south around the outside of Canada's youngest province. And then the *Hudson* pointed for Halifax. On October 16, 1970, the *Hudson* steamed down from the northeast to Chebucto Head, the outer extremity of Halifax harbour, and past the assembled frigates and destroyers and submarines of the Canadian navy and beneath the soaring arch of the Angus A. McKay bridge that hadn't been finished when they left a year earlier but was carrying traffic now. Every boat and ship – even the scow-like Dartmouth ferries – blew a salute in an insane cacophony of sirens, hooters and whistles. Joe Greene, then Minister of Energy, Mines and Resources, was on the dock to welcome home the sailors and scientists and the ship in which they had made one of the epic voyages of man. A message from the Governor General said in part: "You have not only added to our store of useful scientific knowledge of our hemisphere and country, but to the stature of our Canadianism."

The Hudson *comes home*

Joe Greene presents massive commemorative plaque to Dave Butler

This commemorative medal was presented to everyone who took part in Hudson 70.

long abandoned base looked like buildings in a children's farm-yard set. When, later, he was asked why he had left the time capsule he quietly told Bruce Carson: "I felt we just had to leave something to say we had been there. You know, that Base G was unearthly, an inhuman sort of place. I felt we'd achieved something by just being there in a place where man doesn't belong." Foote decided to descend via the far side of the small mountain. He found there was an ice field or small glacier which ran almost all the way down to sea level. It, too, was of old, crumbling ice. He tucked his parka between his legs, sat down on his backside and tobogganed down. He travelled almost a mile in this fashion "and damn near ruined myself."

Down at the huts he found groups of sailors and scientists. In the main hut they had found evidence to suggest the base had been evacuated suddenly. There were shutters on the windows and so the exploration was done by the light of candles found in the cupboard. There were dirty dishes in the kitchen. Articles of clothing lay scattered around. One wall was filled with books, another with pin-up pictures. There were novels, thrillers, scientific tomes, encyclopedias, a copy of *Grimm's Fairy Tales* and a battered edition of *Dr. Jekyll and Mr. Hyde*. All were stamped on the flyleaf: "Falkland Islands Library". With Iver Duedall, Foote expored the attic and found an old gramophone, one that operated with a clockwork motor wound by crank handle. They took it down to the main living quarters, dusted it off and picked up a 45-r.p.m. record lying on a table. It was of Audrey Hepburn singing "Moon River", the plaintive theme song from the film "Breakfast at Tiffany's". They wound the gramophone and played the record, squatting on the floor in a darkened, musty hut lit by the dancing flames of candles held by their shipmates. A hastily abandoned hut at the end of the world . . . a place where man doesn't belong . . . four lonely graves set in a carpet of moss . . . Dr. Jekyll and Mr. Hyde . . . and the small, elfin, yet enchanted voice of Audrey Hepburn: *"Moon River, off to see the world − there's such a lot of world to see. . . ."*

On the crude headstones of the graves were the names of the men who died exploring King George Island:

Dennis R. Bell
Born 15/7/34
Died Accidentally Base G
26/7/59

Eric Platt
Geologist, base leader
Died on duty 10/11/48
Aged 42

Ronald Gordon Napier
Base leader
Born 29/1/25
Lost at sea 24/3/56

Allan Sharman
Born 29/12/36
Died accidentally at Base G
23/4/59

Eric Mills later wrote in his diary: "The hut was large, rectangular, in very good condition though very damp inside. Many of the furnishings were still in place, the pantry well stocked with tinned goods including lots of the old British standby, bully beef. The kitchen had pots, pans, cups and pieces of abandoned equipment like primus stoves, skis, crimpons, books, various ledgers, old clothing and pin-up pictures scattered everywhere. Even the base's electrical generators remained, in surprisingly good condition. It was a ghostly experience to wander with a candle through this hut and to feel that its history was almost clear, the occupants still seemed to linger in the form of their scientific gear, notebooks and items of everyday life. Someone found a package of safes and wondered how they would be used here in the radio cabin, which had a sign over the door in Spanish saying 'Public Pay Telephone', probably stolen in Montivideo. The telegraph key was still fastened to the table and with some guilt Bob Hessler and I pried it off the table for a prize souvenir for me. Many people wandered through the hut, like children in toyland, fumbling, finding souvenirs, most of them the useless abandoned gear of our predecessors. Later this led many of us to feel guilty about our acquisitions and to feel that everything should have been left intact, both because the hut is a refuge and because it is unfitting of the *Hudson* and staff to loot a place like this. All of us feel that our actions were pretty base but that no real damage was done because no one touched the essential stores. Even the crew were being very careful with candles and checked to make sure that the doors were closed as we left."

And the *Hudson* sailed back out again in the part of the world that Charles Darwin saw from the Beagle in the 1830s and described as "enough to make a landsman dream for a week of death, disaster and shipwreck."

The disaster that then befell Hudson 70 was less dramatic than those of Darwin's dreams. In fact, it was not so much the expedition's disaster as the tragedy of Fred Muise, though in one way or another everyone was involved.

Fred Muise was twenty-eight, a big, rawboned Nova Scotian respected as the ship's senior technician and known as a cheerful, comfortingly competent man. He had been overjoyed when asked to join Hudson 70, partly because of a love of travel and partly because it meant he would earn so much in overtime between Halifax and Vancouver, where he planned to leave the ship, that he would be able to make the down payment on a house in Dartmouth, not far from the Institute. And he and his wife Margaret needed a house, badly. They had married young, when he was twenty-two and she seventeen, and now, after six years of marriage, they had a boy of five, John, and a baby, David, and were overcrowded in a small apartment.

The baby, David, had always been sickly, but by the time he was ten months old – eight weeks prior to the departure of Hudson 70 – he was able to say Mummy and Daddy and was beginning to pull himself up on the furniture and take a few faltering steps across the room, proceeding in sudden unsteady dashes before abruptly landing on his backside. It was about then the family doctor, unable to explain David's crankiness and frequent vomiting, sent Margaret Muise to hospital with her baby to have him examined by specialists. The hospital told Margaret and Fred that David had a brain tumour. They would, they said, give him drugs and cobalt treatment. They could not, they said, say whether David would live or die. In

131

the weeks before the *Hudson* was due to sail Fred and Margaret would spend hours talking about whether he should go or stay. It was an awesome decision. David lay in hospital, seemingly in no immediate danger. If Fred stayed, he could do nothing. If he went he would earn enough to make sure the family had adequate housing, and if David were to recover but be sick for a while their own house would be even more necessary. And besides, Fred had already been to Washington for a course in operating and maintaining a new piece of u.s.-made direction-finding equipment to be used during Hudson 70. There was no one else aboard the ship familiar with it, nor was there time for anyone else to be trained in his place.

In the end he went. To save money, he sold his car and Margaret and the oldest boy moved out of the apartment to live with his parents for the duration of his stay aboard the *Hudson*.

The letters from Margaret awaiting him at Rio de Janiero had been comforting. David, she said, was still in hospital, still sick but apparently not worsening. And then, on December 22, had come the cable saying: "David dead." By the time he was able to track down Margaret in Ottawa on Christmas Day, David had been buried. Dave Butler had offered to put into the nearest port so he could return to Canada to be with Margaret, but when Fred spoke to her through the help of a fellow radio ham at midday on December 25 she said that she was all right, that her mother and sister were helping, that he need not dash home. Repeatedly Fred asked: "Shall I come home? Do you need me?" Margaret said no, that everything had been taken care of, that she was able to cope, that she would write so a letter would await him when the ship reached Buenos Aires.

The letter Fred found at Buenos Aires had been even more reassuring. Margaret repeated that she did not need him, and said that if he wanted to stay with the ship and do as they planned, earn enough to be able to buy the house when he returned, then he should stay on. Dave Butler and Ced Mann told him he could fly home immediately. He wrestled with the dilemma for a day and decided to go on.

When the *Hudson* left Buenos Aires Fred was seasick, which didn't surprise him since he usually was the first couple of days out. But this time it grew worse, not better, as the voyage progressed. By Puerto Williams he was vomiting so frequently, his stomach hurt so much, that he began to become obsessed with his own health. He feared he had contracted a disease unknown to ship's surgeon Rustige, of whom he constantly demanded: "What the hell's the matter with me?" As Muise was to remember it later, Rustige could only say that he had the worst bellyache in history and that it was psychosomatic, not physical.

Fred had talked little to anyone aboard about his personal troubles. Even Bruce Carson, with whom Muise was close, did not know the baby had died until two weeks after Christmas. At that point Carson asked whether the ship was putting in early to enable Muise to fly home, and after a long pause Muise had said: "I won't be going home. We've been expecting it for a long time. Look, Bruce, we need the money. We want that house pretty bad." It was easier for Carson to understand than it might have been for many others. The overtime pay earned at sea was important to Carson for the same reasons. He was planning to build his own house, and spent his off-watch hours in the cabin, poring over building specifications and plans and designing the home he would build with the money earned aboard Hudson 70. Even so, Carson noticed that Fred Muise began to behave uncharacteristically. Almost daily he would calculate how much money he had earned in overtime, and he announced repeatedly that when he reached Vancouver he would collect a total of about $20,000, less tax. He never ever talked of David. Even when in agony in the Drake Passage he talked not of his family problems but of his fear that he was dying.

It was in the Drake Passage that Fred Muise's sickness grew to alarm others besides Rustige, Ced Mann and the Captain. The seasickness developed into a sharp, stabbing, agonizing pain. Tranquilizers didn't help. Crewmen and scientific staff took turns to sit with him in his cabin as he raved deliriously. In the middle of one night Eric Mills in the next cabin awoke to hear him pounding on the wall in pain. Rustige told Mills that Fred's illness was psychosomatic and caused by the death of his son and then by his never reacting properly and healthily to the grief and guilt he felt. Wrote Mills: "Guilt and sorrow mixed must be tearing his insides out, and if you listen to Fred you eventually discern that it is the situation and not the physical pathology that has hit him, although he doesn't consciously recognize it. It is a sad situation; a man caught in a vise. I can feel his anguish myself through my love for my own wife and children."

But it wasn't until the day after the visit to Base G on King George Island that Fred Muise agreed to be put ashore. Butler promptly altered course for the South American mainland and, at its top speed of sixteen knots, the *Hudson* steamed back across the Drake Passage to Puerto Williams. There Ced Mann's assistant, Dr. Robert Reiniger, took Muise ashore to the base hospital. The *Hudson* set sail again, and Reiniger stayed while Muise – by now he had not eaten for five days, had lost thirty-five pounds – was fed intravenously. Afterwards Muise told Reiniger: "God, to a man in my shape that was better than a ten dollar steak." Reiniger took Muise on to Punta Arenas by light plane, and there Muise spent two days in hospital, constantly asking the question with which he had assaulted Rustige on board: "What's wrong with me?" The Spanish doctors couldn't tell him either, but they did decide he was physically well, though wasted, and psychologically fit to fly back to Canada. Two days later Reiniger escorted Muise back to Halifax and to Margaret, who met them at the airport. And at last Fred Muise cried.

The dash for Puerto Williams to land Fred Muise changed the pattern of work aboard the *Hudson*. Ced Mann's original intention had been to lay the meters, spend a week or so in and around the South Shetland Islands so biologists could collect samples and other normal station work could be done, and then to turn north back to South America, picking up the four strings of current meters on the way, starting with the one that had been laid last. Now he decided to pick them up as the ship headed south again from Puerto Williams, starting with the first string laid. Again the weather was relatively good as the *Hudson* cleared Cape Horn for the second time in fourteen days and headed south-west. As always when at sea,

134

the ship repeatedly stopped on station for routine work, and it wasn't until 7.30 a.m. on February 11 that they reached the location of the first string of current meters.

The night before Ced Mann had gone to bed early, refusing to join others in the lounge for a drink. As always, he seemed unworried – but to his journal he admitted that "we approached this operation [trying to recover the current meter] with some apprehension." Tom Foote was more explicit. Eric Mills asked him what would happen if the current meter strings could not be located. Foote replied: "We pack up and go home." The task of finding the precise spot in the empty, featureless ocean where two weeks earlier they had dropped the wagon wheels overside was in itself a major problem, but one for Dave Butler and navigating officer Roy Gould. When they were roughly in position it was the turn of Ced Mann and Tom Foote to worry. Were the meters still there? Had the moorings ripped loose? Would the release mechanism respond to signals from the ship? Was it to be the Denmark Straits disaster all over again?

Mann and Foote woke early, ate breakfast in silence, went to the main deck laboratory astern where Jim Murray, a technician working with Foote, had already hooked up the portable transmitter whose sonar signal would, hopefully, first interrogate the transponder and then trigger its release mechanism. Foote sent an interrogative signal. It is not an immediate question and answer process; about sixty seconds – sixty very long seconds this particular morning – must elapse before you can expect a reply from the tiny piece of electronic equipment two miles beneath the surface. Foote and Mann waited sixty-three seconds before they heard a faint signal *bleep* in reply. The two men looked at one another and Mann raised his eyebrows: at least the current meter string was still there. But would the release operate? Foote manipulated the dials again, sent the "release" instruction – and it worked. The transponder replied with the message that indicated it was functioning as planned.

It didn't end there though. It takes five minutes for the buoy to slowly haul the one-and-a-half tons of cable and current meters to the surface. When the buoy reaches the surface a tiny built-in radio begins to transmit a homing signal. Foote and Mann left the laboratory, went to the bridge and turned on the direction-finding equipment which picks up the homing signal from the buoy. The direction finder is, by today's standards, a relatively uncomplicated piece of equipment about the size of a large transistor radio. When the buoy surfaces and when – or, as Foote and Mann were thinking, *if* it did – the buoy's homing signal transmitter begins to work, the unholy racket of the static gives way to a steady *bleep* . . . *bleep* . . . *bleep* of readily identifiable sound. But there is always doubt during this waiting period. As in the other stages of the current meter experiment, there are an agonising number of possible disasters. The buoy transmitter may not function. The buoy may surface too far away for the homing signal to be clearly identified through the static – the range of the direction finder is only twenty miles. The navigator may misinterpret the readings of the direction finder and not come close enough to the floating buoy for it to be seen from the ship. For all its garish red paint, the ten foot long and four foot high buoy cannot be easily spotted from the bridge of a ship ploughing through rough water.

Waiting for the *bleep* . . . *bleep* to cut through the static, Ced Mann began rolling a cigarette. The ship's officers and crew and all the scientists shared the anxiety and lined the decks, looking out to sea. When the signal finally did burst through the static Mann ran to the direction finder and saw its dials indicated the buoy was only two miles away. Within fifteen minutes they had it spotted, were alongside and it was being hauled aboard, trailing the cable and its precious measuring instruments. Although available weather forecasts told of a depression over Cape Horn itself, the weather out in the Drake Passage remained fairly calm – thirty mile an hour winds – and the delicate business of recovering the string, hazardous to both equipment and deck crew in bad weather, went smoothly.

Next morning, February 12, the *Hudson* reached the location of the second string, the one which had not responded when interrogated immediately after it had been laid. Foote and Mann were almost resigned to the fact that this meter string was a loss, and were even more convinced when first there was no reply to the interrogation and then no reply to the "release" signal. In theory, had the transponder been working it would have replied. Foote re-set the dials, sent the "release" signal a second time – and this time there was a faint *bleep* in reply. By the laws of chance Foote and Mann had no right to retrieve this second meter string because even now, with the release mechanism functioning, there was little possibility of ever seeing the buoy unless it popped to the surface almost immediately alongside the ship. It was foggy and visibility was down to 300 yards. Worse, on the bridge the officer of the watch found the direction finder was faulty. Yet he correctly guessed the direction in which the buoy lay and within fifteen minutes of getting under way the buoy suddenly appeared on the starboard bow.

The scientists and crew, by now familiar with all the possible disasters, were elated. For the crew, this was another scientific endeavour which had visible results. If they had to haul two miles of cable up from the oceans, it meant the ship – and they themselves – had been successful. Foote was hugely pleased and smiled for the rest of the morning. Even Ced Mann admitted to being satisfied. His attempt to take the pulse of the oceans had already been fifty per cent successful, which is cause for rejoicing in any oceanographic experiment.

That evening, Mann went to bed early. The next day was, after all, Friday, February 13. He might need to be well rested to cope with the fates. In the event it was a lucky day. The third string of current meters was recovered easily. And now that there was a chance of one hundred per cent success Foote and Mann grew anxious again. Would the fourth and final current meter laid in the south of the Drake Passage be recovered?

February 14 is St. Valentine's Day and Ced Mann's birthday. On February 14, 1970, he was forty-four years old. His gift was the final and total success of one of the most ambitious experiments he had ever mounted – indeed, one of the most ambitious undertaken by any physical oceanographer. When Tom Foote sent the first interrogative signal to the transponder on current meter string No. 4 it failed to answer. The second time it replied with the electronic "yes, I am here" – and promptly operated the release mechanism without waiting for the release signal. Foote, Mann and the others in the laboratory weren't aware it had done so. They were in fact re-setting the equipment to send the release command when Roy Gould piped through the loudspeakers: "Dr. Mann and Mr. Foote to the bridge, please. We have picked up the buoy on the direction finder." They hurried to the bridge. Roy Gould conned the ship to a point where they saw the buoy bobbing on the surface. And Tom Foote – towering, unemotional Tom Foote – turned and grabbed Roy Gould – all 350 pounds of Falstaffian Roy Gould – and started to dance a jig. Gould joined in for a few steps, then stopped and frowned in disapproval and astonishment. Perhaps there was excuse for celebration, but for the officer of the watch to be dancing with another man between the binnacle and the starboard radar. . . .

Ced Mann did celebrate that night. Claude Durin produced a birthday cake two feet across and three feet long, covered in white icing and decorated with somewhat inelegant household candles. Dave Butler opened a case of champagne from the store normally reserved for official receptions in port. Grinning happily, Ced Mann sat at the long oval captain's table; as senior scientist his seat is at one end of the oval, facing Butler at the other. Champagne corks popped and the level of animation grew, and somewhere during a lull in the conversation Mann gazed at his empty glass and said that he didn't know if anyone else realised it, but there were an awful lot of fours involved in that day's activities. "We got back the fourth current meter on the 14th, and the 14th happens to be my forty-fourth birthday," he said irrelevantly. No one remembers whether the usually dour Dr. Cedric Mann burped at that point or not. His celebration had to be cut short however. Two hours later he presided at a scientists' planning meeting, at which point he was once more his usual self.

For Ced Mann the action was over. The films on which are recorded the continuous measurements of current and temperature were removed from the meters and stored because at sea it was impossible to develop them. More than two years later Dr. Cedric Robert Mann, Ph.D., Atlantic Oceanographic Lab-

138

oratory, Bedford Institute, Dartmouth, Nova Scotia, Canada, would produce a scholarly paper for august scientific journals in which he would announce the results of his Drake Passage experiment. There would be no mention of the transponders that didn't work, the foggy day the direction finder began to play up, the hours on a slippery deck in chilling forty knot winds. The prose would be impeccably qualified, cautious and almost incomprehensible to anyone but another physical ocean-ographer. The findings would, however, be startling to the world of science.

From existing knowledge at the time of Hudson 70, Ced Mann had supposed, along with others in his field, that the bottom waters of the circumpolar current would be moving from Pacific to Atlantic. The surface current goes around Antarctica that way, clockwise, following the rotation of the earth. When the measurements recorded on film were fed through the computers back at the Bedford Institute the findings were sufficiently startling for Mann to order the whole procedure to be repeated, a process that takes six months. The second set of findings duplicated the first.

So Ced Mann's scholarly paper would record that in the Drake Passage at that time and over a period of eleven days there was a strong surface current of one-half to one knot – that is, of between three-quarters of a mile an hour to just over a mile an hour – moving in the predicted Pacific-Atlantic direction. At about a mile down there was a current so weak there was almost no motion at all, and what there was was also in the Pacific-Atlantic direction. But – and this was the startling finding that tended to disprove long held assumptions – at two miles down there was a surprisingly strong current for that depth of about a quarter of a mile an hour heading in the reverse direction, anti-clockwise from Atlantic to Pacific. Until Ced Mann's work in the Drake Passage the accepted wisdom was that currents carried water from Pacific to Atlantic all the way down to the seabed, and that therefore between 100,000,000 and 200,000,000 cubic meters of water per second passed from one ocean to the other via the circumpolar current. Mann's find-ings showed that, during the eleven days of his measurements anyway, the reverse flow of the current two miles down was carrying water from the Atlantic to the Pacific just as fast as the surface currents carried water from Pacific to Atlantic. The waters were mixing all the time, but in terms of net volume there was no transfer of water from one ocean to the other.

To Mann, it was a vindication of his thesis about the extent and perils of man's ignorance about the world. Long after Hudson 70 he would tell a seminar of scientists in other fields: "Until 1955 it was generally assumed the deep ocean was a place where the waters were just a slow, sluggish mass of water. We have learned since that the abyssal ocean has currents much stronger than we had thought. Our findings in the Drake Passage show that many of our theories about the circumpolar current, though not necessarily wrong, are at least more suspect than they were. On the surface of the world even elementary knowledge is available. After all, you only have to stand there to know that there's a wind that can blow things around. But in the deep oceans we're still flying blind. We just don't know what's happening down there. Since the oceans make up most of the world and what happens to them and in them influences the life of man – all life, for that matter – then we simply *have* to know. It is not impossible that our survival may depend on finding out."

The scientific community agrees with Mann, which is partly why the results of his Drake Passage work were widely hailed when, finally, they were published. And in his home town of Halifax, where the Bedford Institute and several universities support probably the highest proportion of scientists per capita in Canada, Mann's work was recognized in part by the fact that the Nova Scotia Technical College bestowed upon him an honorary Doctorate of Engineering, citing his organization of Hudson 70 as one reason for doing so.

At the time of the Drake Passage experiment, however, Ced Mann marked the end of the field work by dispassionately recording in his journal that the last of the current meters had been retrieved and the ship was now sailing south again, back to Antarctica to collect more specimens for biologists Eric Mills, Bob Hessler and others.

Behind the work of both Eric Mills and Bob Hessler is the belief of many biologists that all life originated in the deep, colder waters of polar areas – wherever on earth those polar areas may have been at the time of Creation. Mills and Hessler study deep-sea benthic organisms – tiny creatures that live on the seabed itself. It is a rare study and there are only a few biologists involved. Neither Mills nor Hessler place much credence in the belief that all life began in the deeper, colder waters of the earth and their work may end up helping prove or disprove it.

Mills' specialty is the amphipods, minute shrimp-like creatures which are long-legged and have flattened bodies. They are related to Hessler's specialty – the isopods, which have short legs and are flat and squat. Though it would take a biologist to tell them apart, it seems that evolution has dictated that amphipods be tall and slender to enable them to move around the ocean floor more rapidly and to burrow energetically into the mud in their quest for food. Isopods on the other hand crawl slowly across the seabed, scavenging for food on the surface rather than actively hunting for it. Both creatures have been found in the deep, cold waters of the Atlantic abyss at the equator. Hessler believes they originated in the Arctic and were carried around the world in deep ocean currents. Mills argues that they evolved in each area of the deeps from creatures that normally lived in the relatively shallow waters of the nearby Continental Shelf areas. Hessler therefore argues that all isopods had a common ancestry, while Mills claims that the pressures of evolution were the same in many places and produced the same, or a similar, end result: amphipods.

In its detail, the argument is magnificently inconsequential to the fate of mankind. In the broader context of all living creatures being interdependent and vital to the eternal cycle of life, their work is crucial, because from it other scientists can in future draw conclusions about the effects of pollution by man at the top of the life cycle on the tiny life forms at the bottom.

Of more academic interest is that if neither Mills or Hessler do prove their point it will be evidence to show the way in which emergent life forms aeons ago distributed themselves around the earth while the poles changed location and the world was a-borning. But to prove anything Mills and Hessler needed specimens of the varieties of isopods and amphipods that inhabit both the deep waters of the Antarctic and the shallower waters of the Continental Shelf areas nearby. To collect them, the *Hudson* hauled a sledge along the bottom waters in both the deep Drake Passage and the shallower waters to north and south. A sample of one square metre (just over three square feet) of seabed would produce anything up to 500 creatures; isopods, amphipods, sea spiders, sea mice, worms, other shrimp-like creatures related to the isopods and amphipods – in all, scores of other creatures, known and unknown, that when looked at through a microscope often resemble something out of a bad attack of delerium tremens.

The seabed everywhere nourishes a proliferation of benthic creatures. In shallow, warmer waters – in the equatorial belt that girdles the earth, for instance – the few species best able to survive seasonal changes in temperature usually dominate. In polar waters and in the ocean deeps there is a far greater variety of species because the environment is more stable: here seabed temperature varies only a degree or so throughout the year. Freed of the need to constantly fight the changes in the environment, the benthic creatures concentrate on competing with one another for food and space. This competition stimulates evolution because to gain an advantage in the competition for food and space all life forms mutate.

Just where life began is as big a mystery as when and how. But many scientists consider it likely that many of the benthic creatures which Mills and Hessler were collecting are more or less direct descendants of some of the earliest life forms on earth. Thus the question "Where did they originate?" is an absorbing one, because if and when it is answered it will provide a clue to the mystery of where life itself began; where inanimate molecules of carbon, nitrogen and other chemical structures were suddenly fused together into a microscopic organism which – provided the theories are right – led through aeons to the emergence of man. Some biologists believe the ancestors of isopods and amphipods were "born" in shallow, warm Continental Shelf waters and migrated to the deeps, forced out

142

of their home territory by overpopulation. Another belief, to which neither Mills nor Hessler subscribe, is that the isopods and amphipods now found everywhere came originally from the ocean deeps and from polar waters and then migrated to the shallower waters.

Despite Mills' sceptical view of this theory of the origins of life, it was somehow fitting that the *Hudson* should call at Deception Island just before the third phase of Hudson 70 ended. The island, another in the South Shetland chain, reminded him of the way the earth must have appeared as it cooled and life began. Deception was, until 1967, the location of weather observation bases set up by several governments, British, Chilean and Argentinian among them. And then the volcano on the island erupted and the bases were hastily evacuated. The British had returned to the still smouldering island only a few months before the *Hudson* steamed through the great rocks of Neptune's Bellows which make up the entrance to the area known as Port Foster and Telefon Bay, where the weather bases were located. Ced Mann, reluctant to waste time on unnecessary enterprises, had not wanted to visit Deception. Mills led Hessler and other biologists in pressuring Mann to permit the visit on the grounds they wanted to sample the bed of the island bay and to study seabirds. To his diary, however, Mills admitted he had no good scientific grounds for wanting to call at Deception; it was, he conceded, "pure romanticism". Bo'sun Joe Avery was equally happy about the visit, and for equally romantic reasons. Throughout the trip he had spent much of his off-watch fashioning a commemorative plaque to be erected somewhere in Antarctica. The plaque itself was of sheet copper; the lettering painstakingly cut from aluminum and rivetted to the copper. It read: "ccs Hudson 70, Capt. D. Butler." The ideal location for Avery's plaque was Deception Island, which was just about at the other end of the world from Barrington Street in Halifax and looked it besides.

It was February 15 when the *Hudson* arrived. The waters around the shoreline steamed eerily. They are always so hot from the volcano that they have been known to blister the paint on whaling ships. Eric Mills, the man who had led them

143

there, wrote in his diary: "Today we went ashore in Hell."

He added: "It's hard to imagine a grimmer or more forbidding sight than this island with its yellow and grey volcanic slopes suspended between billows of clouds and the cold, grey, sullen sea. Just as we passed by the yellow-banded cliffs of Lavabrua Islet the sun broke through briefly, turning the sea blue and the cloud over the island white, but this in no way lessened the grimness of the scene, only gave it more colour. The ship steamed into Neptune's Bellows and headed into the violent westerly wind blowing from the interior of the island. South of Entrance Point a huge colony of penguins straggled over the bare hillside and where the birds were thickest the ground was yellowish-white with excrement. Cape pigeons came whizzing off the cliffs on the north side of the entrance to meet us. High on the sheer walls patches of lichen were the only sign of life. Once past the Bellows the ship steamed directly up Port Foster towards Telefon Bay and the shores of the island seemed distant for a time as mist and cloud closed in. The shores seemed almost lifeless. Only birds standing on the shore brought life to ash and cinder covered slopes. Most of the hillsides were shades of grey and black but in a few places patches of brick-red ash clashed violently with the dark colours. The British base in Whaler's Bay was quite visible, the older huts looked in poor shape and one large oil tank was on a drunken angle, perhaps because of the earthquake. A wingless aircraft with a damaged tail was parked near a hangar.

"Our aim was to get ashore at Pendulum Cove. The shore there was steaming heavily almost half its length. By chance I had chosen the site of the demolished Chilean base for our shore party landing. We went ashore through a steaming sea to a warm shore of volcanic ash. Ash fields led up to a cross leaning on the remains of a shrine, and the twisted bent skeletons of radio antennae stood sentinel over a pile of twisted sheet metal which had once been huts. Even in the level ash fields we saw the pockmarking of conical depressions. How they formed I can't imagine but they gave me a sense of insecurity even in the flattest parts of this newly formed landscape. It would be hard to feel secure here with the shore steaming and smoke rising from the upper slopes above the camp. The skeleton of

144

the camp itself adds to the feeling of impermanence, impending disaster and death."

Mills was among the party of twelve who went ashore. Tom Foote was along with another time capsule, which he left ashore in one of the huts. Joe Avery returned to the ship disappointed. No rock was clear enough of volcanic ash or lava for him to mount the plaque. Most of the shore party climbed 700 feet up the side of the volcano, slipping and sliding on ash and lava-encrusted rocks, to peer down a smouldering crater. The air reeked of sulphur. It was, thought Mills, "a truly infernal landscape, probably like the earth four to five billion years ago when life began".

The *Hudson* stayed only a few hours, and if the visit to Deception was unscientific Mills' next sample of benthic organisms even more amply demonstrated that scientists are not always men of dogged, dedicated determination. Perhaps because he knew of the theory that polar waters might be the origin of higher forms of life on earth, Dave Butler was more than usually fascinated by the collections of benthic creatures the ship had been dredging up from the bottom of the sea. Throughout this phase of Hudson 70 he had almost always been on deck to see Mills, Hessler and other biologists sorting through their specimens. And now, as the ship steamed back out into the Bransfield Strait and prepared to return to the South American mainland, Butler had Mills piped to the bridge.

"Look, Eric, we've got time to do another station for you people," said Butler. "I know it isn't scheduled, but we can do it. This is a good spot for one of your shallow hauls – around 120 fathoms." Mills groaned inwardly. By then he and the others were ready to quit. He had just finished writing to his wife an analysis of what he called "cruise tolerance level", and he had said that his tolerance had ended. He was sick of the end of the world, weary of donning oilskins and working on deck in cold, howling winds that carried rain or spray and stung the face and left the deck awash. The last thing he wanted to do – and the last thing he suspected his colleagues wanted to do – was to go out into the cold once more, to lower the dredge into the bleak grey sea and, once it was up again, spend four hours on deck sifting through yet another sample, a process even Ced Mann described as "disagreeable". He already had enough specimens to keep him busy back in his Halifax laboratory for the next five years. He was thirty-four then; he would be forty before the last of the Hudson 70 specimens had been dealt with.

Mills stalled for time by calling Bob Hessler to the bridge. On hearing Butler's proposal Hessler, too, looked crestfallen but neither he nor Mills could think of a good, logical reason why they shouldn't dredge. So they went to the lounge to collect Cooke and Michael, their helpers, who had just sat down to a game of chess. Mills said: "Come on, we're going to do another station. The Captain wants us to." Michael looked up and quietly said: "Oh, shit." And four hours later the biologists were forced to admit that what they came to call the Captain's Sample was one of the best of the voyage. Butler was delighted.

On February 18 the *Hudson* set course for Puerto Williams, cruising at thirteen knots. That last twenty-four hours seemed endless. At 3.15 p.m. on the 19th the entrance to the Beagle Channel appeared on the horizon. Astern there was a rain squall and a black, forbidding sky. Ahead the sun shone through mountainous cumulus clouds. Black browed albatrosses staggered clumsily up off the water to avoid the ship; skuas swooped and soared around the deck, and the shores of Tierra del Fuego gleamed green and fecund as the Antarctic islands never would. Next day the *Hudson* reached Puerto Williams – and Butler found himself in the middle of the territorial wrangle that has been going on for years between the Argentine and Chile.

The problem was the presence of the Argentinian naval officer and oceanographer Roberto Rebaudi. On the two previous visits to Puerto Williams the Chilean naval officers had greeted Rebaudi happily, even though Chile and the Argentine were involved in a bitter wrangle over ownership of islands in the Tierra del Fuego archipelago. On this third call at Puerto Williams the officer commanding the Chilean base took a much tougher line about the fact the *Hudson* carried an Argentinian officer in the area which Chile claimed as its own.

146

Talking it over with Ced Mann later Butler began to wonder whether the trouble was his own lack of diplomacy or a deterioration in relationships between the Argentine and Chile during the four weeks between their first visit to Puerto Williams and this last one. When the *Hudson* anchored and set about picking up Ed Bousfield of the Natural History Museum in Ottawa, who had spent the month since that first visit roaming the Beagle Channel area, an aide to the commanding officer was ferried out to invite Butler, his officers and scientists to a party. Butler declined, saying he had to leave in a few hours. He requested a pilot to take the *Hudson* up the inland passage through the Beagle Channel to the Magellan Straits and Punta Arenas, the port at which this third phase of the voyage was scheduled to end.

The aide went ashore – and returned an hour later to say the *Hudson* could not sail through Chilean territorial waters with Argentinian Rebaudi aboard. Such an action would, said the aide formally, be "totally unacceptable." Butler asked: "Will you accept Lieutenant Rebaudi ashore so we can sail through the inside passage?" The aide replied that no, that would also be "totally unacceptable." Since the *Hudson* was then in Chilean waters and couldn't land Rebaudi, this edict simply meant that the ship couldn't sail anywhere. Sitting at his desk in his stateroom-cum-office, Butler suddenly felt glad that he had worn his best uniform to sail into Punta Arenas. It somehow helped him feel able to confront the intransigent Chilean officer. He said: "You place me in an intolerable, quite impossible position. You say I can't sail without him, and that I can't sail with him. What do you expect me to do? Take root here?" The night before the ship's movie had been "Ferry to Hong Kong", the story of a stateless man doomed to spend his life aboard the ferry between Hong Kong and Macao because he was refused permission to land in either place. Wryly Butler wondered whether the *Hudson* and its complement were suddenly being placed in a similar position. He demanded the Chilean officer return ashore and get a ruling from the commanding officer.

Three hours later the aide who had earlier been inviting them to a party returned, stood at attention before Butler and said the *Hudson* could leave but only if she took the shortest course back to Argentinian waters. That meant going out into the South Atlantic to swing around Tierra del Fuego and up to the Magellan Straits. It would take an additional day and be an uncomfortable journey compared with that through the relatively calm waters of the inland route they had used on the way down.

In the event Eric Mills and Fred Cooke were grateful to the Chilean commander of Puerto Williams. They continued to maintain their twice daily bird watches on the way out to the Atlantic and on the morning of February 21, a Saturday, Cooke called Mills to the bridge. There were so many birds he was unable to count them – and that almost certainly meant they had found a hitherto unknown area of upwelling. The great flocks that surrounded the ship on February 21 were located a few miles north of the Le Maire Straits between Tierra del Fuego and Staten Island (named, as was the island in New York, by the Dutch). The two biologists spotted the ubiquitous albatross, the giant petrel with its four-foot wing span, flocks of Wilson's storm petrels, each about the size of a sparrow, shearwaters, terns, jaegers and many others. To Cooke and Mills this discovery alone made the Hudson 70 worthwhile. It indicated an area of the ocean which might be rich enough to be exploited by fishing fleets.

It was, however, a fleeting excitement not generally shared. By now the *Hudson* was once more a weary ship. Ced Mann had written in his journal that "This phase of the voyage seems long, but it has been successful." What was more important was that now, with Punta Arenas and his own departure barely twenty-four hours away, Mann also felt he could write: "Morale on the ship seems good . . . it is a more sober ship than the one that left Halifax three months ago, and a more confident one." In the main deck laboratory aft, biologist Ed Bousfield was painstakingly making the discovery that, while not the most significant of Hudson 70, would subsequently catch the public imagination and help journalists popularize the expedition.

Caleta Wulaia is the name of a small bay on western Isla Navarino and also of a twenty-two-room house, decaying now, that was once a fort of sorts. It housed a garrison of soldiers whose job was to protect the handful of settlers scattered around the western end of Isla Navarino, largest of the Chilean islands north of Cape Horn. The soldiers were Chilean and presumably the enemy from whom they were protecting the settlers were Argentinians, who also lay claim – but thus far not very aggressively – to islands in the archipelago. Puerto Williams is on the north shore of Isla Navarino, and any protecting necessary is now done from there by fast patrol boat, so Caleta Wulaia has been abandoned by the military. When the mini-expedition that Dave Butler called "the pup of Hudson 70" arrived at Caleta Wulaia, the great square house was occupied by Senor Villa Roel, his wife and four children. He is a shepherd, whose flocks graze on the sparse grasses of the bleak land that rises steeply from the sea, and he is also the local radio operator. His nearest neighbours are several miles away and it would be an intolerably lonely life were he not married with a family. As it is, they all live in the sort of isolation the settlers of western Canada and the United States suffered at the start of the century.

When the Hudson's "pup", the thirty-foot launch "Redhead", put into the cove near the house with zoologist Dr. Edward Bousfield, botanist Dr. Jim Markham, coxswain Frank Durnford and official guide Lieutenant Augusto Tapia aboard on the evening of February 2, 1970, Senor Roel and his wife were delighted. Guests were always welcome, especially strangers from a far land. Roel butchered a sheep for dinner. During the meal, Ed Bousfield felt a little uncomfortable because he spoke little Spanish; conversation had to be channelled through Augusto Tapia and the fluently bilingual Jim Markham. Frank Durnford spoke no Spanish either, but seemed less concerned; the casual atmosphere was comfortably like that in parts of Newfoundland, his home. The dinner, however, was magnificent. Bousfield would remember the delicate taste of that roast mutton, garnished with fresh garden lettuce, for the rest of his life.

After dinner the Roel family and their guests sat, trying to

149

communicate. At first Bousfield contributed comments and questions for Markham and Tapia to translate. Then, since such conversations tend to be both confusing and exhausting, he stretched out his long legs and relaxed into silence, watching the four small children cautiously eating the bars of a familiar Canadian candy and gum the visitors had brought. The kids happily played among themselves or watched the visitors in wide-eyed wonder. Bousfield's thoughts strayed to his own family, also three girls and a boy, in Ottawa and the probability that about now they were watching television. He thought it probably better that the children of Senor and Senora Roel didn't have that particular benefit of civilization. Then he wondered whether the word "civilization" was really appropriate. It is said often that all men are born equal, but sitting there half asleep Bousfield decided that they weren't. These children had been born and lived at the end of the world and, lacking education and exposure to the outside, their chances of achieving anything significant to society at large were minimal. But then . . . was achievement as defined in terms of "civilized" technology really desirable? Perhaps this Roel family, simple and charming, lived more contented lives than he or his children did or would. He began thinking, as he did increasingly often now he was forty-four, that biology provided many indications that all was not well with the "civilized" world.

In Ottawa, as men did in cities and urban areas all over the world, Bousfield lived in a society wracked by random, often desperation-paced, change for the sake of change. In nature, random change usually meant extinction. A random change in nature is a mutation, and mutants usually die quickly unless the changes they represent are of value to the organism or the species in its fight to survive. As a scientist, Bousfield could see little permanent benefit to the human race in much of the incessant change of the latter half of the twentieth century. "Civilized" man had almost totally lost touch with his natural environment, was so remote from it in fact that he was destroying it with pollution and population. Despite warnings, man had not fully comprehended that he must stop multiplying at the present rate of 70,000,000 a year and gobbling up his world. If he didn't stop, the decision would soon be made *for* him by the laws of mathematics and nature. Paul Ehrlich, the biologist specialising in population dynamics, performs an experiment by putting a pair of fruit flies into a milk bottle with a small amount of food. Within days the population of fruit flies multiplies to the point where the bottle is black with them. Then the limited food and their own wastes raise the death rate and, equally suddenly, the population drops to zero. The world was the milk bottle, the man the fruit fly.

This part of the world, the very tip of South America, had been spared most of the effects of developing human populations. It was not an accident that life in Tierra del Fuego and the Cape Horn archipelago should be relatively backward when measured against the "civilized" world. Biologically, the whole area appeared backward. That, after all, was why Bousfield had left his large but institutional third floor office in the National Museum of Natural Sciences in Ottawa to explore in the footsteps of Charles Darwin. Here, in the area of the Beagle Channel, evolution seemed to lag behind most of the world.

This phenomenon was easily explainable now that scientists understood – or, rather, believed they did – how the great land masses of the continents drifted around the face of the globe. In this, the Continental Drift theory, the earth's upper crust is seen as several islands "floating" on the plastic rock nearer the core of the world. The theory suggests that, millenia ago, South America was linked to South Africa and Antarctica, but that 150,000,000 to 200,000,000 years ago South America broke free and drifted away. Possibly because of the climate and its separation from more fecund parts of the world, the pace of evolutionary change around its shores was slower than in other places. When the Continental Drift theory was first propounded by Alfred Wegener in 1912, it was then as much a heresy as was Darwin's theory of the Origin of Species in the last century. Bousfield remembered his parents, their intelligence conflicting with fundamentalist religious beliefs, trying to marry the book of Genesis with its doctrine of Instant Creation and the seemingly irrefutable logic of the Continental Drift theory. Bousfield's father had taken a rubber beachball and built the continents on it with plasticine to demonstrate the concept to his son. Both parents had sought to interpret the bible to explain how the seven days and seven nights in which God made the world were symbolic periods designed to represent great slabs of time too vast for a man to get his mind around.

By university, the younger Bousfield had resolved the problem. He disavowed the belief that God, any god, had created all life on earth. He had not, however, discarded the Christian philosophy of life. In fact, at one time he taught Sunday School and gave lay sermons at his church. Even now he sent his children to Sunday School, believing church to be the basis of a civilized society where the children – Marjorie, Katherine, Mary and Kenneth – would meet what he considered right-minded people, those who were prepared to commit part of their lives to working for others and for the community. To Ed Bousfield it was an article of faith that a measure of a man's success as a human being was the contribution he made to society.

It is an abiding paradox of the kind of science in which Bousfield is involved that as he sat there in what was once the guardroom of an abandoned Chilean army barracks, half dreaming and half aware of the sibilant Spanish conversation, he did not suspect that three days earlier he had made one of his own major contributions to society; that because of this collection he would return from Hudson 70 to make an announcement of significance both to biology and to those who seek reinforcement for the Continental Drift theory that had so absorbed his parents.

Ed Bousfield was leader of a part of Hudson 70 in which the *Hudson* played mother ship to its launch "Redhead" and to Bousfield and botanist Jim Markham, of the University of British Columbia. After his performance in handling the lifeboat with Chung Choi aboard during a storm just south of the equator, coxswain Frank Durnford had been left in charge of the launch. The *Hudson* had dropped the launch party ashore at Puerto Williams on January 28, then departed for the Drake Passage and Antarctica. Bousfield and Markham would, during the next twenty-three days, conduct one of the few intensive scientific expeditions in that area since Darwin worked through the archipelago while bound for the Galapagos islands 135 years previously.

Markham's work was largely a general botanical survey of

the flora of the coastline, though his primary interest was the kelp and other marine plants in the tidal zone. Bousfield, on the other hand, was realising a long-term scientific project: to locate and collect specimens of *talitrid* amphipods, crustaceans of the same general type as those that Eric Mills was collecting in the Antarctic deeps. In Bousfield's case, however, the creature lives either in the inter-tidal zone, that area of the beach which the tides cover and expose twice daily, or on the dry land bordering the sea. It dances about the beach on which it lives. If you were to meet one sunbathing you'd call it a beach flea.

The common image of how life moved from oceans to land pictures great sea creatures either crawling up on to land directly from the sea or being trapped inland during some cataclysmic upheaval of earth which abruptly encircled an area of ocean with land. Fish and reptiles, thus trapped in a diminishing land-locked lake, were forced to evolve into land creatures or die. Colonization of land may have happened in these ways; there are no fossil remains that prove or disprove it. There is, however, an alternative version of the history of life, less dramatic but more acceptable to many biologists, Ed Bousfield among them. This interpretation of available knowledge suggests that some seashore creatures adapted over long periods of time, so that succeeding generations moved gradually up across the beaches and shoreline to make use of unexploited food resources in the primaeval forests of the land. No theory excludes any other; the transfer of life from sea to land probably took place in many ways. But, as a group, the tiny amphipods Bousfield studies are even now in the process of abandoning the oceans in favour of the land and thus present a chance to study sea-to-land evolution "on the hoof" in a natural laboratory.

Available knowledge suggests that primitive marine creatures began adapting to land life in pre-Cambrian times, more than 500 million years ago. Since then there has been an interchange of life between land and sea; it wasn't all one-way traffic. But the move in either direction was – and is – so slow that, with a few exceptions, the evidence has long vanished. The exceptions include the whales which have the bone structure of vestigal legs and feet in their flippers, and the penguins and seals of sub-polar areas. The seal, for instance, is related to the

153

entire family of canines, or dogs. Many reptiles also seem to have returned to the sea. Turtles, for example, probably evolved on land. Many now live in fresh water but some returned to the oceans.

Ed Bousfield's theories are in some ways at variance with those of Eric Mills and Bob Hessler, the two other amphipod men aboard Hudson 70. Generally, however, he subscribes to the view that marine amphipods probably first evolved in shallow coastal waters. When these waters became overcrowded with progressively more specialised, competing species, some moved to the deep sea, to eventually come under Mills' microscope, and others moved in the opposite direction to the land, to come under Bousfield's scrutiny. In most places the transfer from sea to land was completed so long ago no evidence remains to prove the belief. Land amphipods are found in forests throughout most of the tropical islands of the world; they are even found in mountain areas of large islands and continents where the rain blowing in off the sea has enough salt in it to enable the animals to maintain body salt balance and survive. They have even been found at 10,000 feet in the cloud forests of Borneo, and in coastal mountain ranges in New Zealand, Australia and South Africa. This dependence on a saline climate marks the amphipods as only moderately successful migrants from ocean to land. Other creatures have totally swapped one environment for another. Land-based isopods, beetle-like creatures which are close relations to amphipods, are, like most insects, descendants of marine creatures that long ago became totally terrestial. Most live inland far from the sea and are not dependent on a salty climate. On the other hand, land crabs have never quite lost their dependence on the water because they must return to the sea or some other body of water to reproduce. Similarly, amphipods also still need the salt in the air that comes from the sea to survive.

Under the microscope it is easy to see the way the long evolutionary journey from sea to land has changed the amphipod. Those found in the oceans still have strong swimming legs, and the male has two pairs of strong forelegs to clutch the female when mating underwater. Those we call beach fleas, and which live in the upper part of the inter-tidal zone, have only vestigal remnants of the strong swimming forelegs. In species that live wholly on the land, the males' mating legs have almost disappeared. But by Hudson 70 what no one had seen was an amphipod in the early stages of change from sea to land creature.

At the time of Hudson 70 there was, in Ed Bousfield's area of research, an unsolved mystery. No wholly land-adapted or terrestial amphipods, common in other parts of the southern hemisphere, had ever been found in South America. Why? Was it because there weren't any? Or was it simply that they hadn't been found? Partly to find them if they were there, or to prove they didn't exist, Bousfield embarked on Hudson 70 and then spent most of three weeks beachcombing in some of the most remote places on earth.

When they weren't out on field trips Bousfield, Markham and Durnford were guests of the Chilean naval personnel at Puerto Williams, staying at No. 10 Beagle Street, a house normally used by single officers. The quarters were comfortable, though somewhat smoke-grimed by the end of their stay because Durnford's clothes caught on fire while drying on the stove. The field trips were less luxurious. One night near a sparsely inhabited island, all four men, including Lieutenant Augusto Tapia, tried sleeping aboard the launch, but it began tossing violently in a heavy swell and everything that wasn't already tied down – pots, pans, clothing, crockery, scientific gear – flew noisily about the tiny cabin. For the rest of the time the group stayed with lonely outpost radio operators and sheep farmers, although Durnford usually slept aboard the launch as a safety measure in case the mooring broke loose. Staying with one shepherd, a man living with four women of indeterminate relationship, Bousfield and Markham overcame the language barrier by playing Chinese checkers with a lady called Olga. Although proud of his skill at chess and other board games, Bousfield was soundly beaten twice. Afterwards the party escaped the kitchen heat by crawling into the wooden guest hut with a tin roof that leaked when it rained.

Several times they found themselves travelling with schools of whales, and whenever they turned on the launch's echo sounder to gauge the depths it would attract dozens of porpoises. Bousfield's Spanish vocabulary improved. "Buenos noches . . . buenos tardes . . . buenos dias . . . chico . . . chica . . . si . . . no . . . caliente (hot) . . . ." They tried to photograph a steamer duck, whose wings are useless for flight but surprisingly effective at paddling through the water at great speed, and chased it at ten knots for several minutes. Steamer ducks travel over the surface at about sixteen knots, seem tireless, and easily outdistanced the launch. In rough weather they lost Bousfield's treasured iron-frame dredge, and in equally rough weather and almost out of diesel fuel, they ran thirty miles for harbour with a following sea that always threatened to swamp the launch. One night they were stranded on an island and dined off cold canned soup. Another they spent at Puerto Toro, the world's most southerly agricultural community. Established by the Chileans to help stake their claim to the island archipelago, Puerto Toro is inhabited by just eighty people. Bousfield and Markham played ping pong there in the community hall. And then Bousfield suffered pangs of guilt because it turned out that Fred Muise's sickness was an unforeseen blessing. The very morning that the *Hudson* made its unscheduled return to Puerto Williams to send Muise to hospital, the launch engine began to overheat. During the ship's brief stay in port, engineers replaced the defective valve of the water-cooling system and Bousfield and Markham were able to continue their work that would otherwise have been brought to a complete halt.

By the time the survey ended Bousfield had, tentatively at least, answered the riddle: why have no amphipods been found above the tide line in southerly South America? He reached the conclusion that it was probably because they weren't there. On all the beaches and shoreline areas he studied, he could find no terrestial amphipods in the tussock grass immediately inland from the seashore. He found many other aquatic specimens, though. In a glacial river estuary he collected a large series of amphipods which subsequently turned out to be of a very primitive, unique species that had been described by a German biologist earlier this century but which could no longer be studied – all available specimens were apparently destroyed during the last world war. In all, he collected about eighty distinct species of amphipods, of which about one-third were unknown in biological literature.

All this Bousfield learned later, when back aboard the Hudson with laboratory facilities at his disposal. It was then that he discovered that on the second day of his mini-expedition he had picked up an amphipod that was to cause considerable excitement among biologists working in his field.

It had happened on January 29th, not twenty-four hours after the *Hudson* had departed, leaving Bousfield, Markham and Durnford in Puerto Williams. They decided to take the launch on a shakedown cruise and tentatively travelled westward for four or five miles. There they stopped at Punta Roballo and, glad to be active at last but not feeling that the expedition was yet really under way, Bousfield worked across the beach. It was stony and he did not expect to find any land amphipods in the upper half of the tidal zone because it was too frequently submerged by the tide. But he did. Back at Puerto Williams he examined his collection with the portable equipment he had available. There were, he saw, three distinct species of amphipod. Two were familiar from the literature, but he was unsure about the third. It caused him no special excitement, however; he had always expected to find hitherto unfamiliar creatures in this region.

Aboard the *Hudson* three weeks later he began routinely examining his specimens through Eric Mills' stereo-binocular microscope set at six-power magnification. One after the other he passed the specimens beneath the microscope, making notes. Then he came to the amphipod of which he had been unsure. He stopped, examined it more closely, then repeated the process. Then he called Eric Mills and Bob Hessler. As Bousfield would later describe it, "we were like three small boys let loose in a candy store. There was a chorus of 'oohs' and 'ahs' from the group of us clustered around the laboratory bench. We all knew that, as biologists, Hudson 70 had given us about ten years' work of identification and description. We wouldn't really know what we'd achieved until we'd finished. But this . . . well, this was something different. We could all see what we had."

What they had was an amphipod that *looked* like a typical beach flea but still had several of the characteristics of the aquatic amphipod. Elsewhere in the world you can only find *talitrides* which have long since lost the characteristics of their marine ancestors. But Bousfield had found a species that was actually at the initial stage of evolutionary change from marine to land-based creature. The beach flea he had picked up was at the point of change from one to the other that, elsewhere in the world and especially in the northern hemisphere, amphipods reached millions of years ago.

The significance of this find in relation to the Continental Drift theory that so concerned Ed Bousfield's parents many years earlier is that it tends to support the belief that South America did part from the South African land mass something more than 150,000,000 years ago. It is believed that at that time fully land-dwelling amphipods had not yet evolved, so the South American land mass would not have carried any with it as it moved across the world to roughly its present location. The land masses of Australia, New Zealand and, among others, Madagascar, all drifted away from Africa after South America had done so. But by the time they did, land amphipods *had* evolved, and were carried along with the moving mass. When South America had gone drifting off westwards from Africa the amphipods' multi-million year march from sea to land had only reached the beaches. And at the tip of South America that's where the march ended. Since life was not abundant around the tip of South America, the intertidal amphipods – along with many other creatures – remained there and thrived. Because of geographical isolation, there was not much competition from other life forms for food and space, and the environmental pressures were not as great as elsewhere in the world. Therefore the evolutionary process was slower. On that stony, boulder-littered beach four miles west of Puerto Williams, Bousfield had found visible evidence of this slower pace of evolution. The unfamiliar amphipod he had found was very probably a case of arrested development – a so-called phylogenetic relict, a veritable crustacean "dinosaur" that having got that far from the crowded ocean needed to go no farther – but, remarkably, survived to this day. Those two pairs of strong legs found on the aquatic male amphipods were still there.

His discovery of other bizarre, unique, or primitive amphipod species during the "Son of Hudson 70" tended to support his thesis of arrested evolution at the tip of South America. He had, for instance, visited one broad, sandy beach where by all the known rules he expected to find a burrowing amphipod "sand-hopper" that spends most of its life in the sands of upper inter-tidal zones. He combed through the sand of this beach for more than an hour and found none. Why? Perhaps because again the evolutionary process in that bleak part of the world was slower than elsewhere, and the burrowing sand-hoppers simply hadn't yet evolved.

As the *Hudson* steamed north to the Magellan Straits and the city of Punta Arenas and the end of the third phase of Hudson 70, it carried a tired but contented complement of scientists. Those doing long-term routine work faced no major difficulties. Ced Mann's bid to take the pulse of the world had apparently succeeded. Eric Mills and Bob Hessler had specimen collections that could only be regarded as a biologist's bonanza. And as part of his own specimen colections, Ed Bousfield had a multi-million year old beach flea.

4

The *Hudson* left Punta Arenas four days late, at 8.35 p.m. on March 5, 1970. It was a grey day. Drizzle softened the silhouette of the Hotel de Cabo Hornos and almost hid the other salient feature of the skyline, the spire of the Roman Catholic cathedral in this, the most southerly metropolis in the world. By mutual consent the two groups of people waving farewell stood well apart on the dockside. One consisted of around twenty women, all somewhat flashily dressed and huddled beneath skimpy umbrellas and improbably gay parasols. They were there to bid the crew goodbye. The second group consisted of perhaps a dozen sober suited men; the ship's agent, local dignitaries, scientists and Chilean naval officers. They were there to bid scientists and ship's officers farewell. The members of each group drew self-consciously, almost defensively, closer because of the presence of the other.

The women all came from Marie Theresa's, a nightclub not far from the docks where the crew spent most of the ten days the *Hudson* was in port. Marie Theresa's is housed in a rambling, single-story wooden building built in Spanish colonial style. The crew discovered the place immediately they docked. Dave Butler found it later.

After two days in port Butler had begun to notice the ship was strangely quiet, almost empty. Half the scientists had departed and others weren't due to board for a few days. Normally when in port the ship is filled with the muffled sounds of music, mostly country and western songs, played by off-duty seamen on the hi-fi sets that abound in the crew's quarters. But it seemed that in Punta Arenas few of the crew were spending much time aboard. And then Butler heard scuttlebutt reports of a battle between his crew and seamen from a German freighter moored nearby. It had, the rumours said, taken place in a nightclub and had been sparked by the fact that a dance hostess sitting with the steward from the *Hudson* had refused to dance with a German sailor because "I am with my friends." The *Hudson* won that particular war, and it caused no trouble with the authorities. Even so, Butler decided to investigate.

Early in the evening of their third day in port, Butler recruited the chief engineer, Sam Lambert, and the two officers knocked at the yellow and white front door of Marie Theresa's. The club wasn't open but a startled girl in a brilliant purple kimono let them in. Butler found Chief Steward Shaw in the kitchen, happily helping the chef prepare the evening menu. Shaw was himself once a chef, and enjoys cooking; one disadvantage of his elevated rank was, he told Butler, that he now rarely had opportunity to work in the galley. A ship's electrician was repairing the wiring in a bathroom in the hostesses' living quarters. Other men were painting a wall. As Butler told chief engineer Lambert: "If we'd looked we'd have probably found the ship's carpenter fixing the plumbing, and if we'd stayed we'd have seen the boys playing in the band as well."

For the crew, Marie Theresa's made Punta Arenas the most memorable stop of the expedition. When the girls turned up at the dockside to wave the ship goodbye, one young scientist complained that it was unseemly for the *Hudson,* the first Canadian vessel to visit that part of the world, to be seen off by a group of dancehall girls. Whereupon Butler, who feels strongly on the subject of sailors and the sea, delivered himself of a lecture. "Look, it's no one's business but the crew's," he said. "These men have a harder life than you, and they do a job that is repetitive, largely manual and always damned uncomfortable if not downright dangerous. They're not absorbed in a scientific project like you, and they're not trying to prove anything, either to themselves or the world. When a sailor gets in to a foreign port after weeks at sea it makes him much more aware than ever that he's helluva long way from home. He's a lonely man in a lonely country and he's looking for love, affection. He hasn't got a snowball's chance in Hell of finding the real thing in three or four days, so all he can do is pay for something that's a pretty lousy substitute. It's shoddy maybe, a travesty of the real thing, but it's no worse than what a lot of travelling businessmen get up to when they're out of town. Prostitutes and sailors . . . you know, for one reason or another they're both looking for love because they don't have much of it in their lives. And here in Punta Arenas my crew and the girls at Marie Theresa's got a bit of comfort from one another. So I don't want to hear any more criticism. One of those girls was actually crying when we sailed. I saw it through the binoculars."

There was another incident at Punta Arenas that demonstrated the effects of a long spell at sea on men – an incident of which Dave Butler was unaware because of a kindly conspiracy or silence. At sea only beer is served in the crew's mess, and so crew parties are relatively sober affairs. Parties in port, where liquor is available, are not. The first night in Punta Arenas there was such a party in the crew's quarters. At midnight a sailor tottered back to the ship from a night on the town, poured a drink, then spilled it. Someone called him a "clumsy bastard", and he lashed out with a wild right that missed. The two men, grappling drunkenly, were parted and the one who had spilled the drink left. The party resumed. Then, suddenly, the door burst open. The drunken sailor stood there unsteadily, flourishing a revolver. "None of you rotten bastards is going to call me a bastard and get away with it," he said. There were a dozen or more men jammed in the cabin. Even a wild shot would hit someone, and perhaps kill. For a moment the party stood paralyzed, Hank Snow wailing mockingly from the hi-fi. And then, with the same dramatic suddenness with which he had flung open the door, the sailor sagged against the bulkhead, the hand holding the pistol dropping to his side. He started sobbing. The nearest man walked to him and, with surprising gentleness, took the gun. From the rear of the cabin Bruce Carson said: "Give the poor s.o.b. a drink." It sounded surprisingly loud, even to Carson. Then the sailor sat down, still crying, and said: "You mustn't call me a bastard.

162

You mustn't" There was a pause, and he looked up and added: "I am one."

Carson reflected that it was almost four months since all of them had seen Halifax and home, and everyone was getting edgy. The drinking aboard was getting heavier, and he thought that that wasn't so bad because it eased the increasing tension among men, who, with thus far only calls in port in Rio and Buenos Aires, had been locked in one another's company since mid-November. He was even affected himself; "going funny" he called it in a letter home. He was scheduled to leave the ship next day and fly with Ced Mann from Punta Arenas to Santiago, and then on to Mexico City, Toronto and Halifax. He had grown obsessed by the fear that the plane would crash and while he dismissed the thought it lay on the fringes of his consciousness, sufficiently disturbing for him to have made copies of his overtime sheets. These he sent by mail to his wife, reasoning that if the plane did crash she would still be able to claim the pay owed him. Irrational, but . . . . At Punta Arenas Ced Mann went ashore and bought a plaid shopping bag in which he loaded all the film from the current meters used in the Drake Passage experiment. He flew home with it in his his lap. "Too precious to risk putting it in my baggage," he told Carson. "Anything could happen."

Dave Butler was aware of weariness and homesickness among the crew and while he was pleased they had become a confident and efficient team, he knew that strange pressures build up in men long at sea and away from familiar surroundings. It was for this reason he was happy the *Hudson* had been adopted by Marie Theresa's. He had, after all, enough problems in Punta Arenas without the crew adding to them.

The *Hudson* had been scheduled to leave on the fourth phase of Hudson 70 on March 1. This was an exploratoin of the fiord system in the Pacific coast of southern Chile with Dr. George Pickard, Director of the University of British Columbia Institute of Oceanography, in charge of a group of Canadian, American and Chilean scientists. But the fiords were largely unknown except to local seamen. Many were not even marked on the charts and where they were marked there were so few soundings Butler could not tell whether there would be sufficient water for the *Hudson* to pass without running aground. Navigator Roy Gould had acquired copies of charts made by the *Beagle* in the 1830s, when it had sailed some of the waters with Darwin aboard. These were more reliable than the local marine charts – and at that weren't really reliable at all.

During the journey through the fiords the *Hudson* would, therefore, have two pilots aboard. One, Lieutenant Fernando Espinosa, of the Chilean navy, came aboard immediately the *Hudson* docked in Punta Arenas. He brought with him a small overnight bag containing one change of clothing. Butler looked askance and said: "Is that enough gear for a month aboard?" Espinosa said: "A month? Two days, I think, to Valparaiso only." Then Butler told him there had been a misunderstanding; that he was taking the *Hudson* through the fiord system. Espinosa was appalled: "The ship is too big," he said. "It cannot be done".

The second pilot was to be a civilian. The ship's agent had engaged a man in advance. He never did board the ship. As Butler would later report to Halifax, he took one look at the *Hudson,* decided she was too big for the fiords – and left town without contacting Bulter or the agent. "His feeling was that with *Hudson's* size and windage and with the unpredictable nature of the weather and the strong currents of the fiords, the ship was unsuitable for the work involved," said Butler's formal report. Since the first civilian pilot had refused the assignment, it meant a delay of five days while a second was engaged. The man who took the job was Hernan Hernandez, a fifty-four-year-old ex-merchant officer. He and Lieutenant Espinosa explained to Butler and his officers that the fiords were frequently sailed by small supply vessels and the occasional Chilean gunboat, but not by ships the *Hudson's* size. Even so, Butler, his officers and the pilots decided to try. They would, later, wonder whether this decision had been wise.

Dr. Pickard, the senior scientist, was not particularly sympathetic about Butler's fears. A veteran of dozens of voyages in the fiords of British Columbia aboard ships smaller than the *Hudson,* he was scornful of Butler's fears and the warnings of the two pilots. "The trouble is, they're all deep sea sailors and don't like working close inshore," Pickard told one of his assistants. "If they were as experienced as the men who take us through the fiords at home they'd have no worries." Dr. Pickard, a small boat sailor, is more accustomed to being carried as a passenger aboard ship than he is to the command of one.

The shadow of big John Tully hung over the entire Hudson 70 expedition. But the scientists were most conscious of his influence in the Chilean fiords because it was in the similar fiord system of British Columbia that Dr. John Tully almost single-handedly gave birth to oceanography as a science in Canada back in the 1930s. And it was largely because of Tully that George Pickard, a physicist whose specialty in the 1930s had been low temperature cryogenics, had begun studying the oceans at the end of the last world war.

Tully had been an oceanographer before the word was invented. Until anti-submarine warfare made a re-evaluation necessary, Canada's involvement in the oceans had been largely dollar-oriented study by the Fisheries Research Board. The study of the oceans had been mostly directed to essentially short-term biological work designed to improve commercial fishing. In the 1930s there were only two FRB scientists studying the physical nature of the coastal waters. Tully was one of the two, and was stationed at the FRB laboratories in Nanaimo, Vancouver Island.

In the late 1930s a paper company proposed to build a pulp mill at the head of Alberni Inlet on Vancouver Island, an area important to the salmon fishing industry. Tully was asked to investigate the proposal and its possible effects on Alberni Inlet, the fiord at the head of which the pulp mill was to be located.

Tully devised ways to study water circulation in the fiord. Any fiord must, by definition, have been cut in the coastline by a receding glacier, and must have the characteristic of either being fed by a river left by that retreating glacier or by the actual remnants of the glacier itself. Because of its salt content seawater is "heavier" than fresh water from the river or glacier, so all fiords have two more or less distinct layers of water – the top relatively fresh and the lower saline. The mixing of these layers with one another and then with the ocean itself is relatively slow. Some smaller fiords on Vancouver Island flush out annually. In other locations on the mainland, where fiords are generally longer and deeper, this flushing process – influenced by winds, ocean currents, the rate at which water flows from the river or glacier, the shape of the coastline and other factors scientists have not yet pinpointed – takes place over periods of years.

Tully's study was among the first in the world to measure and describe this mixing and flushing out process. It was planned that the pulp mill should use sulphite in its manufacturing process, and that the waste water containing this sulphite should be poured in to Alberni Inlet. But sulphite would consume the oxygen in the inlet waters. The assumption of those who planned the mill was that the waters of the inlet were changed so frequently by the mixing of layers and the flushing out process that it would not matter if the sulphite consumed oxygen, since that water and the oxygen would be replenished quickly. What Tully did was to prove that the flushing and mixing process in Alberni Inlet was so slow that the sulphite would probably consume all the dissolved oxygen available in the inlet waters at any given time. And that would leave none for the salmon and myriad other marine organisms that made up the eco-system within the inlet. It was because of this research that the FRB stepped in and virtually ordered that the pulp making process be changed so that it at least does less damage to the marine ecology than it would have if Tully had not been called in at the start. After his report it was decided to use fluid sulphate instead of sulphite in the pulp mill, and whatever else it may do sulphate does not consume the dissolved oxygen.

This exhaustive study of Tully's had a major impact on government and scientific communities. To government it was tangible proof of the practical value of pure scientific study of the oceans. To the scientific community it was a visible

166

demonstration of something only a few people already knew – that the physical structure of the oceans was so complex it demanded investigation by research scientists.

It was at about this time that Bill Cameron, a young zoologist, working on the west coast, first met John Tully. Cameron would remember the occasion for life. An encounter with Tully was an inspiring, almost traumatic experience for a fledgling scientist. Tully had been a basketball hero at the University of Manitoba when the game occupied more of the Canadian consciousness than it ever has since. He was a gay, talkative, passionate Irishman with a flair for the dramatic in speech and gestures and a mane of red hair and a great bushy beard. At that time, he also hopped around with prodigious energy on an unwieldy wooden leg, which, to his enormous disgust, prevented him from going to war in 1939.

Tully spent most of that war working on anti-submarine research on the west coast, and conscripted Bill Cameron as part of his research team. It was Cameron who, after the war, was loaned to the University of British Columbia to set up Canada's first institute of oceanography, and it was through meeting Tully that George Pickard – the English physicist who had spent the war devising ways to make attacks on enemy shipping from the air more efficient – decided to devote his life to oceanography and joined Cameron at the UBC Institute. Tully, however, fired the enthusiasm of many other men who were to end up in oceanography, and he sustained the enthusiasm of many more. Ced Mann was a physicist whose involvement in oceanography can be traced back to Tully through Pickard; it was Pickard who recruited acoustics expert Mann to the cause. In the years since Tully first captured the imaginations of young scientists and taught them the fascination of the sea, the nature of science and of the men in it have changed. Before the war acquiring a university degree was hard enough to require a large measure of dedication; to proceed through master's degree to doctorate was so difficult and required economic sacrifices of such an order that it was almost a guarantee that the Ph.D. had a remarkable measure of dedication to the pursuit of knowledge for its own sake. The post-war – or more precisely the post-Sputnik – education explosion has devalued

167

a university background by the sheer number of people who now have such educations. In oceanography, as in other sciences, the man with a Ph.D. may be just a superior technician whose education was a process of acquiring the tools of a trade, not the ability to think creatively. It was, therefore, inevitable that even though Tully had retired to live in Nanaimo his influence was still profound at the time of Hudson 70, and the middle-aged scientists who, when young, were his disciples are now part of the Canada's scientific and educational establishment. It was former Tully acolyte Bill Cameron who, as Director of Marine Sciences for the Department of Energy, Mines and Resources, was instrumental in expanding Ottawa's commitment to oceanography and who helped make the Hudson 70 expedition possible.

From the start the UBC Institute of Oceanography specialized in the study of the province's fiord and river estuary systems, partly because Tully's pioneering techniques in Alberni Inlet were readily available to them, partly because the fiords were handy and easiest to study, but above all because Tully's work had shown that of all the ocean the world's fiord systems were most likely to be first damaged by man's carelessness. By the time of Hudson 70 the Institute had done pioneering work in British Columbia that was respected throughout the world. But the fiords and estuaries of Canada's west coast, though often remote and frequently desolate, have already been affected by the hand of man. The Chilean fiords, on the other hand, are mostly in virgin areas unaffected by industry, even logging or mining on any significant scale. To Pickard, Hudson 70 represented a chance to study a fiord system before man got there to affect it, as he undoubtedly would in time; to an overcrowded world any habitable space is a vacuum which man must fill. And in the context in which the UBC Institute is working, the more known about Chile's unpolluted fiord system, the easier it is to measure the effect of man's pollution on fiord systems in more populated parts of the world.

George Pickard did not expect to find anything particularly unusual in Chile; just to describe the fiords to other oceanographers would be enough since no one had done so before.

In places they are more glacial than the four other major fiord systems in the world – British Columbia's and those in Scandinavia, Alaska and Greenland – and are more mountainous as well. The Andes rear abruptly out of the shores of the fiords and the shoreline, in the southern half of the system at least, is rocky, scree-covered and largely bald of greenery. Here the tails of glaciers lick down from the mountains, dipping into the fiords, from time to time spawning small icebergs – lumps of glacial ice that go bobbing slowly down to the sea itself. But it was the water, not the terrain, that was of interest. Pickard's team set out to measure the temperature, the salinity, the dissolved oxygen, the nutrient levels and the nature and quantities of zoo- and phyto-plankton. And it was this programme that aroused the interest of the Chilean government to the point where they sent six of their own scientists to work with Pickard aboard the *Hudson*. The information gained would help determine whether the fiords had potential as commercial fishing grounds. This apart, knowing something about the thickness of the layers of fresh water and salt water, the temperature variations and the likely speed at which fiord waters are flushed out by runoff and tides would be important when industry begins to move in, as it will eventually.

When George Pickard sat down with Dave Butler in Punta Arenas and spent a couple of hours explaining much of this, Butler was only partly attentive. As Pickard talked, outlining a scientific expedition that had, in a sense, been twelve years in the making since Pickard decided the Chilean fiords were "my Everest", Butler visualized the charts. One hundred and forty fiords, some of them little wider than the *Hudson* and thirty-two of them ten miles long or more. And all of them shallow, shallow. Worse, tides presumably strong, but how strong? Unpredictable winds that could whip from dead calm to gusts of over one hundred miles an hour within half a day. And the *Hudson* was, so the two pilots said, one of the biggest, perhaps *the* biggest ship, to ever sail the fiord system.

Within four days of sailing from Punta Arenas Butler had dismayed George Pickard and other Canadian scientists seasoned in small ship work around the British Columbia fiords by announcing that he would not take the *Hudson* into any of the smaller inlets they wanted to examine. These explorations would, he said, have to be done in a ship's launch. They tried lowering a launch overside, and one of the eighty-strand wire hawsers on which it was suspended from davits parted at the point where it hooks on to the bow. The launch crashed down the side of the ship and came to rest with its bow in the water and its stern level with the main deck. Butler later found that the material used to weld davit cable to hook had been corroded, that all such fastenings on both launches had been thus weakened. He banned the use of both launches, and thereafter George Pickard or members of his team went off to explore the smaller fiords in a lifeboat.

The night of the fourth day out of Punta Arenas was the worst Butler had ever spent at sea. They anchored for the night in one of the wider fiords which was so deep that they had to sail close inshore until it was shallow enough to drop anchor. And with the anchor down the stern of the *Hudson* swung within fifty feet of a line of rocks by the shoreline. Butler mounted a special watch on the anchor chain that night, but still his fitful sleep was disturbed by visions of weather or tide causing the anchor to slip and carrying the *Hudson* down on to those rocks.

The next day, March 10, was worse. The *Hudson* was to sail up through a labyrinth of islands into the Ultimo Esperanza, one of the largest fiords in the area. Ultimo Esperanza means The Last Hope and was named centuries ago by sailors seeking an inland passage from Pacific to Atlantic. As they sailed south down the Chilean coast the Ultimo Esperanza would have been literally the last hope that they had found one. It was also a forlorn hope because the fiord ends up against the wall of the grey Andes. The entrance to the Ultimo Esperanza is a narrow, cliff-hung channel called Canal Kirke which is at its narrowest between a mainland peninsula, Punta Restinga, and the island of Merino. The gap between peninsula and island is about a hundred and fifty yards; the navigable portion just eighty-two yards wide, which gives a ship the size of the *Hudson* with fifty-foot beam no room for manoeuvre, or for mistakes. The worst hazards, however, are the

170

tides that rip through this narrow channel. They are between eight and sixteen knots and are unpredictable. As Butler and navigator Roy Gould pored over Volume II of *The South American Pilot,* they read: "No two successive tides can be depended upon, also the duration of slack water is very uncertain . . . the west-going stream was observed, on two occasions, running down one side of the channel, with the east-going stream still running up the centre; there was no duration of slack water." And yet the only time to pass through the gap between the mainland and the island was at slack water. If they tried it with the tide running in either direction the *Hudson* would be virtually out of control and almost certain to run aground on the rocks to one side or the other of the channel. Even at top speed of around sixteen knots the ship would be unable to make headway against an ebb tide of the same speed. And on a flood tide the ship would be carried forward so fast that it would again be unmanageable. Thus the only way the *Hudson* could pass through this bottleneck of the Kirke Canal was at slack water – and at that time of year slack water lasted for approximately eight minutes. Eight minutes in which the flood of swirling water slackened . . . eight minutes to get the ship under way at full ahead and through a narrow, rock-littered passage to safety . . . .

The first time they tried it was early March 10. The two pilots, Lieutenant Espinosa and Hernan Hernandez, stood with Butler on the bridge. At what seemed to be the start of slack water they ordered "full ahead". Roy Gould, at the engine console, rang the telegraph. The *Hudson* trembled as all four engines belched smoke – and moved forward so slowly their progress was almost imperceptible. They had mis-timed things. The tide was ebbing now, so fast that within minutes the ship was almost at a standstill, its engines barely holding their own against the current.

The alternative was to use the kelp method of determining just when the slack water began. That meant that Lieutenant Espinosa would have to take a lifeboat into the channel, position himself so he could peer at the kelp which hung in clusters from the rocks, and wave a red flag the moment the weed stopped streaming in one direction or the other and hung

171

limply in the water to signal the start of those precious eight minutes of slack water. The flag would be the signal for the *Hudson*, sitting a quarter mile or so away, to go full ahead through the channel to the other side and comparative safety.

Frank Durnford was given the job of handling the lifeboat. When it was decided he and Espinosa should leave, the tide was again ebbing. They boarded the lifeboat and headed for the channel. They never reached it. The tide was ebbing so fast that even at full throttle, which normally gives it a top speed of nine knots, the lifeboat was swept back towards the *Hudson* at about three knots. Butler and pilot Hernan Hernandez stood quietly on the bridge, dismayed. On the open wing of the bridge Dr. Richard Brown, an ornithologist with the Fisheries Research Board trying to establish a method of taking a census of seabirds, stood making a formal observation. He wrote in his notebook: "March 10 – Kirke Canal – clear, sunny, tide and wind gives surface turbulence – sightings: one giant petrel; 3 blackbrowed albatross; shags – 4 blue-eyed, 2 black and white, one rock; kelp gulls, 3 and 3, probably more; flightess steamer ducks all around ship." Wearily, Lieutenant Espinosa and Frank Durnford brought the lifeboat alongside to climb aboard the *Hudson* and wait until it was time to try again.

Next time the tide was flooding and the lifeboat had no difficulty going ahead, but it did have trouble staying in position in the channel. It was 1,200 feet in front of where the *Hudson* was hove to. On the bridge Butler and Hernan Hernandez stood looking through binoculars at the lifeboat. Lieutenant Espinosa raised the red flag, waved it vigorously. "Full ahead both," said Hernandez, who was standing in the centre of the bridge, chewing a toothpick. Dave Butler stood on the port side of the bridge, uncomfortably conscious that although the pilots give the orders, command was still his. They do what they do with his consent only. Roy Gould, as usual, was impassive. Loren Greek, twenty-four, the quarter-master helmsman, glanced up from the steering console in time to see a great cloud of oily black smoke from the funnel billow out across the bow.

Within minutes the *Hudson's* diesels had brought the ship's speed to sixteen knots. The channel and its threatening rocks surged closer. Ahead, Lieutenant Espinosa ordered Frank Durnford to run the lifeboat down the west side of the channel, which would mean the ship would pass the small boat to port. But Volume II of *The South American Pilot* had been quite right; the currents were unpredictable. Espinosa and Durnford found the current on the west side of the channel was ebbing seawards. The lifeboat was being swept back out of the channel. Espinosa ordered Durnford to head across the channel to the east side, to cut across the course of the *Hudson*. On the ship's bridge Butler watched this change in the lifeboat's course and felt quietly ill. Hernan Hernandez bit right through the toothpick. The *Hudson* was making a six-foot bow wave that could be seen from the bridge. It couldn't stop or change course by as much as a yard for fear of running on the rocks. And the lifeboat was heading diagonally across the ship's bows. Loren Greek at the wheel glanced up again and saw the lifeboat on what appeared to be a course that would bring it directly beneath the bows of the *Hudson*. If the lifeboat weren't actually smashed to matchwood it would be swamped; Lieutenant Espinosa and Frank Durnford would probably drown in the tide that would within minutes start running again. Frank Durnford was Loren Greek's friend. They shared a cabin.

Butler stood watching the lifeboat, now 500 feet away and still on a course that would take it across his bows from port to starboard. He wondered whether the lifeboat was fast enough to get across the *Hudson's* bows in time. He wondered whether Hernan Hernandez would order a change of course to guarantee they would miss the lifeboat. And he knew, coldly, that if the civilian pilot did so, he would immediately countermand it. If it became a choice of a lifeboat and the possible deaths of two men or the *Hudson* and eighty men, then the decision was a foregone conclusion. The men in the lifeboat were the more expendable.

And then . . . the *Hudson* swept past the lifeboat with forty feet to spare. Lieutenant Espinosa and Frank Durnford were looking back at the ship, faces white, as the lifeboat corkscrewed in the bow wave, then danced in the wake.

Hernan Hernandez spat out the toothpick and turned to

Butler, who lit a cigarette. Gould turned from the bridge windows, said nothing. Loren Greek began wondering how he would have felt if the ship with him at the wheel had killed his friend. Butler inhaled deeply and said: "Well, we nearly lost another boat there." That night, asleep, he saw the *Hudson's* icebreaker bow slice through the lifeboat, saw bodies tossed in the sea, then sucked in to the twin screws as the ship passed.

The following day the *Hudson* sailed in Puerto Natales, a town of about 3,000 tucked into a fold in the mountain coast of Ultimo Esperanza. It is not unlike a Newfoundland outport and, like an outport, is supplied by sea.

That day a ship was scheduled to arrive to collect a cargo of sheepskins. As the *Hudson* warped up to the dock, a crane suddenly swung out and dumped a load of sheepskins on the foredeck. When that confusion ended and arrangements had been made to replenish the ship's water supply, Butler took pilots Espinosa and Hernandez out to dinner. Until then the three men had said nothing about the incident in the Kirke Canal. At dinner in a small peasant restaurant rich with the smell of roasting lamb and ancient wine casks, Espinosa said: "You know, all we could see was this big white ship and bow wave. I wondered what would happen, captain. I wondered very much." And Butler said: "If you hadn't made it across the bows you'd probably be dead now. I'd have had to run you down. You do see that I would have had no alternative, don't you?" This last was almost a plea. Espinosa said somberly: "Yes. I know it." All three men got very drunk that night.

Both crew and scientists would look back on the fiord exploration as a month of hard, uncomfortable work hardly relieved by a shared awareness of the dangers of sailing those waters with a ship as big as the *Hudson*. In the open ocean the ship is on station, working, for eight hours at a stretch. Each individual measurement, each plankton tow, takes hours; lengthy procedures are involved in each piece of work – lowering water bottles to take samples at various depths, for instance, when the ocean is up to four miles deep. In the fiords

174

the water was shallower, each individual operation less time consuming. As a result, the ship was on station for perhaps only an hour at a time before steaming on a few miles to repeat the procedure. Between Halifax and Punta Arenas the Hudson did forty-eight deep-sea stations. In the month sailing the fiords they did 207.

The fiords themselves are divided by the Gulfo de Penas, a huge bite out of the Chilean coastline, which is also the demarcation point of two different climatic zones. To the south the weather and land are sub-arctic, and that phase of Hudson 70 was bleak and miserable, and made the more so by simple domestic problems – washing and drying clothes without being able to hang them on deck, for instance. The scientists would wash clothes in their cabins, then hang them to dry on lines strung in the two stern laboratories. Scientific concentration on what could be seen through a microscope became difficult with someone else's underpants dripping down your neck. This apart, laundry created a scientific crisis for UBC technician Murray Storm which jeopardized a major scientific experiment. Storm was analyzing the salinity of the fiord waters. This process must take place in a climate of constant temperature and humidity. Day after day Storm would go to the laboratory to start work and find someone had strung their laundry and turned off the air conditioner so it would dry more quickly. He would have to wait for two hours after turning the air conditioner back on before temperature and humidity returned to optimum level. In exasperation, he finally tore down the hand-lettered sign which read: "Lotus Blossom Chinese Laundry" and kept the laboratory locked.

Once across the eighty-mile-wide Gulfo de Penas the climate and the terrain changed. Rain forests rolled down to the shore and sea otters played in the shallows. Ornithologist Richard Brown grew tanned as he stood, ten minutes at a time, counting birds more numerous and varied than he had seen in the previous two weeks. The crew and off-duty scientists began once more to appear on deck in shorts, stripped to the waist. Strangely, the empty landscape made the crew and scientists feel lonelier than when they were at sea, out of sight of land. Even in the relatively fecund northern fiords people live

175

in isolation, and only occasionally could those on the ship see the fires of the smoke houses of the Chilawayans, the people who are scattered through this land and scratch a living by smoking sea urchins, squid and other seafood delicacies for marketing in distant cities. One sunny day, when the *Hudson* was hove to perhaps eighty miles from the open sea, a small boat was rowed steadily out of the seeming wilderness carrying a man, his wife and three children, a boy of about thirteen and two younger girls. The rowboat did not approach the *Hudson;* the man just sat at his oars, he and the family staring. Chilean scientists went to the side of the ship and held a shouted conversation, relaying information over their shoulders to the watching crewmen and scientists. It seemed the family often went six months without seeing other humans. They had dressed in their Sunday clothes just to go and look at other people. From the stern a sailor tossed a bar of candy to the children. It was the trigger for an amazing scene. Within minutes the rowboat was being deluged with bars of candy. And then crewmen threw down loaves of bread, joints of beef, spare clothes. One seaman pulled off his sweater and tossed that down. Within five minutes the small rowboat was so full of *Hudson* largesse it was in danger of foundering. Yelling his thanks, the man grabbed the oars and pulled hastily for shore, his wife and children waving farewell.

The plan was that when the fiord work was finished the *Hudson* should sail directly to Valparaiso where she would be met by Energy, Mines and Resources Minister Joe Greene, Dr. William Cameron, head of the Marine Sciences Branch, and a contingent of Canadian reporters, all of whom were to be aboard the Canadian Armed Forces plane scheduled to fly a replacement crew to Chile and return with the seamen and scientists due to disembark there. Things went awry. The work was completed three days before the planned reception and Butler was forbidden to take the ship to Valparaiso early. Instead he sailed to Robinson Crusoe Island in the Juan Fernandez Group on what was, for all the scientific justification of additional station work, a sightseeing tour. The island, which inspired Daniel Defoe to write the book *Robinson Crusoe,* has one community, a tiny fishing village whose houses are dotted around the grassy slopes of the shore and where there are neither roads nor cars. The village has two small bars, both little bigger than the average suburban living room. The scientists and crew, eager to walk on land, drank both of them dry. And then the *Hudson* left the island to reach the great port city of Valparaiso as ordered – at precisely 8.00 a.m. on April 7. There they found Mr. Greene had been unable to make the journey, and that J. Michael Forrestall, M.P. for Dartmouth-Halifax East was deputizing for him. There was the press conference, a reception attended by members of the diplomatic corps and dozens of Chilean governmental dignitaries, including the commander-in-chief of the Army and an admiral of the Chilean fleet. For eighteen of the crew, including salty-tongued Chief Officer Mauger, there was leave; they flew back with the Ottawa party to Canada. For Dave Butler there were a few days off while he went sightseeing in Santiago. For Roy Gould, left in command of the ship, there would be the drama of the boy with the bike and an appearance in Chilean court as an advocate for the defence. And for Hugh Henderson, who had been the *Hudson's* chief technician since the departure of Fred Muise, there would be a girl called Iris.

Hugh Henderson was twenty-six, a sturdily built native Haligonian who smiled a lot and said little, and even then would say what he had to say slowly, as though examining each word for its relevance before uttering it. On the second day in Valparaiso he and two other crewmen recruited one of the Chilean scientists who had been aboard during the fiord cruise and went souvenir shopping. In a department store Henderson bought a poncho, an earthenware mug and a wicker basket, then stood waiting while the Chilean scientist conducted the transaction with the cashier, an olive-skinned girl with dark brown hair, dancing eyes and a smile that never seemed to fade. The Chilean explained in Spanish who his friends were, where they came from, where they were going. When the dialogue ended, Henderson took a deep breath, looked directly at the girl, and said: "We're going to the Topsi Topsi at Vina del

177

Mar tonight. Would you like to come?" He hoped that, like most Chileans, she spoke some English. She didn't. She looked blankly at Henderson. Grinning, the Chilean scientist interpreted rapidly. She looked back at Henderson, smiled and said: "Yes please." The scientist then asked her whether she had two friends who would like to make up the party. She said she had; that they would be ready soon before midnight when the Topsi Topsi nightclub opened; that they could be collected at her apartment. She wrote the address on a blank sales slip.

The Topsi Topsi is a nightclub-cum-discotheque-cum-indoor midway. It is built on five levels down the side of a hill. At the upper entrance you can either take the elevator, walk down the stairs or slide down a fireman's pole. On lower floors there are mock rock grottos, an indoor ferris wheel, ponds with concrete platforms shaped like lily pads on which guests dance. There is an incessant cacaphony of hard rock music and psychedelic lights that flash and flicker and make the whole place resemble a figment of Dante's imagination. It is either heaven or hell, depending your age, taste in music, decor and entertainment.

Henderson and the two crewmen went by cab to pick up the cashier and her two friends. All were apprehensive at the prospect of a night on the town with girls who spoke no English while they spoke no Spanish. Henderson reviewed such Spanish he did know as he gave the driver the piece of paper with the address on it. Above the address the cashier had written her name: Iris Godoy. And when they reached her apartment he said "Buenos Noches, Iris." The other two girls were both pretty and to everyone's relief one spoke English well.

They spent four hours at the Topsi Topsi, talking mostly through the girl who spoke English. They also arranged to meet the next day, a Sunday. Before they did so Henderson bought a Spanish-English dictionary. It had a red and white cover with green lettering and it would grow dog-eared during the next week. The party caught a bus to Concon, a small coastal town past Vina del Mar with a magnificent beach and a renowned seafood restaurant. Afterwards, Henderson would remember few details of that day. The restaurant was closed and they had to walk along a sun dappled road to find another.

They got sand in their shoes. They talked a lot, mainly through the girl who spoke English, and they laughed more. Iris was the focus of attention; the gay, always laughing centre of the group. As he tried to explain later, when shipmates questioned the wisdom of his decision: "I felt good, better than I had for years, just being with her."

The six spent much of the rest of *Hudson*'s stopover in Valparaiso together. As the week wore on Henderson began to pick up a few words in Spanish, Iris to learn more English. Struggling through the phrase book, Henderson explained what a technician was, where Halifax was in Canada, that it was an old and gracious city by North American standards. She learned what he meant by saying: "Will you have a drink?" – "Will you dance?" – "Is this a good thing to order?" One evening he worked through the phrase book and cobbled together a sentence which he hoped meant: "Are you interested in getting married?" She thought and laughed and said: "Yes." He went back to the phrase book and, with the pride of a conjurer, produced: "I will return," in Spanish. He used that phrase often, and just as often told her through her girlfriend interpreter that he would come back, that he would write. When Iris waved goodbye to Henderson and the *Hudson* she was still laughing at what she thought were the empty promises of a lonely sailor. And after a couple of days at sea, Henderson began to think that maybe she was right.

In Valparaiso, Roy Gould stage-managed the open-house which was held in every port; a day on which the public was invited to tour the ship and inspect the laboratories. On this day an eleven-year-old boy stole a screwdriver and a pair of pliers. He was arrested by a policeman who saw him carrying them as he cycled out through the dockyard gates. Next morning Gould received a visit from a local police inspector who said that, as commanding officer, he would have to appear in court the following day to give evidence.

For the occasion Gould got out his dress uniform. Aboard any working ship officers rarely wear formal uniforms, and on the *Hudson* only the captain does so even when entering port. Getting into the uniform was a struggle, since Gould, a big man anyway, had grown Falstaffian during almost five

179

months lacking exercise while at sea. In the severe courtroom located in downtown Valparaiso Gould bulked impressive in the witness box and gave evidence through the court interpreter. And then in a burst of frankness he told the interpreter: "Look, I don't want the kid to be punished. He didn't take much of value and it was our fault for leaving the tools around. Just kick him in the rear end and frighten him and then let him go." Before the translator could turn this sentiment into formal Spanish, the judge turned to the witness box and asked in perfect English: "This is how you would do it in Canada?" Startled, Gould replied: "Yes." The judge said: "Well, that is how we will do it here" – and gave the small, frightened boy a stern lecture in Spanish and ordered him released.

Dick Haworth did not begin to lose his resentment at being literally ordered to take part in Hudson 70 until he woke up with a hangover at 3.20 a.m. on April 7 in a Valparaiso hotel room. The evening before he had attended a reception aboard the *Hudson*. No one had actually got drunk, but the stewards had been generous. And those champagne cocktails . . . . Haworth decided it was the lingering effects of the champagne cocktails that made the earth tremble and the room swim. The world always moved when he had drunk well but not wisely. On such occasions he would awaken at night and feel the world moving. The cure was to open his eyes and look at the comforting solidity of the walls and ceiling. When he did this the world stood still again.

And so Dr. Richard Haworth, Ph.D., brilliant twenty-five-year-old geophysicist, half sat up in the bed that was too short for his lanky six-feet-two and opened his eyes and bade the world to stand still. And it didn't. The bed still moved gently. The furniture in the room, all solidly 1930s style, was also moving. The big desk of polished wood, the two uncomfortable armchairs, the Persian-patterned carpets, the nondescript prints on the wall – all were doing a little dance. He looked at the corners where white ceiling met pale walls – and they, too, were moving gently, as leaves might in a breeze. And that was when Dick Haworth felt a sudden excitement, a sudden pleasure that he had had to leave his bride of six months in Halifax and his study of gravity in the Gulf of St. Lawrence to take part in

181

Hudson 70. Because this was not a hangover, this was an earthquake. Or, rather, an earth tremor. And it was his first experience of one. Vaguely content, satisfied almost in the way a small boy is when he finds that his birthday constructor set really does go together to make the model crane in the picture on the box, Dick Haworth went back to sleep. Now he actually knew what an earthquake felt like – and knew firsthand what he had often read; that man had perfected techniques of building that could survive such minor misbehaviour of the earth's crust.

A geophysicist, which Haworth is, examines the nature of the earth by applying the largely abstract laws of physics to the study of the more tangible structure of the earth. His work overlaps that of the geologist. The geologist uses knowledge gained first hand by actually looking at, analyzing, probing the surface and depths of the earth. He goes out and chips at rock and feels it and kicks it and therefore actually experiences the world he studies. The geophysicist takes the readings of electronic instruments, uses what he considers the immutable laws of the universe, applies them to the real world – and often reaches his conclusions without even having left the security of a paper-littered office desk.

Thus it was that Dr. Richard Haworth knew all about earthquakes – what causes them, the significance of the Richter scale of earth tremor intensity, what the consequences may be. But he did not know emotionally, deep down in his belly, just what an earthquake was like. At least, he didn't when he flew from Halifax to Santiago to join Hudson 70 and take part in a u.s.-inspired study of the "shape" of the surface of the Pacific ocean. But then on the drive from Santiago to Valparaiso he saw what life might be like in an earthquake zone like Chile. He saw houses that stood askew, square boxes pushed out of true so they reminded him of those odd-shaped cottages that the children's books always show as the homes of elves and gnomes and fairies of the forest. And then in those early hours of the morning after the night before he actually experienced one, felt the earth move. There was another tremor a few hours later as he stood shaving. It lasted barely three seconds. And he grinned at himself with pleasure in the bathroom mirror. He wondered whether Wilma would understand if he told her that now he had experienced an earth tremor he wasn't quite so unhappy about being separated from her for a couple of months.

Each age has its minor Gods and ours are The Scientists. Of this collective deity the most Olympian are probably the physicists, the men who study the nature of matter and seek to define the immutable laws of the universe. And yet if the layman was fully conscious how little scientists really know – how each new discovery leaves them both excited and humbled by the fresh questions posed by that discovery – there might be less idolatry. An infinite number of questions which must be answered to explain us and the world and universe around us remain unanswered. Of them all the most bewildering and, if man is to continue reaching out into space, one of the most important, may be: Why and How Gravity? Dick Haworth is haunted by gravity.

There are times when Haworth looks up to gaze at the hat-stand in his corner office at the Bedford Institute and lets his mind ponder the fact that between him and that hat-stand there is a gravitational field that links them in the same unbreakable relationship as that which exists between the earth and the moon and the sun. Man can measure gravity – it is one of Haworth's areas of expertise – but he can't explain it.

There is a fundamental law that says any two objects anywhere in the universe are attracted to one another by the force of gravity, the strength of which depends on the mass of both objects and the distance between them. It is the relationship between the human body and the earth below that ordains our movements and their speed; man bounds gazelle-like around the moon because the mass of the moon is so much less than that of the earth. There is a gravitational relationship between you and your wife, you and your television set, you and your car, you and your outboard motor boat. Just as man has known and used the Gulf Stream for centuries without knowing why or how it is there, so we have long known of and used gravity. The axis of the spinning earth is at the poles, and centrifugal force therefore makes the crust of the earth spread outwards, pulling the poles in toward the centre of the earth. Thus the globe has a bit of a belly around the middle; it is about thirteen and a half miles fatter at the equator than it is around the poles.

International shipping and trade agreements have long had gravity built in to them. Because the earth is more compressed at the poles there is a greater mass, or density, beneath the surface of northern and southern hemispheres. Thus the gravity in polar regions is greater than at the equator by about one-fifth of one per cent. A 1,000-pound polar bear captured on the Arctic ice-cap will weigh in at 995 lbs in an equatorial zoo. The gravitational pull of the earth at Halifax is greater than at Kingston, Jamaica, and so a cargo of sugar weighs around one-fifth of one per cent more when unloaded at Halifax than it did when loaded at Kingston. Shipping agreements therefore demand that say a 10,000 ton consignment of sugar from Jamaica shall weigh 10,050 at Halifax. Similar regulations cover most of the world's major ports.

The precise measurement of gravitational variations is to-day made with delicate, easily disrupted and yet beautifully simple instruments called gravimeters. Until recently the equipment consisted essentially of a pendulum, and gravity was measured by variations in the speed of the pendulum's swing. More modern gravimeters shoot a tiny glass "pea" into the air and measure the speed with which it falls down. Using gravimeters, geophysicists use the force of gravity to help find out what might be benath the earth's crust. For example, geologists know that beneath the earth's crust. For example, geologists know that a deposit of, say, gold is of greater density than is a pocket of salt, where oil may have gathered. After seismic tests that indicate thickness, and perhaps type and age of rock, geophysicists survey the area with gravimeters to detect that area of gravitational pull that may indicate an area of high or low density. An area of high gravity might indicate a gold mine, a body of copper ore or the presence of other valuable mineral-bearing rock. An area of low gravity might indicate an area of porous rock or a subterranean pocket of salt – and that might just mean they were sitting on an oil well.

What was more to the point to Hudson 70 is the fact that the variations in the density of the surface of the earth mean that the oceans are irregular in shape. Water is attracted to

184

areas of greater density – and therefore greater gravity – on the seabed. There is a ten-foot high "hill" of water down the middle of the Atlantic, drawn there by the great mass of the mid-Atlantic ridge, the undersea mountain range that separates eastern and western abyssal basins of the ocean. But gravity is not the only natural phenomenon to create such changes in the "shape" of the oceans. Winds, changes in barometric, or air, pressure and, among other factors, ocean currents, all create build-ups of water. The Gulf Stream, for instance, is higher than the surface of the ocean through which it passes. If scientists knew just which of the bumps and hollows in the ocean were there permanently because of gravitational action, and which were caused briefly by barometric, wind and current changes, then it would help weather forecasters to be more accurate. There would also be other scientific benefits, particularly to physical oceanographers like Ced Mann whose concern is ocean circulation.

The only totally satisfactory way of making these measurements would be to send out an armada of gravimeter-equipped ships to criss-cross the oceans for a few hundred years. Since this is impossible, the Americans plan to send up a series of satellites that will measure the precise shape of the earth in general and the oceans in particular. When Hudson 70 began, the first satellite was scheduled to be launched in the summer of 1973. Part of its orbit is to be keyed to the 150th line of longitude, or meridian, up through the mid-Pacific. The main scientific task of the *Hudson* in the Pacific was to steam 7,200 miles up the 150th meridian from Antarctica to the Alaskan coast, measuring the gravitational constants of the oceans to provide a yardstick for the accuracy of measurements reported by that first satellite. This was the project of Dr. William Von Arx, of the Woods Hole Oceanographic Institution in Massachusetts, a man whose name is almost lengendary among oceanographers. Dick Haworth, the Cambridge-educated phyicist then working at the Bedford Institute, was aboard as his collaborator.

It was to take two months for the *Hudson* to steam southwest back to Antarctic waters, find that 150th meridian and then steam north to the coast of Alaska. There are times in a man's life when the demands of his occupation and of his personal life come in to almost traumatic conflict. And it was because Hudson 70 and his personal life were in such a conflict that Dick Haworth had been reluctant to join the expedition. While working toward his doctorate he had spent three summers at the Bedford Institute, an experience which had led them to emigrate to Canada and join the Institute's permanent staff eighteen months prior to his joining the expedition at Valparaiso. Only six months earlier, however, he had returned to Britain to marry Wilma, the Scottish economist-geographer with a smile that, while rare, would turn any man's head. Now he had left her for two months in a still unfamiliar city in an unfamiliar land.

His resentment began to diminish the night of the earth tremor that set the world moving in his hotel room. It diminished farther as he grew more involved in the project; it was one of the contradictions of his life that he had chosen geophysics as his area of study because pure physics was too abstract, and yet it seemed his particular area of interest was to be gravity, in some ways the most abstract area in which a geophysicist could operate. As an undergraduate he had watched pure physicists engaged in the study of ever smaller and smaller particles of matter, following in the footsteps of Einstein. In one research project designed to study the effect of one nuclear particle entering the earth from the atmosphere, graduate students of physics from his university in Durham, England, spent up to a year sitting two miles down in an abandoned mine in India waiting for their instruments to detect such a particle. To Haworth, such pure physics was the study of unreal, head-in-air abstractions. It was because he wanted something more tangible to work with – the rocks and the earth – that he had chosen geophysics. And now he found himself measuring gravity, in itself far more intangible and abstract than particle behaviour. But his initial disenchantment with Hudson 70 vanished completely after he met the legendary Von Arx, a man he would describe in a letter to Wilma as "a great eclectic scientific mind, and a wonderful man." In fact, Von Arx became Haworth's idol.

The process of acquiring his doctorate had been for Ha-

186

worth, as it was for all doctoral students, a period of dedication to one specific area of science, one corner of the jigsaw. At the time of Hudson 70 Haworth was beginning to look up, to get glimpses of the whole puzzle. Von Arx was the kind of man that Haworth was slowly perceiving he himself would like to be; the renaissance man that truly great scientists must become. His knowledge and understanding of the world went far beyond his own scientific disciplines, and he could talk with great expertise to scientists in many fields. He did so in the lingering evenings of the Pacific, where he set up once more the Green Flash Club that Ced Mann had founded in the Atlantic months earlier. Later Haworth would get an even greater bonus from the expedition, sadly at Von Arx's expense. The American scientist's wife fell ill soon after his return to Massachusetts, and the lingering illness before her ultimate death in 1971 would make it impossible for him to process the gravimeter work done aboard the *Hudson* in the Pacific. Haworth would do most of the work needed to help the satellite on its way.

The *Hudson* was in Valparaiso just a week, and when she sailed on April 14 there were those who thought the stopover should have been longer. Most of the officers and a large slice of the crew, plus a few scientists like chemist Iver Duedall, had been aboard for so long that they could have used sufficient time ashore to grow weary of the place before setting out for another two-month spell at sea. Duedall and the other veterans began talking with awe of the early explorers – men like Henry Hudson, for whom both the ship and the bay were named – who made great voyages in cockleshell sailing ships, perhaps spending a year or more at sea at a time.

Valparaiso is on latitude 34. The *Hudson* was scheduled to sail around 3,000 miles south and west to the point where 65th latitude south meets the 150th meridian of longitude. Back down into the Roaring Forties the weather was foul, and it it stayed that way. The wind rarely dropped below forty-five knots, and often howled much faster than that. The ship pitched and yawed through the long Pacific rollers which come more widely spaced than those of the Atlantic swell, and therefore produce a slower, more sickening roll through an arc of around forty degrees. There was driven snow for much of the time, and this congealed on deck. As the ship went farther south – down farther south than it had been when exploring the tip of Antarctica – they began running into the Antarctic winter. The spindrift – stinging, wind-borne spray – froze where it landed, and with the snow coalesced into ice on winches and rigging and decks so that the crew were kept busy chipping it clear for fear its added weight would make the bow sit lower in the water and the ship harder to handle. It came to be that a Force Five gale on the Beaufort Scale was a calm day. In the laboratories equipment was bolted to the benches. Chairs were turned back to front and lashed to the bench supports, and the scientists clung to the chairbacks while trying to work. After one particularly stormy day – a Force Nine gale; that is, between forty-seven and fifty-four m.p.h. – biologists Dr. Ray Sheldon and Dr. Bill Sutcliffe sat relaxing with Dr. Peter Wangersky, of Dalhousie University. The topic was, inevitably, the weather. Suddenly Wangersky pulled a slim volume of John Masefield's poetry from his hip pocket, opened it and began to recite: "I must down to the seas again, to the lonely sea and the sky . . . . " And the weather was a problem of such magnitude that no one laughed.

Through all this the new equipment shipped aboard at Valparaiso for Von Arx's work measuring the shape of the Pacific up to the 150th meridian had been kept operating, partly because little is known about the seabed in the South Pacific and any findings were useful and partly as a warming-up exercise before the major work along the 150th meridian began. The *Hudson*'s depth measuring bathymetry equipment operates constantly, charting the contours immediately beneath the ship and these findings are reported to the international hydrographic bureau (GEBCO) in Monte Carlo for inclusion in future charts of the oceans. The graphs produced by this depth sounding equipment were always closely watched by Hudson 70 scientists, who constantly hoped that at some point the *Hudson* would find something – a hitherto unknown undersea mountain, perhaps – that would be marked on international charts and could be named after the expedition. On this leg of the voyage it was Dick Haworth's job to inspect

188

those graphs, along with those produced by gravimeter and magnetometer. And in the South Pacific he belatedly found the unsuspected mountain that would leave the ship's name on the charts.

The data from depth sounder, gravimeter and magnetometer was fed into the ship's computer, and it was found that Bill Von Arx's u.s. gravimeter couldn't "talk" to the Canadian-owned computer. On April 20, six days out of Valparaiso, Haworth radioed the Bedford Institute to ask computer expert Dave Dalby to prescribe changes in the computer's programmed vocabulary so that gravimeter and computer could communicate. Two days later Dalby cabled the needed admonition to the computer and Haworth was able to correlate the records of all three pieces of equipment. With Dalby's amendments to the computer's programming, he ran the records of depth sounder, gravimeter and magnetometer through the computer and then began to examine the results. It wasn't a job he enjoyed. Either the swell or the food aboard left him feeling constantly queasy (for the first time there were complaints about the food on this leg of the voyage), and anyway all available charts indicated the seabed was fairly level along the *Hudson*'s course, so it seemed a tiresomely routine exercise.

By midday on Sunday May 3 he was studying the records of April 20 and 21. On those days the *Hudson* had been about 2,000 miles south-west of Valparaiso. The records for 6.00 p.m. Greenwich Mean Time (it would have been noon aboard the *Hudson*) on April 20 showed that the relatively level sea bed had started getting rough. There was a range of what appeared to be undersea hills. They were not particularly big and not worthy of being dignified by actually being named on the charts, but nonetheless the hills were not supposed to be there. Haworth grew interested. He worked through the records for the next six hours of April 20 and all the while the hills got bigger. And then he found that at midnight Greenwich Mean Time on April 20 the *Hudson* had passed over an undersea mountain that rose 6,000 feet out of the ocean floor and reached to within 9,000 feet of the ocean surface. Then the *Hudson* had immediately passed over a massive valley – a great rift in the seabed that plummeted down toward the centre of the earth. The records showed that this valley was at least 3,000 feet deep.

By the time he found this Haworth had worked through the afternoon, through dinner and into the early evening of May 3. He had even forgotten he felt seasick. And at about 9.00 p.m. he tucked the rolled computer plots beneath his arm, went to the lounge, took a beer from the bar fridge and walked over to Russ Melanson, chief scientist for this leg of the voyage, and quietly said: "Russ, I think we've found it. I've got a beautiful profile with a large free air gravity anomaly. There's a big trough amplitude of 1,600 fathoms. I think maybe we've got the name *Hudson* on the charts." The next day Haworth found himself besieged by scientists, officers and crewmen who wanted to see the computer plots. Those plots would later form the basis of a scientific paper by Haworth published in *Earth and Planetary Science Letters,* a prestigious publication, which described this ocean mountain and valley as The Hudson Peak and Deep. And that name will duly appear on future charts of the world.

At 10.26 p.m., on April 26 the *Hudson* reached the 150th meridian at 63 degrees south – 130 degrees short of the schedule – and turned north. And it was then that spirits began to lift. If they weren't exactly on the way home to Halifax, at least they were heading in the right direction. And if Vancouver wasn't Halifax, was in fact about as far from Halifax as Halifax is from Europe, it was after all part of Canada. Iver Duedall wrote to his wife: "Literally, I feel I have been on this ship for years. We have been through so many different weather and climate conditions that my body keeps telling me that years are passing by instead of months." There was to be another abrupt weather change. Within five days of turning north the *Hudson* was out of the Antarctic winter and into the balmy South Pacific, where the nights were soft and long and lingering, the days sunny and hot and the sea temperature around eighty-five degrees. Oreste Bluy, who had rejoined the ship in Valparaiso, once more began waking everyone for breakfast with his underwater bombs. The Green Flash Club set up shop again on the wing of the bridge. And even the food began to improve, though biologist Ray Sheldon stayed on hunger strike, refusing to eat the products of the galley. Instead he produced his own meals from supplies in the scientists' private pantry: fruit, bread and cheese, canned tuna – anything he could find that *wasn't* cooked aboard. "I don't claim to be a gourmet," he said. "But when I travel my stomach is always upset, and the swill they're serving on this ship would ruin my digestion for life."

Sheldon was doing more than ruining his digestion; he was in the process of probably dimming the hopes of those laymen who believe the sea is so rich in potential food that if the worst comes to worst we can always turn to the oceans for sustenance. A small, volatile and impatient English palaeo-ecologist, Sheldon had emigrated to Canada in 1965 because he, like others, had observed Canada's new commitment to ocean sciences and decided that "Canada was where the action is in oceanography." To Canada he brought the germ of an idea which, two years after Hudson 70 and as a result of work done during the expedition by himself and colleagues from the Marine Ecology Laboratory of the Fisheries Research Board, Dr. Anand Prakash and Dr. William Sutcliffe, seemed to have produced a new and more precise way of measuring the total of marine life in the oceans. From it may come methods for measuring the potential productivity of the sea. Although it had its genesis in the hard work involved in incessantly sampling the phyto- and zoo-plankton down the Atlantic and up the Pacific, the Sheldon hypothesis is an abstract scientific theory which in time may set the world of science on its ear.

Dr. Prakash had been doing the basic sampling work aboard the *Hudson* from Halifax, but Sheldon joined the expedition at Valparaiso. At the time he was thirty-five, and for much of his life had been studying the behaviour of particulate matter in the oceans. From this had come theories about a possible way of measuring the total bulk of living matter in the oceans with unprecedented accuracy.

Until Sheldon's hypothesis is tested in the crucible of analysis by scientific critics, the accepted scientific wisdom is that there is a ten-to-one relationship between each link in the marine food chain. That is, the prey organism is ten times greater in numbers and total quantity, than the predator organism which lives off it. This belief has always been broadly supported by the known fact that any living, moving creature, whether on land or sea, uses only about ten per cent of the energy it acquires in food for its own physical growth; the balance is used to supply energy needed for movement, hunting, mating, brain functioning or is excreted as fecal matter.

Sheldon's growing conviction before Hudson 70 was that the total biomass – total weight, or bulk – of the creatures in one link of the food chain was equal to that in the next link up. There may be billions of phyto-plankton organisms, but Sheldon believed their total biomass was about the same as that of the creatures in the next link in the food chain; that is, the millions of zoo-plankton that feed on the phyto-plankton. By extension, the total biomass of the baleen whales, biggest known creatures on earth, is only equal to that of the millions of shrimp-like creatures called krill on which they feed. Other scientists have often measured the populations of specific links in the food chain, but they had hitherto not been correlated with precision. During Hudson 70 Sheldon and his colleagues set about making such precise correlations using phyto- and zoo-plankton samples as their yardstick. Their work ultimately produced new studies about the sizes of phyto-plankton in Arctic, sub-arctic, tropical and Antarctic waters which indicated that there may be more small phyto-plankton in tropical waters than had been thought, and that therefore these areas of the oceans – now regarded as relatively unproductive – may contain more life forms than hitherto suspected, or at least may be able to support more life than is commonly believed possible. But to Sheldon this finding, although significant, was of secondary importance.

The problem here has always been that a sample of seawater – on Hudson 70 the sampling was done by simply dipping a bucket over the side – produces great quantities of particulate matter as well as plankton. It is difficult to distinguish between the smaller phyto-plankton and this non-living particulate matter as well as plankton. It is difficult to distinguish had devised techniques for doing this. Once that was achieved it was relatively simple to count the amount of phyto-plankton in a sample. Then they measured the amount of zoo-plankton in the same sample. Predictably, there were far fewer zoo-plankton organisms than there were phyto-plankton organisms. But further tests showed that, as Sheldon's hypothesis claimed, the total biomass, or weight, of both phyto-plankton and zoo-plankton was about the same.

It would be much later, in his painfully cramped trailer-laboratory at the Bedford Institute, that Sheldon would be able to take the next step in proving the hypothesis. That is, to measure the biomass of the zoo-plankton against the next link in the food chain – the micronekton; small fish, tiny crabs, shrimp and any marine life about the size of a minnow that feeds on zoo-plankton. Other scientists had already done this work in equatorial waters, and when the figures were correlated Sheldon again found that the total biomass of micronekton was about the same as that of the zoo-plankton. On and on up the food chain, Sheldon did similar calculations involving even the giant blue whales and their food, the krill. Here he had to depend heavily on the work of marine biologists who had taken a census of the whales in the 1930s, before most of them were killed off during a frenzy of whaling immediately after the last war. But using Dr. Prakash's sampling of krill during the Antarctic legs of Hudson 70, Sheldon correlated the krill biomass to the biomass of the whales in the 1930s, when there was a normal population. And yet again the hypothesis stood up.

For years after Hudson 70, Sheldon would remain scientifically cautious about these conclusions. At no point would he concede that his hypothesis could produce conclusions about the total numbers of any marine creature with anything less than a fifty per cent margin of error. To land-based scientists, such a margin would be horrifying. But our knowledge of the oceans is so slight that many other commonly accepted measurements involve a 1,000 per cent margin of error, and marine scientists are forced to use them. All that Sheldon would concede was that – *"If I'm right"* – he had reduced the margin of error a hundredfold.

The scientific benefits may be obscure to a layman, but it could be vital to marine biologists if the Sheldon hypothesis – exquisitely simple as it is – helps predict the rough growth rate of any marine organism. If, say, zoo-plankton eat ten times their own weight in phyto-plankton, then the phyto-plankton must ncessarily reproduce ten times faster than zoo-plankton to maintain the balance of nature. This theory, too, can be applied up the food chain. The potential practical benefits of the Sheldon hypothesis are breathtaking to those concerned with the need to locate new food sources. If, for instance, you want to fish for herring you could, in theory, measure the biomass of phyto-plankton in a given area and by simple multiplication could come to a reasonably accurate guess of how many herring there should be in that area of the ocean. Then you would know whether trawling there for herring would produce enough fish for it to be worthwhile. It would also be possible to set ecologically "safe" limits on how many herring could be caught before the species is endangered.

This safety factor has already been exceeded in the case of many species. The blue whale was so overfished immediately after the last world war that there are only about 2,000 left in the world, and that may not be sufficient for the species to survive; to "come back" in healthy numbers, as scientists put it. Twenty years ago, when areas of upwelling were discovered in equatorial waters, the Japanese found such waters were rich in tuna and began fishing for them with typical, and frightening, efficiency. They first did so in the Pacific, and in the early 1960s began sending fleets of tuna boats to the Atlantic as well. Their success as fishermen has led many marine biologists to fear for the survival of the tuna. But if it were possible to put quotas on the numbers of tuna – or any other species, for that matter – that may be taken from the sea, the problem of endangered species would end. Similar quotas have been set for many land creatures, and the penalties for exceeding them are at least a deterrent. However, quotas can only be set if there is some reasonable way of determining the approximate population of, say, tuna or blue whales or herring, and the likely rate of each species' reproduction and growth. If Sheldon's hypothesis is right it will enable quotas to be set simply by determining the place that the tuna, for example, occupies in the food chain. It is now generally believed that you must leave two-thirds of the total population of any species intact at all times to ensure the species maintains its growth rate in harmony with other creatures in the food chain.

His own work apart, there were for Sheldon – as there were for all scientists who took part – other excitements on Hudson 70. Sheldon may have disliked the food, but he enjoyed the conversation with scientists of other disciplines. In the main, however, the scientists split into social groups of their own kind; biologists with biologists, geophysicists with geophycicists, electronic engineers with electronic engineers, chemists with chemists. Observing this social phenomenon one evening in the lounge, Sheldon hungrily munched an apple and thought of the question often asked, only half in jest: when is a scientist going to be elected President of the United States? And then he decided that if that ever did happen, it would be a disaster.

Science is amoral. The really good scientist is a man whose passions are channeled into answering one question, just as Sheldon's own energies had for years been almost totally devoted to his own project. If his hypothesis was right, it would be of considerable benefit to mankind as a whole. But it wasn't because of those possible benefits that he did the work. The uses to which any piece of new scientific information, any new truth, could be put were purely incidental to the work itself. It was the desire to find out, the passion to answer one of the thousands of riddles of nature, that drove the scientist. If he or she were to ever stand back and look at the total scheme of human endeavour and human need, then that piece of work might never be done.

In a sense, Sheldon decided, the scientist is a social misfit. The world itself is not a place of moral absolutes, but of grey areas between a pragmatic right and wrong. On the other hand, the scientist's world was either black or white; there was no such thing as a half-successful experiment. He might half convince himself, but the most important thing was to convince others. And so, in his blinkered dedication, the scientist was of necessity like the photographer whose picture of a pathetic beggar woman in Paris earned praise from a man who, moved by the woman's poverty, asked: "What did you give her?" The photographer replied: "A thousandth of a second at f8." This kind of mono-mindedness bred arrogance. The scientist had to believe he was right, and that his science was also right. Sheldon was only glad that his work was not in the same league as that of, say J. Robert Oppenheimer who stage-managed the development of the atomic bomb and was wracked with conscience thereafter. And yet Sheldon's pursuit of an answer to a problem was of the same order as Oppenheimer's; it was simply that the results were different.

His own work might help man catch more fish – and at the same time make man realize he must catch fewer fish since in some cases the Sheldon hypothesis would inevitably demonstrate that to do so would imperil a species and destroy a food source for future generations. It would also destroy the myth of the inexhaustible oceans. His job was to acquire knowledge, and all knowledge – the development of nuclear fission for instance – was a weapon for either good or ill.

The arrogance that led to discovery also led to unwise intolerance of humanity. Overdependence on scientific wisdom – which was often indistinguishable from scientific arrogance – was as dangerous as the other extreme, the refusal of politicians and community to pay heed to the scientist. An ecologist could say the use of the pesticide DDT was dangerous to the environment. He could say that with certain levels of carbon monoxide in the atmosphere x people out of a hundred would probably die, and y would suffer agonies. And yet it must be left to the politician to measure the immediate consequences of banning DDT against the future benefits of not doing so. To ban it might cause millions to die of malnutrition or malaria in India, but might help preserve the world for some shadowy future. Where did the priority lie? In the here and now, or tomorrow? That was a moral decision – and science was necessarily amoral. An arrogant, amoral Ph.D. president would be rather worse than a politician whose personal morality might be questionable but who was, perforce, controlled by the morality of the community.

And having finished such sobering thoughts at the same time as he finished eating the apple, Ray Sheldon – quietly cursing all ship's cooks as adulterers of good food – went back to the stern laboratories where colleagues Prakash and Sutcliffe were doing work that would enable Sutcliffe to test his theory that ribonucleic acid in zoo-plankton was yet another way in which the productivity of the oceans can be measured.

Sheldon and Sutcliffe are neighbours in the untidy trailer camp hidden behind the dockside warehouses at the rear of the new, but spartan, Bedford Institute building. Their physical closeness is convenient, since their work is in many ways complimentary; both, for instance, can make use of the same analyses of seawater samples. In the end – though at the time of Hudson 70 neither knew when the end would be – the work of each man may be enhanced by that of the other.

Dr. William Sutcliffe was for much of his forty-eight years an administrator of science. For seventeen years he was director of the Bermuda Biological Station, one of the world's small yet renowned oceanographic laboratories, and was also director of marine science studies at Lehigh University in Pennsylvania. Toward the end of this period as an administrator he began to formulate a theory about a possible way to measure the rate of zoo-plankton production in the oceans. Two years before the Hudson 70, while Canada was scouring the world looking for top men to join its revitalised oceanographic programme, Sutcliffe abandoned administration and went back to original research in the Fisheries Research Board laboratories at the Bedford Institute. The voyage of the *Hudson* was his first opportunity to acquire data which might enable him to extend his theories to the point where they would be accepted as proven by the scientific community. It is hardly an accident that Sutcliffe and Sheldon and many other marine biologists devoted so much of Hudson 70 to studying what Sutcliffe, a burly man who looks and dresses like a fisherman and deliberately eschews the esoteric language of most scientists, calls "the bottom of the barrel"; that is, the plankton life forms and other creatures near the bottom of the food chain. As Sutcliffe is fond of saying: "We know hardly anything about what happens to life in the oceans, and we're not likely to find out unless we start with these critters down at rock bottom where it all begins." Sutcliffe always says "critters" for creatures. It's a refreshingly anti-scientific affectation.

On land, man knows enough about his environment and the inter-relationship of the food-web, or food-chain, involving all living creatures to be able to manipulate the world to suit his needs. We may have mismanaged things to the point of disaster, but because he knows how plants grow and how animals feed man can still farm the land and make it grow as much as possible and raise cattle and sheep and pigs and chickens in what almost amount to production lines of tasteless protein pap. Conversely, we know so little about the food-web in the oceans that man at sea is still a hunter, not a farmer. And now that man faces increasing dependence on the sea for food it is vital to know more about the bottom of Bill Sutcliffe's barrel, where the original nutrients come from. Moreover, such knowledge is vital to the survival of the world since all life is presumed to have begun with phyto-plankton, and it is the phyto-plankton which, some scientists believe, produces over half the oxygen needed to keep the eternal cycle of life on earth in motion.

Of the two experimental programmes Sutcliffe led during Hudson 70, the one involving his theory about ribonucleic acid (RNA) and the rate of zoo-plankton production was dearest to his heart. In recent years biologists have been able to measure the ocean's approximate production rate of phyto-plankton because it grows easily in laboratories. Zoo-plankton don't, and therefore the oceans' productivity of the tiny (they're mostly invisible to the naked eye) creatures that are the next link in the food chain can only be guessed at. It was Sutcliffe's belief that the amount of RNA in zoo-plankton would be a reasonably precise productivity measurement.

It is usually accepted by scientists that the more RNA in any living creature the greater its protein synthesis, or growth rate: protein is a fundamental building block of any life form. By Hudson 70 Sutcliffe had taken many samples of zoo-plankton, freeze-dried them so that while all moisture was removed the chemical structure remained the same, then analyzed that chemical structure to determine the RNA content. His early results were exciting, persuasive enough for him to have proffered his theory as a hypothesis in several scientific papers. But still it remained just that – a hypothesis. While the relation between RNA and growth rate was accepted in principle by scientists, Sutcliffe's findings were on zoo-plankton samples from limited areas of the oceans, and therefore scientifically inconclusive. Hudson 70 gave him a chance to sample a great stretch of the oceans. The long haul up the 150th meridian of the Pacific was particularly valuable; he could sample the ocean from Antarctic to Arctic. It would take several years to analyse all the samples and correlate them, but in the end his evidence would compellingly prove him either right or wrong.

Early in his analysis of his findings Sutcliffe would be encouraged because they showed that there was more RNA in the "critters" he caught in the tropics than in those collected in arctic or colder boreal waters. And since everyone knows that almost everything grows faster, and dies faster, in the tropics than in colder climates, this tended to support his theories. It is a measure of the frustrations of marine science that even if Sutcliffe is right, the RNA method will only provide a rough measure of the zoo-plankton productivity of any area of the oceans. But as Sutcliffe said at the start of the expedition, "any measurement is better than none at all."

The other research programme which occupied Sutcliffe and his team on Hudson 70 had its beginnings in the summer evenings of St. Louis, Missouri, with small boys bounding around river banks catching fireflies. They sell them for fifty cents a dozen to a chemical company. It's an after school job that produces far more pocket money than delivering the St. Louis *Post-Dispatch,* and if they didn't do it scientists like Sutcliffe would be in difficulty.

In this second research project Sutcliffe and his associates were really scraping the bottom of the barrel of life. They wanted to measure not phyto-plankton but the amounts of non-living organic matter in the surface waters. If phyto-plankton is the grass of the oceans, and zoo-plankton the insects, then this non-living organic matter is the dust. It is fecal matter from zoo-plankton and fish; it may be pieces of any dead marine life form, animal cells left over when one creature has eaten another and not swallowed everything. It can also be the "sweat" of phyto-plankton that Chung Choi was studying in the Atlantic when adrift in a small boat with the three Newfoundland sailors who introduced him to the rules of the mating game as played in port. But, wherever it comes from, this "dust" is a fundamental source of the nutrients which in the end stimulate all life – and science knows little about this non-living organic matter beyond the fact that there's a lot of it.

Since the techniques for measuring it weren't developed until 1965, Hudson 70 provided the first chance in history to do a major two-ocean survey of this nutrient "dust". The technique involves filtering a sample of seawater through a net of almost unimaginable fineness: each hole is 160-microns (or one sixth of a millimetre) square, so small you couldn't get the point of a needle into it. When the water sample is strained through this mesh almost all the zoo-plankton are trapped and what is left is microscopic phyto-plankton and "dust". Like all living organic matter, the phtyo-plankton contains the high energy molecule adenosine triphosphate (ATP). The "dust" does not. Aboard ship, Sutcliffe and assistants spent days preserving samples of phyto-plankton and "dust" for final laboratory tests back at the Bedford Institute.

Back in those trailer-laboratories at the Institute the fireflies from St. Louis get into the act. A chemical company buys the fireflies from small boys and chops off the tails that glow at night. They are ground down to become a powder which, when mixed with the sample of plankton and "dust", causes the high energy ATP molecule from the phyto-plankton to glow. By measuring the degree of glow Sutcliffe can tell just how much of the sample is phyto-plankton and how much is non-living "dust". Again, it would take years before the results of this work were known, but a few months after Hudson 70 Sutcliffe was able to say that it seems there is almost always twice as much non-living "dust" as there is living phyto-plankton "grass". Indeed, in some parts of the ocean he found there was up to thirty times as much "dust" as there was "grass".

Each in their own way, both Sutcliffe and Sheldon were helping measure the potential of the oceans as a source of food for man. And neither is particularly optimistic; at least, neither thinks that the oceans are likely to be as productive as many laymen would like to believe.

200

And then there were the dogs. By now Nicodemus, the pup Dave Butler brought aboard at the start of the voyage, was almost full grown – a big, black and beautiful German Shepherd; an endearing animal, still deferring to Mark, the doctor's Doberman Pinscher from whom he had learned how to be a dog. He had been taught to sit and to beg by Larry MacDonald, the steward who served the captain and officers and who left the ship at Valparaiso. He was high-spirited but not vicious. In port he would stand wistfully by the gangplank, mutely pleading with shorebound scientists and sailors to take him walking in the strange environment of dry land. But he was still not house-trained and when he and Mark began romping up and down the companionways they were a threat to anyone passing nearby. At a formal reception in Tahiti, where the ship stopped for fuel and supplies, a French-speaking local official expressed admiration for Nick and Dave Butler reluctantly gave him away. When the *Hudson* left to continue the run up to Alaska they left behind a seadog better able to stay upright on a pitching deck than on a hilly street, who didn't understand the French commands of his new master.

Tahiti, a name synonymous with South Seas' Paradise, was a disappointment to both crew and scientists. They drank in the famed Quinn's bar, rented Honda motor bikes and went roaring around the richly vegetated mountains behind Papeete, stayed at hotels to rest from the cramped quarters aboard ship. One sailor, Neil Gray, crashed his Honda, broke his leg and was left behind in hospital. Within two hours of arriving in Papeete at 8.30 a.m. on May 12 Ray Sheldon had left the ship to end his month-long diet of cheese and fruit and canned sardines. He found the best restaurant in Papeete – not a difficult task, since Papeete isn't big – and ordered a medium rare filet mignon, French-fried potatoes and a small bottle of wine. That night some sailors got into a fight, which they lost, and two spent the night in the local jail.

But a South Seas paradise Papeete wasn't. The beaches are rocky, and the consensus was that Papeete itself was both unfriendly and unlovely. The *Hudson* set sail on May 16, on what was described as Phase Seven of Hudson 70, though the major work was a continuation of that begun in the Antarctic.

Typically, Frank Dobson was by then weary of the sea, of Hudson 70 and of ports where he could not communicate because the local language was either Portugese, Spanish or French. Dobson had been senior of the four quartermasters, or helmsmen, since the ship left Halifax. Older than the others – he was thirty-nine – he was the union spokesman for the crew, a fact which pleased Butler since he considered Dobson "a sound, reliable, intelligent and sensible man." He looks like a bespectacled clerk rather than the sailor he has been most of his life, and had signed on for the entire expedition because, as he told his wife Mayola, "it's a once in a lifetime chance to see these places; to have such an adventure." But by Papeete the adventure had worn thin.

And then about 350 miles south of Hawaii – that other Pacific paradise that is a little less than Nirvana since it became part of the u.s. and was invaded by the Coca Cola culture – Dobson and bo'sun Joe Avery heard Anne Murray singing. The effect on them, and on the crew, was startling. As he told Mayola later: "It was only a radio show, but it lifted everyone's spirits." It happened this way: Coming off watch at 8.00 p.m. one evening, Dobson was walking past the bo'sun's cabin when he heard an English voice on the radio. That in itself was a milestone; for six months the radio programmes had all been in either Spanish or Portuguese in South America or in French in Papeete. All the music had been Latin American, and as Dobson had told cabin mate Denny Fraser: "South American music is okay, but it makes you realize how far you are from home." This evening, however, bo'sun Avery was fiddling with his massive radio, a multi-waveband Eddystone, and had picked up a Hawaiian radio station as Dobson was passing his open cabin door. The first thing they heard was a raucous commercial for a used car dealer. And when that ended, there was Anne Murray singing "Snowbird": The Canadian singer had just been "discovered" by the Americans, and her version of "Snowbird" was at the top of the u.s. hit parade.

Within minutes Avery's cabin was crowded. Anne Murray on a Hawaiian station. . . . "Y'know Joe," said Dobson to Avery, "I think I'm beginning to understand how the French Cana-

202

dians feel when they have to talk and listen to English all the time and not their own language. I never really understood what all the fuss was about until now." That first sound of English on the radio from the 50th state of the u.s. made a major impact on everyone aboard, as chemist Iver Duedall noted in his journal – a journal which was, in fact, probably the longest letter from husband to wife in the history of written language.

Hawaii, however, was to produce a more profound excitement for Duedall. Of all the scientists, he had spent the greatest amount of time aboard. His work, carrying out the basic chemical sampling programme designed by he and the Institute's senior chemical oceanographer, Art Coote, had been uneventful, even dull, though at times exhausting and uncomfortable; lowering cables with water bottles on them down through a few miles of ocean in mid-storm is at least tiring, and sometimes hazardous. Even though Hudson 70 represented the fulfilment of an ambition born when he chose oceanography over teaching or industrial chemistry, he had grown weary by the time the ship was passing Hawaii. His love of the outdoors was such that when he acquired his masters degree in Oregon, he had chosen to work at the Bedford Institute while taking a doctorate in chemical oceanography and Hudson 70 had presented the first opportunity to spend more than a few days at a time at sea.

Taking the job of the *Hudson*'s resident chemical oceanographer meant delaying his doctoral thesis by a year, but at the time he knew so little of the sea he felt somewhat like an airplane designer who had never flown, or a composer who had never played an instrument. The first psychic rewards had come early in the expedition. To prevent seasickness he had taken pills prescribed to cure his wife's morning sickness when she was pregnant with their only child, Paul. They had worked, and while most of his colleagues lay in their cabins, nauseous because of the heavy Atlantic swell that greeted the *Hudson* when she first left Halifax, Duedall was up and about on deck. He stood for hours gazing at the immensity of the ocean and for the first time sensed the finite nature of man. In an urban society, man was surrounded by himself and his own achievements, and it bred the arrogance that had led man to think of himself as the ultimate creation. Out in the North Atlantic, watching the endless sea splutter against the bow and heave along the hull of the ship, Duedall recognized emotionally what he had known intellectually for years; that he was just one example of one form of life amid myriad other creatures, all interdependent. In that chronicle of his experiences written for his wife, he talked of it as being almost a religious feeling; a searching for an answer to the mystery of how he, Iver Duedall, human animal, came to be where he was when he was, shaped as he was, functioning as he was.

His precise function was to produce analyses of ocean samples that were "internally consistent" – that is, to provide data collected, analyzed and tabulated by the same person using the same equipment – through three oceans. That meant the data, while a repeat of much that had already been acquired by other scientists, could not be suspect on the grounds that it had been produced by different people using different techniques. Duedall's job was to measure the quantities and concentrations of oxygen, nitrate, phosphate and silicate in the oceans. His work will eventually provide the world with an invaluable yardstick of pollution. Future generations will take Duedall's findings – and those of other scientists as well – and be able to measure the degree to which man's activities have changed the evnironment. The normal life cycle of earth generates prodigious quantities of nitrogen and phosphate compounds, most of which end up in either the oceans or the atmosphere. In the process of photosynthesis – of producing oxygen – phyto-plankton absorbs much of the nitrate and phosphate compounds, and so "cleans" the atmosphere, in which a delicate balance of oxygen and nitrogen must be maintained to make life possible. The industrial society generates unnatural quantities of nitrate and phosphate compounds and may have already upset the natural balance of these elements in the oceans. No one knows for sure whether this is so, though doom and gloom environmentalists claim that man has already so damaged the chemical balance of the oceans that the end of the world is at hand. In 1968 man was dumping pollutants into

204

the seas at the rate of 48,000,000 tons a year, and French ocean explorer Jacques Cousteau claims that the oceans are now so polluted they can produce one-third less oxygen and consume one-third less of the alien elements in the atmosphere than they were able to at the start of this century. There may be conflicting views on the subject now, but because Iver Duedall spent seven months of 1969-70 analyzing the chemistry of three oceans at 247 locations over 20,000 miles future generations will not be beset by such uncertainty. They will know whether the chemical structure of their oceans has changed, or at least will be able to find out by using Duedall's findings as the basis of comparison. There were other reasons for the chemical ocean-ography that took place during Hudson 70, and one of the most important is that knowing the chemical nature of layers of the oceans helps physical oceanographers like Ced Mann to reach conclusions about the ways in which the waters of the earth circulate.

As so often with the science of Hudson 70, it would be months, even years, before the results of the work by Duedall and Coote – he was aboard for part of the voyage – would ap-pear as a reportable achievement. It would not be until 1972, for instance, that they could say that their findings demon-strated that oxygen levels in the oceans had not changed since 1961, the year in which the most acceptable earlier chemical analysis had taken place. But they also announced they would be another year or so trying to determine whether there were more or less of the other potentially damaging nutrients, not-ably nitrate and phosphate compounds.

There was, however, some excitement as the *Hudson* worked its way past Hawaii. The chemical analyses – done aboard ship by a Technicon autoanalyzer of the kind used by hospitals to analyze blood, urine and other bodily secretions – showed some unexpected variations. At the end of months of routine work, this in itself was exciting, though it would not be until long afterwards that they would realize they had de-tected a previously unsuspected extension of a known deep-sea current. A few years earlier chemical oceanographers from the Scripps Oceanographic Institute in California had worked across the same area and found that part of the so-called "boundary current" that runs up the Pacific around Hawaii actually headed round the east end of the islands. They concluded that it continued eastwards. The work of Duedall and Coote proved that it turned north instead.

That, then, was how scientists and sailors ended the long haul up the 150th meridian to Vancouver – in pursuing an uneventful routine that was necessary, but boring. It was the *Hudson* herself who provided the only excitement. On the way into Victoria on Vancouver Island one of the four main engines burned out. And then, at 10.15 p.m. on June 10, as the *Hudson* once more steamed back into Canadian waters, the port radar set failed. Dave Butler, who would never publicly admit to emotional feelings about his ship, privately decided that the *Hudson* was as tired as he and the rest of the crew were. It took a day for customs and quarantine clearances to be completed, and most of it the crew spent reading letters that had accumulated during the two months since leaving Valparaiso. Hugh Henderson, the technician, had a letter in unfamiliar handwriting. It was from Valparaiso; from Iris Godoy, the girl he had left behind in Chile; the girl he had promised: "I will return."

At 6.00 p.m. on June 11 the *Hudson* sailed from Victoria, bound for the Canadian Pacific Dock in Vancouver harbour. She steamed slowly in to berth at 8.10 a.m. on June 12. It was so early the dockside was almost empty. There were three people standing waiting to greet the expedition's return to Canada. They were Iver Duedall's wife, Dave Butler's wife and Dr. George Pickard, from the University of British Columbia. They stood apart from one another, and looked very lonely.

At the time the men of Hudson 70 felt their return to the Canadian mainland was something of an anti-climax, but within hours they were made to feel so welcome that Peter Reynell, the young junior officer from England, was to say that he thought all the pained agonizing about Canadians not having a sense of identity was a lot of nonsense – though he didn't say it quite that politely. Joe Greene was on hand for an official welcome home, and provincial and civic officialdom turned out in force. The departure of the *Hudson* in November the previous year had attracted little public attention, perhaps because the world was infected with moon-shot fever at the time. The expedition's return to Canadian soil was a different matter. Vancouver newspapers, television and radio stations devoted a great deal of attention to the return of the *Hudson* and as a result the "open house" days aboard the ship, when the public were invited aboard, seemed at times in danger of degenerating into riots. They had expected perhaps 500 through the ship each day; they got a staggering total of 8,000 a day. On the second day in port Dave Butler, in civilian clothes and accompanied by his wife, tried to return to his ship from a shopping trip. He went to the head of the queue of people waiting to get aboard. Two very large men turned on him and snarled: "Get in back and wait like the rest of us." He found himself surrounded by a milling crowd sceptical of his repeated explanation: "Look, I'm the captain. Really I am. It's my ship. I want to go aboard, *please.*" The sailor on watch at the gangplank rescued him.

Vancouver was the pause in the expedition before the big push north to the Arctic and the Northwest Passage. Butler took leave with his wife for six weeks. Chief Officer Mauger, who had left in Valparaiso, flew from Halifax to assume command. Coxswain Frank Dobson's wife Mayola was on the same plane, and she and Frank spent their second honeymoon in seven years of marriage touring the British Columbia Interior. Officer's steward Larry MacDonald, who had returned to Canada from Valparaiso, rejoined the ship a changed man. Two days after flying back to Halifax he had caught a plane to Calgary where Jean Sampson, the girl he left behind to go on Hudson 70, was then living. In Calgary they had got engaged. "You don't know what you've got until you haven't got it," he told cabin mate Art Carroll, a fellow steward. He even considered having another tattoo added to the impressive array on his thick, hairy arms, already covered with hearts and flowers, Indian maids sitting before teepees, and the inevitable Grave of the Shipwrecked Mariner. Hugh Henderson, who was staying with the ship, bought four *Teach Yourself Spanish* books and settled down to really learn Spanish because, after all, Iris Godoy down in Valparaiso had written that she was learning English. Besides, it was embarrassing having to take her letters in Spanish to a friend for translation.

Roy Gould, still acting chief officer under acting captain Mauger, left the ship briefly to spend a few days at the luxurious Bayshore Inn near the Vancouver waterfront. For Gould, an ex-Royal Navy officer with few personal ties since his wife died in an aircraft crash in the early 1960s, this was an almost routine performance when in port. He takes both work and his pleasure in large doses. In Rio de Janeiro, Buenos Aires and Punta Arenas he had spent his shore leave in the most elegant, and expensive, hotels available. The Gould that lives, however briefly, in such splendour would be unrecognizable to the *Hudson* crew. Aboard he wears old, almost scruffy clothes. Ashore he is immaculately tailored. Aboard he'll eat whatever is placed before him, usually two helpings of it. Ashore the food is epicurean, the wines are vintage, the women exquisite. The only clue to this schizophrenic aspect of the man is his cabin, which has a Degas print on the wall, an Iranian rug on the deck and a well-handled collection of books ranging from the complete works of Maugham to Stendhal.

For the *Hudson* herself, the stopover was the time for a minor overhaul and engine repairs, which meant the next phase of the expedition would be cut short. And while the ship was laid up at Victoria, Chief Steward Bill Shaw quietly and at length cursed Peter Beamish, the whale man who had been aboard in the Atlantic. The porpoise he had killed in Rio harbour and then stored in the big specimen freezer was still aboard. They had tried to find ways to ship it back to Halifax from every port at which they had called, but there had never been any way of guaranteeing that it would stay deep-frozen on route. Shaw had hoped he would be able to ship the carcass east from Vancouver. He found he could not. So the dead dolphin would have to stay with the ship, and the specimen freezer – so little used by scientists Shaw had grown accustomed to having it available for reserve food storage – was still in use. There would be no ice cream in the Arctic.

6

Somehow the next stage of Hudson 70 lacked the drama and excitement of that which had gone before and was to come in the next three months. Until now the ship had been in strange and often unknown waters, and the scientists had been clearly working on the frontiers of available knowledge. In the months ahead there would be the drama of completing the Northwest Passage, of scientific discoveries that would ultimately effect the fate and face of the world. But what was officially designated as Phase Seven of the expedition involved relatively routine work in known waters barely a day's steaming from Vancouver. The only real diversion was the disgust of the crew of the Canadian Naval Auxiliary Vessel *Endeavour,* with whom the *Hudson* was working, over what came to be called the Great Movie Con Trick. *Hudson*'s movies had been supplied nine months earlier in Halifax. They were all old, the prints faded and the film itself broken in many places, so they were hard to run through the projectors. The *Endeavour*'s movies were all recent issues, with the prints in good condition. Roy Gould arranged a swap – and when the two ships were at sea and the inequity of the deal was exposed he received several rather bitter radio messages, including one from Fred Muise who, now fit again, had rejoined the expedition and was technician aboard the *Endeavour.*

For all its apparent lack of drama, however, Phase Seven involved exploration of – scientifically speaking – a relatively new but almost totally accepted concept of how the world came to be in the shape it is today. There have been many theories about how the physical shape of the earth came about, beginning of course with the early beliefs that a deity set things down the way they are for better or worse. The most recent theory, and the one most likely to stand the test of time and future science, is that of Continental Drift. It was first comprehensively advanced in 1912 by Alfred Wegener, a German meteorologist, and popularized by Dr. J. Tuzo Wilson, of the University of Toronto, in 1963 with a brilliant analysis of the several versions of the Drift theory.

In very simple terms, the accepted wisdom at the time of Wilson's publication was that as it coalesced from a ball of gases into a more substantial form, the earth was fixed in roughly its present shape, with the continents "frozen" in place as the cooling process continued through a few billion years. Isaac Newton first put this belief into words and a great many scientists, geologists included, still believe it.

But the actual shape of the continents has for centuries fascinated early explorers and their spiritual descendants, the scientists who explore the unknown. The coastlines of Europe and Africa and of North and South America, for instance, would fit together much like the pieces of a jigsaw. If you were to swing both land masses out to mid-Atlantic, Canada and the u.s. would tuck neatly in against the coastline of the Low Countries, France and Spain, and South America would fit snugly in under the bulge in the North African coastline. That bulge itself would nicely fill the Gulf of Mexico.

The two topmost layers of the earth are the crust and the mantle. The crust is the time-toughened part of the world on which we live. It is believed it is made up of seven major "plates" containing continental land masses, plus an unknown number of smaller ones, one of which contains the Caribbean Islands and another of which fits into an area between the North American plate and the Pacific Ocean plate just south of the Queen Charlotte Islands off Canada's west coast. It was this area that Phase Seven of Hudson 70 was to explore.

While the earth's crust is of ancient rock with an average thickness of thirty-three kilometers (just over eighteen miles), the mantle beneath it is around 2,500 kilometers (1,500 miles) thick and consists of solid matter near the surface and probably molten rock at the bottom, near the core of the earth. The most popular version of the Continental Drift theory holds that the plates that make up the crust have probably bumped together and swung apart over and over again and that they are in the process of doing so even now. The ninteenth-century Austrian geologist Eduard Suess played with maps and assembled all the land on earth together so it fitted neatly, coastline to coastline, and gave it the name Gondwanaland, after Gondwana in East Central India which was roughly at the centre of this artificially assembled land mass. Around 180,000,000 years ago, give or take a few million, this great land mass broke up into its component parts and they began drifting apart. That, for instance, is when the Atlantic Ocean began to be formed, which is why it is said to be the second youngest ocean of all; the Red Sea is thought to be younger.

Man's existence has lasted but the flicker of an eyelid in the measures of time the Continental Drift theorists are talking about. At present, Europe and North America are drifting apart at the rate of three centimeters a year, or roughly six feet in the lifespan of an average man. For this reason those who believe that an advanced civilization existed on a land called Atlantis in mid-Atlantic, subsequently swallowed up by a cataclysmic contortion of the earth, are daunted by the Continental Drift theory. There may have been a land mass between Africa and the Americas at some point, perhaps even an island on a breakaway portion of one of the plates, but present scientific evidence suggests it would have to have been several million years ago, and so far as anyone knows mankind isn't that old. They've dug up fossils of some pretty remarkable creatures that did roam the earth around then, but none of them look much like a two-legged anthropoid.

The irony of mankind's abiding belief in the reassuring stability of terra firma is that it isn't very firm. The whole thing is far more plastic than the layman realizes. The giant tides that sweep past Saint John, New Brunswick, up the Bay of Fundy, place so great a weight of water on that part of the North American plate that at high tide it buckles inward – and New Brunswick to the north and Nova Scotia to the south tip down by a measurable amount. And though the drifting of the plates is immeasurably slow in the terms of a man's life-span, their grinding together set up the pressures that created the mountain ranges and is still doing so. Canada's west coast mountains are part of the crust that may once have been beneath the sea and reared upward because of the stresses set up by the Pacific plate moving eastward and grinding against the North American plate moving westwards. This was why Hudson 70 included a seismic investigation of the seabed south of the Queen Charlottes.

The mantle on which the crust plates "float" is a great reservoir of rock substances between the crust and the bowels of the earth. It appears to be solid, but the temperature is 500 degrees Fahrenheit at its coolest just beneath the upper crust, and the moment any of it escapes through the faults in the crust or gaps between the plates it liquefies into molten rock. In this sense the earth is a massive pressure cooker; the mantle remains solid because, despite the great heat, it is under pressure from the lid above. A volcanic eruption is the best and most visible example of what happens when the lid lifts briefly, but such eruptions of liquefied rock happen on a far less dramatic scale almost continuously as the plates grind together and drift apart. Molten rock oozes up from the mantle to fill the gaps, cools and becomes part of the crust. In a sense the earth's crust is like a self-sealing, puncture-proof tire.

The meeting points of the plates are called faults. They are weaknesses in the earth's crust, and the earth is a spider's web of this global, timeless varicosity. There is, for one, the great Rift Valley fault in western Africa from Ethiopia down through Kenya and Tanzania. To the east of the fault the plate is moving eastwards; to the west it is heading westwards. In a few thousand years western Africa from Aden in the north to Madagascar in the south will have parted company, and a new sub-continent will have been formed. The San Andreas fault which bisects California may be the most famous of all. This is a continuation of a fault that begins in the South Pacific off the coast of Chile. There the Pacific Ocean and American continental plates meet. The fault runs up the Gulf of California and into the land mass to become the San Andreas Fault. It was a particularly violent interaction between plates

212

along this fault that caused the great San Francisco earthquake, and the continuing grinding action between Pacific and American plates makes the west coast of South America an earthquake area where tremors such as the one Dick Haworth experienced in Valparaiso are an almost daily fact of life.

In an area of their science called plate tectonics, geophysicists are just beginning to learn how to measure the interaction between the plates of the earth's crust. Sound waves, for instance, travel faster through rock under pressure and are therefor useful in measuring the direction of the interaction, and in pinpointing those places where the plates are grinding hardest against one another. It was seismic work of this kind that the *Hudson* and the CNAV *Endeavour* were doing south of the Queen Charlottes; the *Hudson* sat still while the *Endeavour* ran circles around her, letting off undersea charges as she did so. The speed and angle at which the sound entered the earth and bounced back up to the *Hudson* provided measurements about the interaction between the Pacific and American plates and the smaller plate that fits in between them at that point.

The *Hudson* was also making gravity and magnetics measurements, since the polarity of the various stratas of rock in the earth's crust are major clues to the history of the earth. The north-south polarity registered on the *Hudson*'s compass – on any compass, for that matter – is vastly different from that which has existed through the ages. During the past 10,000,000 years, which isn't very long geologically speaking, the earth's polarity has reversed itself, or has been reversed, no fewer than twenty-five times. That is, the magnetic north moved from one end of the earth to the other. These reversals of polarity have followed no nicely regulated time pattern. At one point around 7,000,000 years ago it seems to have reversed in the space of 50,000 years, though as a rule the reversals seem to have taken place every few hundred thousand years. Geologists are able to determine this by drilling into the earth's crust and taking a core sample of the rock. Palaeontologists use radioactivity to define the ages of the levels of rock from the fossils they find within it. And then modern technology is able to unravel another, less visible, secret locked into the rock; the magnetic polarity that existed on earth at the time the rock was formed, probably from new material that came from the mantle. Science is fairly certain it has measured the reversals in polarity accurately. Scientists say, for instance, that we are currently in the longest period in the earth's history during which polarity remained stable. That is, the north pole has been in roughly the same place for almost 700,000 years.

What science cannot explain, however, is why or how the reversals of polarity took place. This particular mystery in natural science has sparked many theories. It may, for instance, lend some credibility to the theories of Immanual Velikovsky, the Princeton man who suggested that Mars and Venus entered our solar system as comets and, before becoming fixed in orbit, passed so closely to the earth that they set our world tumbling base over apex. He uses this hypothesis as the basis for explaining how similar cultural-religious patterns crop up in all cultures of earth, cultures formed long before there was any apparent means of communication between the continents.

According to Velikovsky, it was the abrupt dislocation of the natural order of things created by the passing of Mars that caused the waters of the Red Sea to conveniently slosh out of the way so the children of Israel could be led to safety by Moses when they fled Egypt. He points out that not only the Judaic-Christian god is said to have created the world in seven days and seven nights – the "barbaric" gods of, among others, the Mayas of Central America also go down in legend as having worked overtime for seven days to make the world. Velikovsky suggests that Mars and Venus upset the natural order of things on earth on seven separate occasions, thus cementing the number "seven" in the hand-me-down history of almost all races on earth. There are other indications that the world has moved abruptly on its axis from time to time. Certainly the polar ice caps were once not far north of the present equator and tropical forests existed in what are now frigid polar regions. Sudden and cataclysmic changes in the location of the poles would conveniently explain several mysteries, such as the discovery in Siberia a decade or so ago of a quick-frozen mammoth, a creature which was always assumed to have roamed tropical forests. Its death and subsequent freezing were so sudden that the flesh of the mammoth could still be eaten when the body was uncovered.

For all these theories, however, conventional scientists point out that magnetism is even more of a mystery than gravity, and that magnetic fields may spontaneously reverse themselves. There is, they argue, no known immutable law that says the north should be "positive" and the south "negative" in terms of electro-magnetic energy. But for all that little is known about magnetism, it does seem certain that variations in the strength of the earth's magnetic field over the millennia had profound effects on the evolution of life forms that now exist. From fossil remains, it is known that of all the species of life forms that have ever existed on earth, less than ten per cent survive today. And those may exist in their present form in part because of mutations caused by the periodic weakening of the earth's magnetic field.

Gamma radiation from either the sun or from any nuclear activity produces mutations in life forms. The rays from the sun are kept at a "healthy" level because they are largely absorbed by a belt of charged particles that girdles the world on the outer edge of our atmosphere. The strength of the earth's magnetic field is responsible for the distance of this belt of charged particles – the Van Allen Radiation Belt – from the earth at any given moment. When, back in time, the earth's magnetic field weakened or strengthened, either more or less of the sun's gamma rays were able to reach the surface of the earth and influence the life forms that lived on it at that time. What did that do to the shape of the creatures on earth and the law of the survival of the fittest? No one will ever know. In any event, this belt of charged particles is responsible for one of the most astounding sights on earth: The charged particles which leak out of the Van Allen Belt into the earth's atmosphere are drawn to the magnetic north and south poles. They cause a number of natural phenomena, most notably the incredible vision of the Aurora Borealis in the polar night sky.

In one way the Aurora Borealis symbolically represented an underlying impatience among the crew of the *Hudson* during the work south of the Queen Charlotte Islands. The scientists, led by Dr. Charles Maunsell aboard the *Hudson* and by Dr. Keith Manchester on the *Endeavour,* were in the main attempting to refine known techniques of studying the interaction of the plates that make up the earth's crust. They were not measuring the movement taking place; rather, they could only be concerned with movement that has taken place. And plate tectonics is still sufficiently in its infancy that such measurements pose more questions than they answer. The *Hudson* and *Endeavour* found that the plates that meet south of the Queen Charlottes are not only grinding together, but that there is a seventeen degree difference in the directions in which the plates and the mantle beneath are moving. Since crust and mantle are in fact both part of the same whole, enormous stresses are set up by this difference in the way each is heading

To scientists this was an exciting discovery that raised many more questions for future investigation. To the officers and crew it was largely meaningless. What was of great significance to them as sailors was that they were soon to sail north to the Beaufort Sea and then to attempt to make the fabled Northwest Passage. In the maw of time the earth might be a shaky, insubstantial place. But in the here and now of the sailors' world was the prospect of attempting to do what sailors had tried to do for years – to sail across the roof of the world.

7

Like Ced Mann, Dr. Bernard Pelletier is a small man. As with Ced Mann, too, his lack of stature is irrelevant because he has about him an ineffable air of substance, of authority. He is plumper than Ced Mann, and more communicative; indeed, by comparison Pelletier is almost jovial. He is head of the Bedford Institute's marine geology division, and when the *Hudson* left Esquimalt harbour on Vancouver Island on the evening of August 13, bound for the Arctic, Pelletier was aboard as chief scientist, heading back to part of Canada that was both familiar and well-loved. He was then forty-six, and much of his earlier life had been spent in surveying the north. He had been part of the Canadian Geological Survey task force which, in 1959, begun a crash programme studying the resource potential of the Arctic, including both Canadian mainland and the islands in the great northern archipelago that stretches up to the North Pole and to which Canada has long laid a sometimes tenuous claim. The north was an old enemy, and one with which Pelletier was comfortably familiar.

This last phase of the Hudson 70 expedition had largely been made possible by Pelletier's ambition to fill in a yawning gap in the geological maps of the Arctic. The Geological Survey task force had done most of the needed work east of the Mackenzie Delta, and the Americans had investigated their part of the Arctic north of Alaska, though not as thoroughly as the Canadians. In between these areas of work lay a 700-mile-wide gap that included the Mackenzie River Delta itself and the Canadian Continental Shelf of the Beaufort Sea. This part of

217

Canada is largely unexplored by geologists and geophysicists who would be able to at least indicate whether it, too, might hold reservoirs of oil, natural gas and other mineral wealth.

Two years earlier, when Ced Mann had been tentatively planning the expedition, he had offhandedly asked Pelletier: "Bernie, d'you have anything you want to do in the Arctic?" Pelletier later felt that Mann's casualness had hidden an urgency. There were by then good scientific reasons for taking the *Hudson* down the Atlantic, round the Horn and up to Vancouver, but for the expedition to be the dramatic enterprise that Mann and Atlantic Oceanographic Laboratory director Bill Ford hoped it would become they needed the grand finale of a trip through the Northwest Passage. And Pelletier had instantly provided justification for it. In terms of geologic science, the Beaufort Sea was unknown territory and in the political and social climate that had persisted for a decade its exploration was at least necessary, perhaps vital. At first, Pelletier was allocated two weeks for his work. And then that political and social climate warmed up to the point where instead of being a valid rationale for sending the *Hudson* through the Northwest Passage, Bernard Pelletier's work was to become a major – perhaps the major – part of Hudson 70. As the *Hudson* rounded the southern tip of Vancouver Island and headed north west to the Aleutian Islands, Pelletier knew that he would spend a month in the Beaufort Sea and would virtually be admiral of a flotilla of four of Canada's fleet of scientific ships. Even so, he anticipated no drama; Ottawa might have decided to mount a massive effort, but it was essentially a barnstorming attempt to do a monumental amount of relatively routine work in the space of a few weeks. Six weeks later Bernard Pelletier would remember having had that thought and grin wryly. By then he had begun smoking again for the first time in five years, was ten pounds lighter, the future of the world had been changed and he was wondering whether he would one day regret ever having had a hand in Phase Eight, Hudson 70.

The search for the Northwest Passage from Atlantic to the Orient began in the sixteenth century and produced some of the epic stories of heroism and hardship in the history of man. Even so, the Arctic itself was, until the end of the last world

218

war, a largely neglected land. Bleak, inhospitable to most life and almost inaccessible, it bulked large on the map and small in the minds of men. But when that war ended and the Cold War confrontation between east and west started, both Russians and Americans showed a renewed interest in the roof of the world. They discreetly placed bases on the great islands of ancient ice which drift slowly around in the ice-pack of the Arctic Ocean, and set up complex electronic equipment to monitor one another's activities.

In 1959 the Geological Survey of Canada, founded in 1842 and the nation's oldest government scientific establishment, was instructed to focus a task force on the Arctic. At the time it seemed a logical outcome of the 1957 election of John Diefenbaker as prime minister after a campaign in which he dramatically and repeatedly spoke of his Northern Vision.

This apart, events elsewhere had already created an awareness that the Arctic was vital to the future of the world – the western world in particular. Through the chill that froze the world into aggressive attitudes during the 1950s, the Americans were convinced that their technological superiority made them invulnerable. The cracks in their sundry alliances in Europe, Asia and elsewhere in the world had not yet begun to show. Fortress America seemed invulnerable. Sputnik I changed all that. It caused Washington to begin a desperate reappraisal of the world, and the western nations to examine the state of their technology. Part of the reappraisal which Ottawa watched with more than usual interest was the study by a group of powerful u.s. geologists who pointed out that America did not have an inexhaustible supply of the fossil fuels on which the economy, and u.s. security, depended. The u.s. Geological Survey pointed out in the mid 1960s that while major oilfields in Texas, Oklahoma and Louisiana were still producing, they would run dry long before the year 2,000. Other resources were also dwindling. There was, for instance, only twenty to thirty years supply of copper, zinc and lead ores to be found in the continental United States itself. Coupled, these facts increased the awareness that the supplies of oil and other minerals from the Middle East and Latin America were jeopardized by the changing social order and burgeoning nationalism

219

in these areas. Washington and Ottawa grew worried, though for slightly different reasons. The u.s. is long on people and short on resources. Canada is long on resources and short on people. It may be an overstated politician's point, but it remains true that Canada is like the mouse that shares a bed with a friendly elephant. The elephant might shift in the night because it needs more room and an unwary mouse could get hurt.

Until this point Alaska had been the Cinderella state of the union. Geologically, it was little explored, largely because in a vast, sparsely populated land such exploration was expensive, uncomfortable and likely to be unprofitable: If there was oil in Alaska the problems of setting up drilling rigs on permafrost that softened in summer, and then of getting the oil to market, were technologically awesome, and if they were solved it would only be at great expense. Now, however, the oil companies found themselves being pressured into looking north to Alaska for new reservoirs of oil to guarantee the future of the u.s. economy.

Canada was ahead of the game at this point. u.s. oil companies began a relatively modest survey of the Alaskan Arctic a couple of years after the Geological Survey of Canada task force had begun its work in the north. By the time the first major survey of Alaska began, teams of Canadian geologists, working with dog sleds on the one hand and miniature submarines on the other, had already explored much of the Canada that no one knows and few would care to. They had drilled through the ice pack to take seabed cores, bored through the permafrost for the same reason, chipped at ice-sheathed rocks, flown millions of miles in helicopters and light planes. Bernard Pelletier had been part of the task force from the beginning. Three times he had been in aircraft that had crashed. Once a plane in which he was a passenger plunged through weak pack ice and he and three others had spent two days in a pup tent waiting rescue. He had survived a unique accident while over 1,000 feet beneath the ice pack in the archipelago islands. He was in a miniature submarine, from the portholes of which he could see evidence of ancient smears of oil on the undersea rocks. Then the submarine sprang a leak; the seawater dribbled in and short-circuited an electrical wiring circuit, starting a small fire.

No exploration work by geologists and geophysicists can say for sure whether oil, gas or other mineral or fossil wealth exists in a particular area. What Pelletier and others of the task force were looking for was rock of an age and nature that it might be a potential source of these resources. Such rock must be between 25,000,000 and 400,000,000 years old – and that 400,000,000 years represents less than a tenth of the time that has elapsed since the earth began to cool and the rocks of its crust began to form. Since oil and gas were formed from the remains of once living organisms of some kind, there is no point in looking for it in rock formations that were created long before life appeared on earth.

By the time Hudson 70 was being planned, the pressure was off both private oil companies and the Geological Survey of Canada. Arctic surveying was still intensive, but the political climate had changed again and the pressure had eased. It was the u.s., coming from behind, which had actually put man on the moon and so reaffirmed its technological superiority. New offshore oilfields had been found around the coasts of America. There had been changes in political stances. It was still vital to know whether the Arctic was a potential bonanza of mineral goodies, because if the world is to survive in its present form it must find new sources of fuel. The u.s. particularly must know whether it can remain self-sufficient. But the post-Sputnik panic had ended and exploration had slowed to a more normal pace. Ced Mann and Bill Ford had decided that Pelletier's geological work in the Beaufort Sea, while important, could occupy only two weeks of Hudson 70.

That, however, was in 1968. In early 1969 the Atlantic Ridgefield oil company found exploitable quantities of oil at Prudhoe Bay in Alaska, just a few miles in from the Canadian border. Within six months natural gas was found on Melville Island in the Canadian archipelago. In the summer of 1969 the Humble Oil supertanker *Manhattan,* aided by the Canadian icebreaker *Sir John A. Macdonald,* bulldozed its way through the Northwest Passage to demonstrate both u.s. determination to

221

exploit Arctic oil fields and that it was possible for tankers to get the oil out. And then, in January 1970, Imperial Oil brought in a rich well at Atkinson Point in the Mackenzie Delta, 200 miles from the Alaska border. By now everyone knew for sure what had until then only been suspected; that oil and gas were there in commercial quantities. And one of the most likely places to find it would be beneath the Continental Shelf of Canada that stretches seventy miles out into the Beaufort Sea beneath water that is rarely deeper than 300 feet. Man had spent centuries looking for a passage through the Arctic to reach the riches of the Orient. In an age in which the world runs on oil, the riches have turned out to be in the Arctic itself.

The effect of all this on Bernard Pelletier's Beaufort Sea programme was almost instant, and dramatic. He was given four weeks of Hudson 70 instead of the originally scheduled two. The *Hudson* would also be part of a fleet that would include the Canadian Scientific Ships *Baffin, Parizeau* and *Richardson*. The *Baffin,* principally a hydrographic ship, shares a berth with the *Hudson* in Dartmouth and is about the same size, 296 feet long. The tiny *Richardson,* sixty-six feet long, and the bigger *Parizeau,* 212 feet, are based on the west coast. All four ships would explore the Mackenzie Delta and the Beaufort Sea. Pelletier's geology would now be a major part of a massive scientific probing and charting operation.

If Pelletier was in a sense the admiral of this fleet, then the *Hudson* was the flagship and Dave Butler the senior captain. In itself, however, that meant nothing to Butler. The earlier stages of the expedition had been fascinating, important, challenging. His ship had carried the Canadian flag to parts of the world where it had never been seen before. But to Butler, and to his officers and crew, the Arctic phase of Hudson 70 was the most important partly because they were working in Canadian waters, but mostly because they were to attempt the Norhwest Passage. In the epic history of man versus the sea the Northwest Passage has always been a dream to conjure with, and was still. Butler thought it strange that, with man now almost routinely commuting between moon and earth, the passage should still be the golden ring that sailors hoped would one day be passed to them, an ultimate achievement for a master mariner. He understood clearly how the late Captain Kettle, his predecessor as master of the *Hudson,* had fought to add the Passage to Hudson 70. Long afterwards he was to say, with rare poesy: "It hung there at the top of the world and the end, or almost the end, of the whole expedition as the ultimate challenge to me, the *Hudson* and to all the men aboard."

Part of the challenge for Butler was actually working in ice. He had often sailed through icebergs, but never tried breaking through the ice pack. The *Hudson* was built to do just that, with steel plates three times the thickness of those in a conventional merchant ship hull and an icebreaker bow. Butler, who found there was little literature on the subject to learn from, wondered how he would fare, and on August 23 as the ship neared the ice pack that closed in around Point Barrow in Alaska he determined to make his first encounter with the ice by daylight. His estimated time of arrival at the edge of the ice pack was late afternoon.

The previous day they had passed through the Bering Strait, seeing the ghost-like outline of Siberia off to the west, and were now about a mile off shore steaming for Point Barrow. Near Wainwright, the location of an Eskimo community and a u.s. air base, a small outboard motor boat shot out from shore and pursued them. It contained two Eskimos who, as their boat bobbed up and down in the swell alongside the *Hudson,* yelled up a request for help. That, however, was all that Butler could make out; neither man spoke English well enough to make it clear what kind of help they needed. At Victoria a helicopter had been loaded aboard for the Arctic leg, and Roy Gould heaved his considerable bulk into the fragile-seeming plastic bubble of a cabin and was flown to the Eskimo village on the coast by ex-Battle of Britain Spitfire pilot Wilfred Pinner. They landed on the black sand of the beach not far from the cluster of shack-like houses built on stilts so the heat from inside would not melt the permafrost beneath. Gould clambered down, said: "Take me to your. . .er, headman, please," and was led to a house more spacious than the rest. The village chief spoke good English and was tinkering with his two-way radio, trying vainly to raise either the civil authorities at Nome, Alaska, or Wainwright air base to report that two men were missing. They had left three days earlier in a small outboard motor boat to go sealhunting. Gould tried to operate the faulty radio and failed, so he returned to the *Hudson* where radio officer Phillip Rafuse reached the Alaskan authorities on the distress waveband. They said they would launch a search immediately, and Butler offered the services of the *Hudson*. The U.S. radio operator said: "Well, you can go looking if you want but we won't pay for the gas." To his astonishment Butler found himself becoming very formal, almost music-hall British. "I don't think fuel is an issue when men's lives are at stake," he said stiffly.

Eventually satisfied the *Hudson* could do nothing to help, Butler ordered the ship to get under way again. Because of the delay the *Hudson* reached the ice pack around Point Barrow at 8.50 p.m.; soon it would be twilight and then the brief Arctic night would descend. August is the time the Eskimos talk of the Death of the Midnight Sun; during the brief summer it never grows dark, and in winter it is rarely light. Butler faced ice for the first time in the twilight zone.

Butler collected two additional packs of cigarettes from his cabin and wedged himself into his flip-down seat on the bridge. It would be a long ride through the ice, and he planned to be on the bridge throughout. On his orders, the ship headed for the shore lead – that gap of open water which usually exists between the land and the ice pack at that time of year. It was perhaps three-quarters of a mile wide. For three hours they steamed at half speed, hugging the edge of the ice pack since the inshore waters there are poorly charted. Then, at midnight, the shore lead began to narrow; the ice pack extended closer and closer to shore and the shallows. With the ship less than half a mile offshore and the lead closing, Butler began to consider turning around and heading back to the edge of the ice pack to seek an alternative route. Then the radar picked up a gap in the ice that glowed milky white in the gloom on the ship's port side. It was another lead in the ice heading due north. Butler ordered the change of course, and the *Hudson* headed into the ice pack proper.

At 4.00 a.m. it was light again, and the lead petered out.

Ahead was pack ice; to both port and starboard was pack ice. The ship stopped. Butler lit one cigarette from another and was uncomfortably aware that once again he had only three of the main engines working; the fourth had failed in the first few days out of Victoria. The *Baffin* had passed this way six weeks earlier to begin her work in the Beaufort Sea, and at that time – high Arctic summer – she had spent ten days battering through this same Point Barrow ice pack. "Half astern all," said Butler. And then, from a quarter mile away, he ordered "Full ahead, all." The *Hudson* charged the ice.

At first it was easy. The idea is to either smash the ice on impact or to ride the bow up onto the ice pack so that the ship slithers sideways until it finds a weak point at which its weight will break through the ice. The ship inevitably follows this line of least resistance, which may not go in the same direction as the course the ship is supposed to be following. After two hours of relatively easy icebreaking, the *Hudson* suddenly stopped dead. The ice had grown so thick it had stopped 4,800 tons of ship travelling at ten knots. The *Hudson* backed up again, and again charged the ice. The bow rose up on the ice; the ice creaked, groaned and split with an almighty wail, and the *Hudson* continued on her way.

Butler left the bridge to go to breakfast at 8.00 a.m. next morning. He was strangely exhilarated. He looked around the bridge at the officers, the quartermaster, the lookout, and realised that they, too, were elated. The adrenalin was running. He thought ruefully that they were all like kids on a roller coaster, and he handed over the bridge to Gould and went below. The *Hudson* cleared that ice pack at 3.00 p.m. on August 25, a total of forty-two hours after it had entered the shore lead at Point Barrow. The new course was almost due east, to Herschel Island on the edge of the bay that is part of the Mckenzie Delta.

At 8.00 a.m. on August 26 it was cold on Herschel Island, and there was a heavy, clammy fog. At dawn a big helicopter had flown a group of scientists and technicians about to board the

Hudson from the relative comfort of Tuktoyaktuk to the barren landing strip on Herschel. They were waiting there to rendezvous with the *Hudson*'s smaller helicopter and then fly out to the ship herself. Bruce Carson was among them, rejoining the expedition which he had left in Punta Arenas. To keep warm he and a few younger members of the group played touch football. Others huddled in the warmth of the radio shack. Dr. Bosko Loncarevic stood looking in the direction of the sea that was hidden in the fog and thinking that from the viewpoint of his employers, the Canadian government, he would probably be better employed back in his office in the Bedford Institute. As assistant director of the Atlantic Oceanographic Laboratory, second in command to Bill Ford, his role in Halifax would be more useful than the job he would do aboard the *Hudson*. He would be one of several operating the geophysics console aft of the bridge, watching the complex electronic equipment measuring gravity, magnetics and scanning the contours of the seabed.

The rationale behind his presence was that, like Bill Ford, he had to go to sea occasionally to be able to stay in touch with the original research that went into oceanography. Bill Ford himself had intended to be aboard during the Valparaiso-Tahiti leg of Hudson 70, but had been prevented from joining the ship because he had been conscripted into the massive effort made to clean up the disastrous oil spill from the tanker, the *Arrow,* in Chedabucto Bay, Nova Scotia, at about that time. Dr. William Cameron, the Director of the Marine Sciences Branch of the Department of Energy, Mines and Resources, also got into the act by being chief scientist on the Tahiti-Vancouver leg of the expedition. All had had the same rationale for leaving their desks: they must keep in touch. But Loncarevic was obliged to admit that he wanted to join the voyage so he would be able to say he had been part of it, that he had made the Northwest Passage. His enthusiasm wasn't explained by a love of the sea, because he had spent three of the previous twelve years at sea and long since learned that he had no emotional involvement with the oceans at all. In fact, he recognized that he didn't much like the sea, and that may have had something to do with his first acquaintance with it.

Loncarevic was a Yugoslav who had been raised by an uncle, a professor at the University of Belgrade. After the war the uncle, his family and Bosko wanted to go west. But Josif Broz Tito had already undergone the metamorphosis from resistance hero to Communist dictator and they were locked behind what Winston Churchill was to later name the Iron Curtain. The only possible route of escape was across the Adriatic to Italy; the only craft available were fishing boats – and anyone who tried it was caught by fast government patrol boats and interned. The boats were always missed before they had outdistanced the patrol boats, and the fishing fleets themselves were well policed. The professor's escape took two years to plan. The first summer he took a house in a fishing village, cultivated the image of an eccentric academic and demonstrated a passion for the sea by sailing with the fishing fleet.

The second year he took the same summer house and again went out with his friends the fishermen. But he insisted on being helpful – and clumsy, deliberately displaying incredible ineptitude by snarling lines and nets and damaging equipment. The exasperated fishermen decided that if he were so fascinated by the sea he should restore an old hulk that lay on the beach near the village. He had earned their friendship, if not their respect for his seamanship, and so they helped with the work. At the end of that summer the family had its own functioning boat and would putter up and down the coast, accepted by local officialdom as well as the villagers.

By the third summer the professor's family – which included the then lean, nineteen-year-old Bosko Loncarevic – had become part of the village scene. Their sailing activities were unremarkable; they would often stay away overnight on an island up the coast, but it was known they always returned. And then one mid-summer day they marched gaily down to their boat carrying camping gear, started the auxiliary engine – and waved goodbye to Yugoslavia. The cockleshell voyage across the Adriatic to Italy took three days. They momentarily expected a grey-hulled patrol boat to come leaping out of the horizon or a plane to swoop overhead. But the worst that happened was that they were all seasick, young Bosko included.

From Italy he had emigrated to Canada. In Toronto he

worked as a hospital orderly, had installed television equipment in surburban homes, had worked in an electronics factory on the production line. He had also studied at the University of Toronto. When he left the production line to continue his university studies his fellow workers threw a big party. At first he was astonished, and then he realized that there were many immigrants and working people among them who saw their lives limited only by their lack of education. They were overjoyed that one of their own, as they perceived him to be, had made it out of the grind, was going to university, would become one of the elite. In his going they were all going. It was as though his departure was a reaffirmation of their flagging faith in the strangely durable Horatio Alger myth that the boot boy can become bank president.

But, if anything, he was thinking of that trip across the Adriatic over twenty years earlier as he stood in a cocoon of fog on Herschel Island and the tiny red and white dragonfly helicopter from the *Hudson* crept in along the coastline carrying Bernie Pelletier to welcome the newcomers. He suspected Pelletier would not be exactly overjoyed to see him. There was, inevitably, an undercurrent when either he or Bill Ford were aboard one of the ships serving as juniors to the senior scientist aboard who was in charge of the major project. In the event, however, Pelletier was to be glad that he had another senior member of the government scientific establishment aboard. What they were to find could best be talked over by two senior men with an understanding of the broader implications of scientific discovery.

The three other ships of the fleet had been working in the Beaufort Sea for several weeks before the *Hudson* arrived. The *Baffin* was doing magnetics, gravity, geological sampling and hydrographic survey work, charting the contours of the ocean floor. The little *Richardson* was doing geological sampling and hydrographics inshore and in the Mackenzie Delta. The *Parizeau* was doing bottom sampling, magnetics and hydrographic work in Mackenzie Bay. The *Hudson*'s load was the biggest. Its job was to sail back and forth in closely paralleled lines between the shore and the edge of the ice pack, covering the Continental Shelf and that part of the deeps that was clear of ice. They would sample the seabed by dropping a mechanical grab overboard to pick up great gobs of the sediment. They would take cores by lowering the corer – a forty-foot-long, three-inch-diameter pipe with a 1,200 pound weight on top – to within twenty feet of the seabed, then dropping it. The weight drives it into the sediment; the sample brought to the surface is of the layers of that sediment as they have been laid down through the ages. From the fossils within the sediment palaeontologists can tell the age of those layers of sediment. Thus the task was to determine the depth and age of the sediment as well as the shape and age of the rocks beneath it. In the event, however, it was the actual charting of the contours of the seabed that would provide the drama. Jim Shearer, a geologist with the Geological Survey of Canada and a lean, undemonstrative man given to long, comfortable silences, provided Pelletier and Loncarevic with the first hint of what was in store when he boarded the *Hudson* from Herschel Island.

He had been working aboard the *Richardson* whose inshore work had been done in part with side-scan sonar. The name itself is almost self-explantory; conventional sonar equipment sends a beam of sound bouncing directly down ahead of the ship and delineates the depth and shape of the area of the ocean immediately beneath the vessel. It is a one-dimensional measurement. Side-scan sonar bounces sound at an angle to either side of the ship, sees a greater area of the seabed and provides a three-dimensional "picture". When Pelletier greeted Jim Shearer on Herschel, Shearer was carrying a box containing side-scan sonar records collected aboard the *Richardson*. He tapped it significantly. "Wait until you see what I've got," said Shearer. Pelletier knew Shearer well, and sensed he was bubbling over with some suppressed excitement.

Aboard the *Hudson*, Shearer, Pelletier and Loncarevic went to the laboratory aft of the bridge and on one of the massive glass-topped tables began laying out the side-scan sonar records. As the long rolls of paper were unwound the whole face of northern development began to change. John Diefenbaker's Northern Vision dimmed, and the world's expectations of the Arctic as an accessible treasure house of vital oil and gas were diminished, if not exactly dashed.

What Shearer was showing Pelletier and Loncarevic was visible proof that the ice pack that covers the Beaufort Sea for most of the year builds up to become so thick and under such great pressures that it develops "keels" – massive lumps of ice that hang beneath the surface and often reach down to the seabed itself and gouge deep valleys in the sediment there. The implication of the side-scan sonar records would have been obvious to any layman. The gouges were easy to see – long straight indentations that criss-crossed the seabed. The three men unrolled tube after tube of the side-scan sonar records. They showed that the gouges in the seabed were sometimes twenty feet deep in places where the Continental Shelf was 150 feet beneath the surface. If an oil well were located in such an area it would probably be impossible to run a pipeline to shore to carry the oil because at the time the icepack covered that area of sea it could rip open the line and send crude oil bubbling into the ocean. It was not inconceivable that man could devise some way of setting up an inshore oil rig that could somehow withstand the pressures of the ice pack; to Pelletier, Loncarevic and Shearer it seemed virtually impossible to find a way of protecting the needed pipeline from the ice keels gouging the seabed. Pelletier broke the silence by saying: "'Perhaps it just happens inshore. That's where the *Richardson* has been working. When we get out over the Shelf a bit, and in deeper waters, you might lose the gouges. Anyway, perhaps they're all old."

At 6.20 p.m. that evening, August 26, the *Hudson* raised its anchor and set out for the first run between land and the ice pack. Pelletier stayed in the general purpose laboratory on the main deck, watching the automatic pen of the side-scan sonar chart trace a picture of the seabed beneath. As the *Hudson* steamed slowly northward the continuous picture of the ocean floor confirmed the *Richardson's* findings. There were ice gouges everywhere. But the depth was 150 feet or less, and Pelletier still retained the hope that they might be confined to shallow waters. At midnight the ship steamed into the deeper waters of the Continental Shelf. As it did so the side-scan sonar picked up the deepest gouge of them all – a miniature valley cut thirty feet into the seabed. With Pelletier in the laboratory were geologists Gus Vilks, Jim Shearer and Chris Yorath, and technicians Tony Hardin and Vernon Coady. Bosko Loncarevic sat in the console room just off the laboratory aft of the bridge monitoring the gravimeter, the magnetometer and the conventional depth-sounding sonar. The *Hudson* steamed on and the water deepened. At 200 feet the gouges were still there. They were at 250 feet as well. And at *300* feet. And this was only fifty to sixty miles offshore, still over the Continental Shelf where oil wells might one day be located – oil wells whose product could not be pumped ashore by any pipeline technique then known.

At 1.00 a.m. Pelletier and Loncarevic met in the lounge for coffee. They discussed the possibility the gouges were old, then promptly discarded the theory since, as Pelletier pointed out, the seabed was latticed with them and while some seemed to have been partly silted in, others were as sharp and clear as the lines of an etching. It seemed certain the gouging was a constant, current process. There was, they decided, insufficient time before the ice pack closed in to ship a miniature submarine to the Beaufort Sea for closer inspection. They decided to depend on the underwater cameras, both still and television. In the event these were to prove useless, since the still camera saw only about twenty square feet of the seabed at a time and they never were able to drop it precisely into one of the gouges. The television camera simply didn't work in the extreme cold of the deeps.

The next week may have been the most dramatic of the entire Hudson 70 expedition, since the evidence of electronic equipment probing the seabed is immediately assessable by the scientists aboard – and it was Pelletier's policy to make sure officers and crew knew what was happening. But that was only partly the reason for shipboard excitement. On August 30 the *Baffin,* operating in the eastern end of the Beaufort Sea, radioed the *Hudson* with the news she had found another "Admiral's Finger". And that was the second blow to the prospect of the Arctic becoming a second Texas within the predictable future.

The previous summer, while the *Manhattan* had been clearing the western end of the Northwest Passage sixty miles east of Tuktoyaktuk, the *Sir John A. Macdonald* had been danc-ing attendance a couple of miles to the north. As the *Man-hattan* headed into Mackenzie Bay the *Sir John A. Macdonald* passed over what on the sonar record seemed to be a shoal that came to within fifty-three feet of the sea's surface. The *Manhattan* was drawing fifty-six feet. Rear Admiral A. H. G. Storrs, director of the Marine Operations Branch of the Department of Transport, was aboard the icebreaker. He looked at the sonar record, saw the abrupt peaking of the line which records the sea depth and poked his index finger at it in astonishment saying: "Christ, look at that!" He poked rather emphatically and his finger went through the chart, so there-after that hitherto unsuspected shoal was known as The Admiral's Finger. Had the *Manhattan* passed that way she would have run aground.

Thus the first report from the *Baffin* that another such shoal had been found indicated another place that supertankers should avoid if and when they started making the Northwest Passage regularly. Then, within twenty-four hours, the *Baffin* sent increasingly urgent radio messages to Pelletier aboard the *Hudson*. They had passed another shoal. Then another. And yet another. And they were all straddled across the western end of the Northwest Passage – the Gulf of Amundsen.

Three days later, at station 382 at 11.00 a.m., the *Hudson,* working at the opposite end of the Beaufort Sea to the *Baffin,* found her first Admiral's Finger. In one thirty minute period, during which the slowly moving ship steamed just 6,000 feet, they passed over seven more – and saw scores of the inevitable ice gouges as well. But the *Hudson*'s more sophisticated side-scan sonar demonstrated something else: these "Admiral's Fingers" were very aptly described, since they were not shoals at all but wicked geologic shards poking upwards toward the surface of the sea. They are a phenomenon called pingoes, anti-deluvian ice at the core and around that layer upon layer of sedimentary debris. When Dave Butler looked at the charts that Pelletier had drawn up he said, awestruck: "God, the *Manhattan* was lucky she didn't have her guts torn out." The pingoes in themselves do not present an insuperable naviga-tional problem for tankers, since they can be charted and, in theory, avoided. But in the Arctic a ship cannot always go where it wants to. The ice pack is in large measure the arbiter of just how any ship goes from point A to point B. And if a tanker became locked in that ice pack, as would inevitably happen, it would be carried around as the ice moved. It might be slowly swept across one of the pingoes and, as Butler put it, "have her guts torn out."

It was to be months before palaeontologists back at the Bedford Institute could analyze and examine the cores and sediment samples that, along with recordings of Bosko Loncarevic's geophysical equipment, would provide a total picture of the Beaufort Sea. But on board the *Hudson* it was then important to have some indication of how long the gouging of the seabed had been going on. Dr. Frances Wagner, forty-two-year-old palaeontologist and one of the two women aboard the *Hudson* on this leg of the voyage (it was the second time women took part in the expedition), made what proved to be a remarkably accurate guess. On September 2 they brought up a seabed core that on preliminary examination was found to have in it, twelve feet from the surface, a fragment of the shell of the *Baccinum,* a creature of the whelk family of molluscs. Frances Wagner told Pelletier she thought that it was around 4,000 years old. Long afterwards, the laboratories of the Geological Survey of Canada were able to carbon date this fragment of shell, and demonstrate that the *Baccinum* had died and fallen to the bottom of the sea 3,500 years ago, give or take a margin of error of 240 years. Carbon dating is a procedure which measures the quantity of Carbon 14 in a fossil. Carbon 14 exists in all living creatures at all times since it is a form of carbon created by the radioactive rays of the sun, and has a known rate of decay. The presence of a piece of whelk shell twelve feet down in the seabed sediment was relatively conclusive proof that the sediment in the Beaufort Sea built up at the rate of one meter, or slightly less than forty inches, each thousand years.

Frances Wagner's tiny scrap of shell demonstrated to Pelletier that the ice gouging had probably been going on for 12,000 years – in fact, ever since the Arctic Ocean had been open water. Then the glaciers inched their way northward –

no one is sure why, though it may have been because of a gradual shift in the earth's polar axis – and the oceans were covered with ice as the land itself was exposed. Although this phenomenon can be studied by geologists, many mysteries remain. It is known that it was as the glaciers moved north that the Great Lakes were formed, and it is believed that at about the same time the northern edge of the continent subsided to form the Beaufort Sea and other Arctic waters close to the continental land mass. Ever since the glaciers receded the earth has been springing back; slowly rising because it is no longer weighed down by the masses of those great sheets of ice that once stretched down almost to the Gulf of Mexico. The bed of the Beaufort Sea is also rising.

Like the gouges, the pingoes were an entirely unexpected discovery. The *Baffin* alone found and plotted seventy-eight pingoes, while the *Hudson* found fifteen. All seem to average around 1,000 feet across at the base and narrow, spike-like, as they near the surface. At the eastern end of the Beaufort Sea, in the area supertankers would have to navigate if they used the Northwest Passage, the pingoes were between forty-five and sixty feet beneath the surface of the sea.

As September wore on and these blows to Arctic development continued showing up, Pelletier found himself working incessantly. The implications were awesome, and for the first time in five years he found the lust for a cigarette irresistible. At first he begun borrowing one here and one there from colleagues. Then, when they wearied of his habit at their expense, he bought a carton of his own. Within two days he was again smoking twenty-five a day. But while the significance of his discoveries weighed heavily, Pelletier the scientist was also excited at breaking new ground and his excitement – and that of the other scientists – communicated itself to the crew. As the month allocated to this phase of the expedition neared its end, the evening gatherings in the lounge grew more spirited. Peter Wadhams, the young Englishman who had been working aboard throughout the voyage as a scientific maid-of-all-work, once more got out his guitar and he and Frances Wagner, an expert on the harmonica, would lead communal singing. Pelletier even joined Wagner in duets playing his own harmonica, but steadfastly refused to play his accordion. That was his private avocation. He would stay up late of an evening playing the accordion as he sat on the couch in the chief scientist's cabin. Over and over he would play his favourite song, and the one at which he was most practised; the German biergarten favourite "Du, Du Liegst Mir Im Herzen" – "You, You Lie In My Heart." Mostly, his neighbour Gus Vilks did not object. He said it helped him to sleep in self defense.

"Du Du Liegst Mir Im Herzen. . . ." As he spastically squeezed and tugged at the accordion on September 22, the work of the Beaufort Sea ended, Dr. Bernard Pelletier, Ph.D., took stock of what was perhaps the most dramatic month in his career. Some argue that science must be amoral; that man's right to know and thus to investigate, to experiment with the building blocks of nature, was a measure of the ultimate transcendental character of man and must never be stopped. And yet there were times, and this was one of them, when Pelletier began to wonder if man was not a little like a child playing with fire. He has to do to find out whether it burns, but his game can be a threat to the rest of the house and the people in it. A wise parent watches the child's game and teaches it that fire should be treated with respect and caution. Was anyone watching over mankind's little games?

The implications of the work of the past month were prodigious. On the one hand they had demonstrated that yes, all the Arctic, and now including the Beaufort Sea, was a potential bonanza of oil and presumably natural gas. The reservoirs of both could not even be guessed at, but given the probable geological history and nature of the area they were likely to be immense. This could mean new resources to feed the oil industry which in turn fed the industrial, technological society in which we live. And yet . . . and yet . . . . Knowing those reservoirs were there would mean that man would delay – perhaps delay too long in terms of the present ecological crisis – the need to find an alternative source of power less damaging to the environment than the fossil fuels. Apart from which, to be able to go back and tell the world – in this case Canada and the U.S.

– that they had more mineral resources than they had thought might well influence the balance of power in the world. That meant that for essentially political and economic reasons the Arctic oil could not be left in the ground, but must be exploited. That might lead to perilous haste. One super-tanker load of oil spilled into the Arctic, one broken oil-filled artery from offshore well to land, would destroy a large slice of the fragile ecology of the north.

On the other hand, scientists simply had to believe as an article of faith that all knowledge serves humanity. But knowledge was a weapon, and weapons weren't always wisely used. The crossbow, gunpowder, ships, flight, chemistry – all had been used for, and some were developed expressly for, man's destruction of man. Nuclear power might still not have been developed had it not been for the need for a bigger and better bomb, and even though the bomb was a sword that had stayed in its sheath for a long time there was good enough reason to wonder how long it would stay there.

Bernie Pelletier stopped playing; he put the accordion back in its case. He decided that if Canada and the Bedford Institute hadn't done this work and pointed out both the potential benefits and the dangers of the Beaufort Sea Continental Shelf area and the Arctic in general, then someone else would have. That someone else would then have the knowledge, and if knowledge was a weapon it was as well to have it in your own hands. And yet, as he fell asleep, the thought remained: Would he one day wish he had never had a hand in the entire undertaking?

There was other scientific exploration in the Beaufort Sea that would affect Canada's national stance on the subject of world pollution controls, though this would not be known until later. Pre-eminently, geologist Gus Vilks, backed up by the research of Frances Wagner, demonstrated that the flow of water through the Arctic is from Atlantic to Pacific, and that therefore any pollution in the North Atlantic could ultimately affect the Arctic environment. When, two years later, he came to make his point Vilks used photographs that look like something out of a book of science fiction; an artist's dream of a space station, perhaps. In fact, they were the photographs of a

236

creature smaller than a pinhead which had been magnified up to 100,000 times.

Vilks' work was among the first done by a new breed of scientist – a man with qualifications in widely disparate disciplines that overlap in the field of oceanography. He had begun life as a geologist, but was most fascinated by the fossils in the rocks he examined. Thus he went on to take a master's degree in biology. And with him in the Arctic he carried books on the subject of physics, or that part of physics that relates to ocean circulation, or physical oceanography. For Gus Vilks was working towards yet another qualification – a doctorate in biology and physical oceanography. He knew that when he was finished he would be one of a rare breed of scientists. Biologists work in oceanography. So do geologists and phycisists. Rarely is expertise in all three fields concentrated in one man. Oceanography is a bastard inter-disciplinary science; Gus Vilks was an inter-disciplinary man.

More than that, he was the odd man out among the scientists whose careers, in the main, had taken conventional course of high school graduation to university and then, much later, to work in research.

There was a strange cause and effect relationship that had led to Vilks being at work in the Canadian north as a senior and highly respected scientist, a circumstance of which even he was only dimly aware the day the ship had steamed through the Bering Strait and he had stood on deck and seen the misty, almost unreal blobs on the horizon that were the coast of Siberia. Butler had thought of the stories of Russian slave camps in Siberia; other scientists had thought of the theory that there was once a land bridge linking Siberia and Alaska and that it was across this bridge that the wandering tribes of northern Eurasia drifted into North America to become Indians and Eskimos. But to Gus Vilks that distant darkening of the horizon represented the fears that had haunted the people of Middle Europe since the October Revolution in Russia that had swept Lenin's Bolsheviks into power. Siberia was the place where the Russians shipped the unwanted, the unruly, the non-conforming, and Siberia was as much as anything the symbolic reason for the course Gus Vilks' life had taken.

Siberia represented the reason why he was studying a miniscule creature called *Orbulina universa* instead of ploughing fields in Latvia.

As the war ended Vilks' farmer father had fled the prospect of living under Russian rule. He packed the family into a fishing boat and set sail from Riga to Sweden on the first leg of a journey that led to a farm near Hamilton, Ontario, worked by the father and his sons, including teenaged Gus. But the farmer's boy grew restless and went west, first to farm again and then to be a carpenter of sorts. Then, fiddle-footed, he drifted east again to mine gold in Kirkland Lake, northern Ontario. When the mine closed, his mining skills took him back to Hamilton, where he helped dig sewers. And when that ended he settled down, took a training course and became a diesel mechanic. It was a steady, skilled job, one that many post-war immigrants from Europe would have been glad to have.

And then Gus met Ruta.

The Latvians, like other ethnic groups, cling in close community to form part of the vertical mosaic Canada is perversely proud to be. Ruta was Latvian and had been younger than Gus when she arrived in Canada. Thus she had profited more from the educational system and had gone to McMaster University to earn an arts degree. Meeting and loving Ruta had made Gus aware — uncomfortably at times — that life could and should have broader horizons than those he had seen. And so he went back to school. By the time their second boy was born he was in his freshman year in the science course at McMaster. Calculus and colic were his twin problems when he got his exam results. His best marks were in geology which, ultimately, became his main area of study as an ageing undergraduate; a broad-bulked, heavily-muscled ex-miner on a campus full of fuzz-cheeked young students.

Geology led to the fascination with fossils found in rocks and seabed sediments — scraps of shell and skeletal remnants of fish mostly — which are the footsteps in the sands of time left by life in all its many changing forms during the history of the earth. By carbon dating these fossils it is possible to tell the age of rock, or the rate at which sedimentation occurred.

Palaeontologists can often add another dimension to this work. If they can identify the fossil as being the remains of a cold water or tropical creature, they can tell how the climate has changed in any particular area in the course of the ages. Theoretically, one ten-foot-long core taken from the bed of the Atlantic should enable palaeontologists to tell with what is believed to be remarkable accuracy just how and when the climate changed on earth over the past million or so years.

Of these fossils the forminifera are among the most revealing. So small that even a few thousand of them look like a layer of dust, the formanifera (foram) is the tiniest and one of the most primitive life forms to leave a fossil. Other zooplankton do not leave fossil remnants; on death they are either eaten or totally decomposed. But the foram has a shell, even though it cannot be recognized as such unless looked at through a 25-magnification microscope. (Forams are not, however, the smallest life form; nunno-plankton cannot be seen with the naked eye and won't even show up until viewed through a microscope at 100-magnification, and yet they are vital to the ocean life-cycle.)

With the development in 1967 of the scanning electron microscope it became possible to study forams in detail for the first time, since they could now be viewed and photographed at up to 100,000 times life size. The Bedford Institute spent $60,000 on such a microscope in 1968, and Vilks began his work on the foram species *Orbulina universa*.

Orbulina is probably the most ubiquitous of all amoeba zoo-plankton and is found almost everywhere in the world. A creature that has existed since soon after the dawn of life, it became possible with the scanning microscope to see that the forams found in different parts of the world are similar in size and that all have minute spines projecting from the orb-like shell to make them unappetizing to bigger creatures that might otherwise feed on them. This shell, in fact, may be an ultimate demonstration of successful evolution; at least the foram has survived through time where millions of other species have not.

There are slight differences between those forams in the Atlantic and those in the Pacific, between those in tropic waters

239

and those found in the polar regions. When Vilks began his work it was believed these differences delineated different species. The Pacific and sub-tropical forams, for instance, have spines that grow out of little bumps in the outer shell, while the spines of those found off Nova Scotia and in the Drake Passage grow out of "shoulders" of a different shape. Vilks' contention is that forams are all of the same species, the "shoulder" differences being caused by climate. If this hypothesis is proved it means foram shells found in seabed sediments will provide a more accurate indication of how the earth's climate changed through history than any other fossil yet discovered. Examining the cores taken in the Beaufort Sea, Vilks found what he considers to be the fossils of tropical forams *beneath* fossils of cold water forams, and that tends to prove what geologists have long believed – that the now barren Arctic was once a fecund area with great forests of vegetation. He also found forams and other creatures indigenous to the North Atlantic, which indicates that water flows in from there, going east to west across the roof of the world. Thus pollution in the North Atlantic is probably carried into the Arctic.

In one sense, Vilks is trying to see into the future by studying the past. If scientists can more accurately determine changes that have taken place in the world's climate in the past, they can perhaps more accurately predict the future. And as with many other Hudson 70 projects, Vilks' work also had relevance to measuring pollution levels: Forams are particularly sensitive to subtle changes in climate and water quality that man cannot yet detect, so determining how many of these creatures are in any given area of the oceans in 1970 will provide a yardstick to measure the impact of pollution by, say, 1990. The foram-sampling programme had taken place throughout the voyage, though Vilks himself was aboard only in the South Atlantic and in the Arctic.

Vilks' work was to continue through the Northwest Passage itself, but before that was to be attempted the *Hudson* returned to Tuktoyaktuk for re-fuelling and to collect, among others, Dr. Cedric Mann. As with Loncarevic, there was little scientific justification for Mann's presence aboard at that time.

But who more deserved to be there for the grand finale: The Northwest Passage itself? Ced Mann flew out in the ship's helicopter. Bernie Pelletier met him on the stern flight deck as, looking bulky in his Arctic parka, he clambered down to rejoin the expedition he had fathered. The two men shook hands, and Mann looked around the ice-encrusted ship and said: "Last time I saw her it was a bit warmer." Then the two men went below, where Mann said: "You know, Bernie, it's amazing. That schedule I worked out. It worked. Everything is bang on time." And he moved his gear into a junior scientist's cabin, ready to spend the rest of the voyage working on deck doing plankton tows and taking bottle casts. Science, at least aboard the *Hudson,* is very democratic.

With him Ced Mann had brought mail for the ship. Unlike the mail the men had received when Mann was last aboard in South America, this batch did not generate a mood of melancholy, or homesickness. Rather, the result was to produce a feeling of elation: The Northwest Passage lay just ahead, and soon afterwards Halifax and home. There were two letters for Hugh Henderson. Both were from Iris Godoy in Valparaiso. By now his Spanish was good enough for him to be able to read them unaided.

From west to east, the Northwest Passage is generally considered to begin with the Prince of Wales Strait between Banks Island in the north and Victoria Island in the south. This leads to Viscount Melville Sound which in turn leads to Lancaster Sound and thence through to Baffin Bay and the open Atlantic. The Prince of Wales Strait is not a major hazard, but Viscount Melville Sound is. It is a large, exposed area of sea almost entirely landlocked by islands. For that reason, even during summer, the ice does not break up and drift away. The ice builds up year after year, coalescing into a lid that is twenty-five feet thick, sometimes thicker, over that part of the ocean. It is there that men have died through the centuries, their tiny ships locked in ice that builds up, hits the surrounding land and then sits there under unimaginable pressure until the Arctic summer, when the pressure sometimes eases. It is there that the great bulk of the *Manhattan,* one of the biggest ships ever built, and the powerful *Sir John A. Macdonald* had their greatest struggles with the ice. It was there the *Hudson* would almost founder.

At 7.45 p.m. on September 22 Butler ordered the anchor raised, and the *Hudson* set sail for the Northwest Passage. At 9.40 a.m. on September 24 they entered the western end of the Prince of Wales Strait, heading north-east. Almost everyone was on deck for the occasion. Bo'sun Joe Avery had a particular interest in the Prince of Wales Strait. At about the halfway point between the Beaufort Sea and Viscount Melville Sound lay the Princess Royal Islands. It was here he planned to erect the plaque he had so carefully made almost a year earlier in the Atlantic. Having been unable to erect the "css Hudson – Capt. D. Butler" plaque in the Antarctic, he had chosen the Arctic as second best. Bosko Loncarevic had suggested the Princess Royal Islands, uniquely important to Canada, as an appropriate site.

The islands are three desolate hummocks of rock, the biggest of them scarcely three-quarters of a mile long and half a mile wide. But because they're there, almost bang in the middle of the eleven-mile-wide Prince of Wales Strait which is the only possible route for ships making the Northwest Passage, Canada has control of traffic across the roof of the world. For navigational purposes, international law says Canada can claim only three miles of territorial offshore waters. The claims for Banks Island in the north and Victoria Island in the south total six miles. That means that for most of its length the Prince of Wales Strait has a belt of "international" waters in the centre. Any nation can send ships through. But midway along the strait it is all Canadian territorial water because Canada can claim a three-mile limit around the Princess Royal Islands as well. Thus the territorial waters of Banks, Victoria and Princess Royal Islands all overlap, and Canada has a tollgate on the Northwest Passage.

The *Hudson* reached the Princess Royal Islands at 5.00 p.m. on September 24. It was cold, damp and foggy – so cold the helicopter could not take off since within fifty feet its rotors would ice up. Winter was creeping in on Hudson 70. Joe

Avery could not go ashore on the largest island and place his plaque by the cairn of rocks that marks the grave of an RCMP constable who died on duty here. The disappointment of the crew was the keener because that morning the *Baffin* had been able to send a party ashore. From the deck of the *Hudson* Avery saw, through binoculars, the Canadian flag the *Baffin* party had left flying by the grave. He went below, got the plaque and was on his way to toss it overboard when he met Bernard Pelletier. "It'd be bad luck to take her back to Halifax," said Avery. Pelletier talked him out of it, and suggested the plaque should be erected on Beachy Island by the Franklin Memorial.

Franklin was an Englishman who mapped much of the shoreline around the Mackenzie Delta and the Beaufort Sea. He was knighted for his work, and in the 1840s led the Royal Navy's last thrust in a thirty-year effort to find the Northwest Passage. He and his crew vanished. Looking for them, the Royal Navy mounted eleven expeditions and at one point there were fifteen British ships in the Canadian Arctic – more than there have ever been at one time before or since. Independently wealthy, Lady Franklin mounted two expeditions of her own, and it was the second of these that found the remains of Franklin's expedition on King William Island. By then it was seven years after the expedition had disappeared and, being a practical woman, Lady Franklin had sent the second expedition off carrying a memorial to her husband to be left in the Arctic if it was proved that he had died. Francis Leopold M'Clintock, leader of the expedition, erected it on Beachy Island north of Viscount Melville Sound.

But before Avery's plaque could be erected, there was the Northwest Passage, which was now represented by the time-toughened ice of Viscount Melville Sound. Early on September 25 the *Hudson* rendezvoused with the *Baffin* and the icebreaker *Sir John A. Macdonald*, which would escort both ships to Resolute on the eastern edge of Viscount Melville Sound. It was a slow passage. The convoy could travel only by daylight, and since the *Hudson* still had scientific sampling to do she would often fall behind the two other ships, then follow them through the passage the *Sir John A.* had smashed in the ice. At night the scene was eerie and magnificent – three ships seemingly locked in a desert of ice, their lights glittering across space in the chill of the Arctic air. Even Butler, who had earlier tried to get permission for the *Hudson* to make the passage unescorted, conceded that there was something comforting about seeing the lights of the two other ships barely a quarter of a mile away. Not for the first time did Butler think of the adventures in the Arctic of Henry Hudson, and feel inadequate.

Henry Hudson's *Discovery* was a vessel of fifty-five tons and had a crew of twenty-one. The ship that bore his name 360 years after his death had a crew three times as numerous and weighed in at almost 5,000 tons. Butler, on his bridge going through the Northwest Passage, thought that in a sense Henry Hudson had made it at last. But even in that sense he nearly didn't.

On September 27, at dusk, the *Hudson* was breaking through the ice to catch up with the rest of the convoy. Suddenly the ship was brought to a halt by the ice pack. Butler ordered: "Half astern both" and the *Hudson* backed off to take a run at the ice. In the main deck general purpose laboratory Bernard Pelletier and Gus Vilks paused at the change in the engine note. Pelletier said: "Oh, oh – he's winding up for something." Both men ran out on deck as the ship surged forward on all three functional engines. The *Hudson* reared up on the ice pack – and suddenly canted crazily over on its port side. Pelletier grabbed the starboard guard rail and, as he told Vilks later, felt as though he hung vertically from it, parallel with the deck. Also on deck, steward John Carroll clung to a stanchion and would later say the port guardrail had been just a foot above the ice. But then the weight of the ship crashed down through the ice and the *Hudson* righted herself. Pelletier went to the bridge and Butler, visibly shaken, said: "That ice must have been harder than a whore's heart."

The weather remained bad and it proved impossible to fly Joe Avery to Beachy Island to erect the plaque. But a day later, while the ship was near Resolute on Cornwallis Island, the weather cleared and Avery flew to land a couple of miles outside the settlement. With him he carried a portable pneumatic drill. He chose a large rock, named it Hudson Rock, mounted two steel posts in cement and fixed the plaque to them. On September 30 the *Hudson* steamed through the ice into Resolute to drop some scientists and pick up Dr. David Ross and his party who would be responsible for the next, last and shortest leg of Hudson 70.

Bosko Loncarevic, Gus Vilks and Frances Wagner were among the party landed at Resolute to fly back to Halifax. These three trekked out to Hudson Rock where Avery had erected his plaque. Loncarevic found and pocketed the piece of wood which Avery had used to mix and lay the cement around the steel posts. He carried it back to Halifax, explaining to Vilks: "You have to be aware of history when it's happening, Gus. Some day this piece of wood will be an artifact of the past, and valued because of it." Back in Halifax he drew up a codicil to his will stipulating that Joe Avery's makeshift cement spatula was to be passed on to his eldest grandson and that the grandson should donate it to the Dartmouth Heritage Museum. It was a reasonably safe bequest; his own son or daughter, aged two and four at the time, were almost certain to provide him with grandchildren.

When geophysicist David Ross moved to Halifax from New Zealand in 1965 he was twenty-six and fascinated by Baffin Bay, that broad swathe of water separating Canada and Greenland. It seemed to him likely that the description "bay" was a misnomer. He suspected it should be called Baffin Sea or Ocean.

The scientific definition of an ocean is that body of water between two land masses on separate and distinct plates which make up part of the earth's crust and which, presumably, are still moving either apart or coming together. One accepted wisdom that justified describing Baffin Bay as such was that Greenland was still part of the North American plate and that there had been a split, or fissure, in this plate which had caused Greenland to pivot away from north-eastern Canada. The fissure in the southern section of that area of the plate had permitted the sea to flood in and create the lower part of Baffin Bay. This pivotal action had – so this theory goes – also set up stresses that caused the remaining part of the plate to subside and form the northern part of the bay.

There was, however, another theory about the bay, and it was this that most intrigued Ross. This theory argued that Greenland had become totally severed from the North American plate and drifted north-east. If right, this theory would mean the bay was, in fact, more accurately described as an ocean, since Greenland was now on a separate and distinct plate of its own.

It was not until Hudson 70 however that Ross had risen sufficiently in the scientific hierarchy of the Bedford Institute to try to prove which theory was correct. Until then he did not have sufficient staff at his command to undertake the necessary experiment. Besides which, Hudson 70 also coincided with the recruitment of Dr. Charlotte Keen, a seismic expert who was also convinced that Baffin Bay was not a bay. It was the last task of Hudson 70 to find out whether Ross and Charlotte Keen were right.

The experiment involved three ships, the *Baffin* and the U.S. coastguard cutter *Edisto* as well as the *Hudson*. The job of scientists aboard the *Baffin* was to work across the bay with gravimeters and magnetometers to take readings that would provide a counterpoint for the seismic work of the *Hudson* and the *Edisto*. Although there were initially fears that these two ships would have difficulty finding one another on schedule in the middle of the bay itself, the experiment was to prove simple and conclusive. To rendezvous on time was, however, vital since winter had begun and within days there would be so much floating ice the experiment would be impossible.

On October 5 the *Hudson* and the *Edisto* began work. Ross already knew that gravimeter readings suggested that the floor of the bay was so thin that it had probably been formed by new material seeping up from the plastic mantle of the earth as two distinctly separate plates drifted apart. This suggested that Greenland had in fact broken cleanly away from North America and that the crust of the earth beneath the bay was a relatively new rock formation. The seismic work of October 5 and 6 was designed to provide conclusive proof. At midday on October 5 the *Edisto* began steaming away from the *Hudson*,

246

setting off underwater explosions that sent sound waves down into the seabed and into the mantle before they bounced back up to the surface to be received by the *Hudson*. Twenty-eight hours and fifty-four explosions later Charlotte Keen, a tiny woman in her late twenties whose determined efforts to be one of the boys fail to hide her femininity, sat down with Ross to examine and interpret the seismic records. Their findings were conclusive. They had proved that Baffin Bay wasn't: it was an ocean. The radio message they ordered sent to the Bedford Institute reflected jubilation. It simply said: "Baffin Bay now an Ocean." And that night there was a party in the senior scientist's cabin which Ross occupied for this leg of the voyage. Bernard Pelletier loaned his precious accordion to Donny Barrett, who plays like a virtuoso, and several men tried, most unscientifically, to kiss Charlotte Keen.

Hudson 70 had ended – the scientific part of it anyway. There remained ten days of sailing south to Halifax, and a minor mutiny among the crew which began amiably enough in the lounge one evening when Dave Butler explained that the *Hudson* was on a course to take her through the Strait of Belle Isle between the mainland shore and Newfoundland. Abe Granter, the burly ex-army sergeant who was the ship's writer, or administrator, mildly pointed out that this would mean they would circumnavigate the Americas but not Canada. To do that, he said, the ship would have to take the seaward route and go round the outside of Newfoundland. Someone else told a particularly scurrilous Newfie joke, and the subject was forgotten. But the next day there were rumblings among the crew, at least one-third of whom were Newfoundlanders. It grew serious enough for Roy Gould, by now again acting as Chief Officer, to raise the subject with Butler and Ced Mann. The three men realized that to take the inside route and by-pass Newfoundland would generate considerable ill-will. There was the spectre of volatile Joey Smallwood, then premier of Newfoundland, making it a public issue and, more seriously from Butler's standpoint, of affronting men who had manned the *Hudson* on one of the epic voyages of the twentieth century.

With Halifax three days away and the ship headed directly for the Strait of Belle Isle, Butler ordered an abrupt change of course due east so they would pass round the outside of New-foundland.

And then they were home again.

On October 16, with the *Baffin* in the lead, the *Hudson* steamed down from the north-east to Chebucto Head, the outer extremity of Halifax harbour, and down past Never-fail Shoal and then past the assembled frigates and destroyers and sub-marines of the Canadian navy and beneath the soaring arch of the Angus A. McKay bridge that hadn't been finished when they left but was now carrying traffic. Every boat and ship in harbour – even the little scow-like Dartmouth ferries – blew a salute in an insane cacophony of sirens, hooters and whistles. On the dock that juts out into the Bedford Basin from the Bedford Institute stood Joe Greene and Bill Ford and Bill Cameron and Dick Haworth and Iver Duedall and Bosko Loncarevic and a thousand others. On the bridge in his dress uniform, which had been altered again to accommodate an-other increase in girth, Butler gave the orders attendant upon bringing a ship the size of the *Hudson* alongside, and quietly prayed that this would not be the one occasion when his ship handling ability deserted him.

And then he and Ced Mann walked down the same gang-plank that they had mounted eleven months and 57,956.5 miles earlier. Joe Greene welcomed them with a speech that waved no nationalistic banners and was free of ringing rhetoric. It was a speech of quiet pride. He departed from the prepared text to point out that the *Hudson* returned to a troubled country, for only that day the federal government had invoked the War Measures Act to deal with the latest Quebec crisis, this one caused by separatist terrorists kidnapping first a British diplomat and then a provincial cabinet minister, who they murdered. Greene had himself been up all night at the Ottawa cabinet meeting at which it was decided to invoke the War Measures Act. It was a bleak day in the nation's history, and Greene looked bleak as he said that for him and for Canada the success of Hudson 70 was the more important at this point in history because it was an achievement of which the whole

248

nation could be proud, Quebec included. There was a message from the Governor-General, His Excellency Roland Michener. It said in part: "You have not only added to our store of useful scientific knowledge of our hemisphere and country, but to the stature of our Canadianism." Greene presented the *Hudson* with a commemorative plaque, and Dave Butler and Ced Mann with commemorative medals struck for the occasion. And there was the inevitable press conference, which ended when one reporter asked Butler whether there had been any memorable dramas or crises during the expedition.

Butler sat quietly for a moment, then said: "Yes, there was one crisis I remember particularly well. On September 30 in the area of the Northwest Passage we ran out of tea."

Epilogue

The baccalaureates came first. They stood in a line down the side aisle in the crowded convocation hall, unnaturally subdued and gowned, even the most unruly hair curried neatly for the occasion. A middle-aged man in a black gown slightly grey with use at elbows and hem – who was he; the Registrar? – intoned names, and on cue the young man or woman at the head of the queue stepped forward to give that anonymous name a face and form and to receive the document that conferred upon them a Bachelor of Arts or Sciences degree from Brock University, St. Catharines, Ontario.

Dave Butler at first looked intently at the parade of faces – beards, sideburns, occasional crew cuts, long curtains of centre-parted hair, modest make-up, trim ankles beneath black gowns – and thought they were all innocent of the lines that come with living. Then he thought of the irony of the fact that he, who had left school at fourteen to go to sea, should be sitting there in a gown himself, awaiting his turn to have bestowed upon him a degree, an anointing that would be a major part of this university Convocation in the Spring of 1971.

When it ended he would be Dr. Captain D. W. Butler, LL.D., honoured for his part in Hudson 70. It was, he thought, one of those moments in life that from his deathbed would shine through the mists of memory, an occasion matched by few others, with the exception of his wedding day and the day he had stepped on the bridge of his first command, the *Limnos,* the Canadian government's scientific ship in the Great Lakes.

He knew the honorary Doctorate of Laws was being bestowed upon him in good part because he was the handiest human symbol of the odyssey that had ended on October 16 the previous year. He thought that if he ever wrote his memoirs he would have to say that the shades of two hundred or more other veterans of Hudson 70 sat with him on this day as he awaited the ritual bestowal of an academic honour with his wife glowing with pride in him and pleasure at her new outfit. As it usually did when he had a passive role in formal occasions, Butler's mind wandered.

When asked a few weeks earlier to assess the results of the expedition, Ced Mann had written with characteristic lack of emotion: "Looking back, the expedition was far more successful than might reasonably have been expected at the outset. This was due to good fortune with the weather, to the efforts of the 122 scientific staff who at one time or another sailed on the ship during her passage through four oceans, and not the least to the efforts of a dedicated crew. The expedition provided an opportunity for marine scientists across Canada to join together in common venture and extended their investigations to relatively inaccessible areas of the oceans at a time when assessment of the marine environment on a global scale is becoming of increasing importance."

It was, Butler knew, quite impossible for Mann to say more at that time. The government's public relations people had grown almost apoplectic with frustration when the ever-cautious scientists had refused to make grand and sweeping announcements about their work during the voyage. All science seemed to belong to a world outside the ken of more ordinary mortals who were accustomed to an immediate cause and effect relationship between their efforts and the tangible or at least visible results of them. But for most of the scientists who had come and gone during Hudson 70, the real work did not begin until they returned to their laboratories. In the world of science there is one major totem of achievement – publication of scientific conclusions in a learned journal. The vital questions at the end of any research project are: "Can you publish?" and "When?" Butler had already heard gossip that the first Hudson 70 man to publish would probably be Dr. George Pickard, who had mounted the study of the Chilean fiord system. (In fact,

251

the gossip was accurate; Pickard delivered his fiord paper to a world symposium of oceanographers in New Zealand at the end of December 1971. It was described as "masterly".)

But there were other sequels to Hudson 70 which, generally, were of more consequence to the individuals involved than to the world at large.

When the *Hudson* returned to Halifax, technician Hugh Henderson had found two more letters from Iris Godoy in Valparaiso awaiting him. He had collected his accumulated pay and overtime and promptly flew back to Chile. Iris met him at the airport in Santiago. By now he knew she was twenty-seven, almost a year older than he, that she was the third youngest in a family of ten, that her father was a construction worker in the town of Serena almost three hundred miles from Valparaiso. From Serena he wrote friends in Halifax: "I didn't really know what or how I felt when I got on the plane in Canada, but the moment I saw Iris again I knew I loved her. Just being with her feels right." Hugh Henderson, of Halifax, Nova Scotia, married Iris Godoy, of Serena, Chile, in the Casa Municipale of Serena on December 23, 1970.

Iver Duedall and his wife had the first Hudson 70 baby. He had spent six continuous months aboard before she had met him on June 12, waiting on the dock as the *Hudson* tied up. In mid-February Mr. and Mrs. Iver Duedall proudly announced the birth of a second child, a son. Duedall was under pressure to name him Henry Hudson Duedall, but he refused.

On learning of the existence of almost a hundred "Admiral's Finger" pingoes in the Beaufort Sea, the Canadian government firmly announced that they would not readily give permission for tankers to use the Northwest Passage ever again. Coincidentally, Ottawa's commitment to Arctic development and conservation increased by several thousand per cent, and the government firmly staked a claim to more of the north than they ever had before, and it was decided to move oil south by pipeline rather than tanker. Bernard Pelletier was delighted.

Bruce Carson's plans for his new house, so laboriously drawn up in off-duty hours aboard the *Hudson*, were discarded soon afterwards. The house was built, but to a different plan.

His wife didn't like his design for the kitchen, the location of the fireplace or the size and number of the storage cupboards.

Frank Durnford, the coxswain who became a small-boat hero during Hudson 70, left the ship after passing examinations for a mate's ticket. He became an officer aboard a ferry plying between Nova Scotia and Newfoundland.

Just before leaving Halifax to attend the Convocation of Brock University, Dave Butler had seen Fred Muise, whose sickness after the death of his baby son had led to an unscheduled dash across the Antarctic, out shopping with his wife. She was pregnant again, and Butler found himself quietly praying to a God about whom he was sceptical that this time the child would be normal. (The baby was born in the summer of 1971. It was another boy. They called him Robbie.)

Chef Claude Durin had left the ship within days of return to Halifax. He had said that he now had enough saved to marry and have a good house and perhaps to even open his own restaurant. Ray Sheldon, the biologist who refused to eat what he had called "swill" in the Pacific, said that he did not think Escoffier would approve. Everyone else, however, wished Durin well. No one had heard from him since.

Larry MacDonald, the officer's steward who had so carefully checked Butler's dress uniform for the honorary doctorate ceremony, was married now. He had told Butler that five months at sea aboard the *Hudson* had shown him that he had foolishly taken his girl friend Jean Sampson for granted. It was for this reason he had flown from Chile to Calgary, whence she had moved, and almost immediately proposed.

Mark, the Doberman Pinscher owned by ship's surgeon Rustige and the only dog to have ever circumnavigated the Americas, was dead. Soon after the return of the *Hudson* he was killed by a car. Butler thought that after eleven months at sea Mark had probably lost the keen edge of his instincts for survival on land. He wondered how Nicodemus, the German Shepherd he had raised from a puppy and then presented to a French official on Papeete, was faring. He felt guilty about that dog.

And then the Convocation neared its end and it was the

turn of Captain David W. Butler to stand and be honoured by the Chancellor for his part in the Hudson 70 expedition. He said that he accepted the Doctor of Laws degree not only on behalf of himself, but for his crew and the scientists who had taken part. Afterwards, outside the hall, people stood in groups, smiling happily, and Butler's wife took his photograph with an expensive and complicated camera he had acquired during one of his voyages and which neither he nor she felt competent to use.

In the next few days they dawdled around southern Ontario, visiting the lakeshore towns and cities he had known when commanding the *Limnos* as it undertook research projects in the Great Lakes. The day after they returned to Halifax, Butler went back to the ship to catch up on the administrative paper work that is a large part of any captain's job. As he walked through the almost deserted companionways of the *Hudson* Butler accidentally eavesdropped on two of the crew talking in an empty cabin. They were talking about him. They no longer referred to him as "The Captain" or even as "The Skipper", which were the formal titles they used when the Hudson 70 expedition began and he was the new boy among the crew. In fact, what Dave Butler overheard was one crewman saying to the other that "the old man isn't a bad old sod."

Somehow that made him even more proud than his honorary doctorate.